THE

ANABASIS OF XENOPHON

BOOK IV

THE
ANABASIS OF XENOPHON
BOOK IV

EDITED

WITH INTRODUCTION, NOTES AND VOCABULARY

BY

G. M. EDWARDS

CAMBRIDGE:
AT THE UNIVERSITY PRESS.
1967

CAMBRIDGE UNIVERSITY PRESS
Cambridge, New York, Melbourne, Madrid, Cape Town,
Singapore, São Paulo, Delhi, Tokyo, Mexico City

Cambridge University Press
The Edinburgh Building, Cambridge CB2 8RU, UK

Published in the United States of America by
Cambridge University Press, New York

www.cambridge.org
Information on this title: www.cambridge.org/9781107600218

© Cambridge University Press 1898

First published 1898
Reprinted 1899, 1922, 1935, 1952, 1959, 1967
First paperback edition 2011

A catalogue record for this publication is available from the British Library

ISBN 978-1-107-60021-8 Paperback

PREFACE.

THE Fourth Book of the *Anabasis* is an excellent subject for school reading. The Greek is simple even for the *Anabasis*. I know no portion of Xenophon's works where there are fewer difficulties of construction ; and there are fortunately no speeches more than a few lines in length. The contents of the book are of great and varied interest. We have remarkable examples of Xenophon's tactical skill in the capture of strong mountain positions and the passage of rivers ; several stirring battle scenes ; the hardships of the Greeks on the mountains of Kurdistan and the wintry table-lands of Armenia ; entertaining episodes, such as the luxurious life in the underground dwellings and the disastrous effects of the intoxicating honey. The interest of the book culminates in the graphic description of the first view of the sea from Mount Theches.

In the text I have adopted only a few of the many changes which Cobet and his followers have introduced with a free hand. For the topography of the book Mr Tozer's recently published *History of Ancient Geography* is a most valuable guide. I am also indebted to the works of Grote, Mure, Curtius, Vollbrecht, Rehdantz, Hug, R. W. Taylor, Pretor, and Dakyns.

The student is recommended to read at least pages xiii–xxi of the Introduction before beginning the Greek text of the Fourth Book.

G. M. E.

CAMBRIDGE,
    10 *March*, 1898.

CONTENTS.

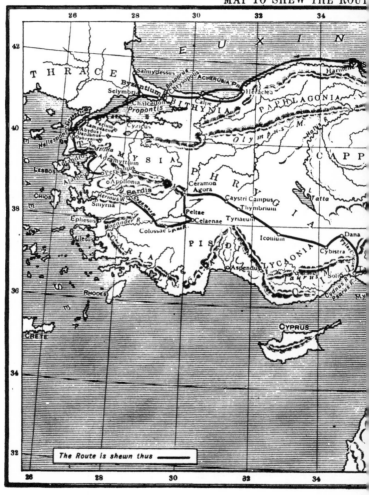

The Route is shewn thus _____

F THE TEN THOUSAND.

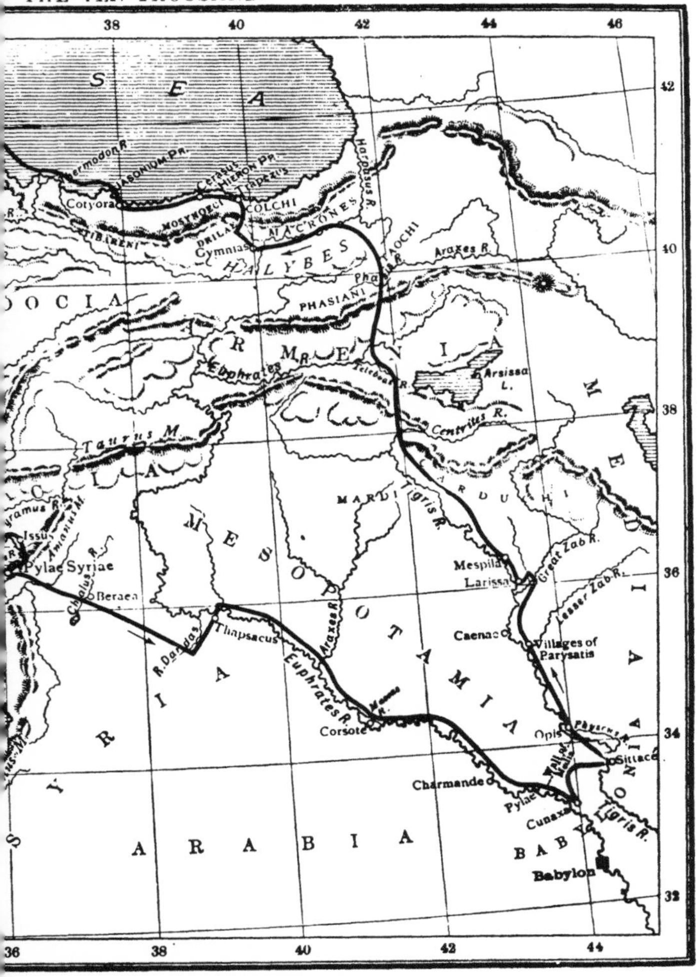

INTRODUCTION.

XENOPHON was the son of Gryllus an Athenian of the deme of Ercheia. Our information about his early life is extremely meagre and uncertain. The date of his birth is entirely a matter of conjecture ; the slender evidence available seems to point to the year 435 B.C. The date usually given, 444 B.C., is unquestionably incorrect.

In his boyhood he made the acquaintance of Socrates, who, it is said, one day met the young Xenophon in the street and proceeded to catechise him after his fashion, enquiring of him where different articles could be obtained. He then asked him where men were made good and noble ; and, the boy being unable to answer his question, Socrates bade him follow him and see. Henceforth Xenophon became the devoted disciple of the philosopher, whose *Memorabilia* (*Memoirs*) he afterwards wrote. When still a boy, he was present with his master at the banquet given by Callias in honour of Autolycus, 'Victor among the boys' at the Panathenaic games. The story of his preservation from death by Socrates at the battle of Delium in 424 B.C. is evidently a fiction, like many other stories in Greek literary biography.

When Xenophon reached the age for military service, Athens was suffering severely from the stress of the Peloponnesian War; and he doubtless took part in the defence of the city down to its capture by Sparta in 404 B.C. He seems to have belonged to the 'Knights.' Several of his books manifest a keen interest in horses and horsemanship. Any one familiar with Aristophanes' picture of the 'Thousand good Knights' and their aristocratic contempt for the demagogue will to some extent appreciate that strange feature in the life of Xenophon, his antipathy to the Athenian democracy and his enthusiastic admiration for Sparta and all things Spartan. Still it is very remarkable that one who evidently owed his success in life mainly to his training in democratic Athens should display a marked preference for the Spartan system of education and government.

Before Xenophon left Athens in 401 B.C. he had probably completed the first two books of his *Hellenica* or *History of Greece*, a continuation of the unfinished work of Thucydides. These books describe the closing scenes of the great war, the tyranny of the Thirty and the restoration of the democracy by Thrasybulus in 403 B.C. The extremely interesting essay *on the Athenian Constitution*, ascribed to Xenophon, is the earliest remaining specimen of Attic Prose; it must have been written when Xenophon was quite a boy, and cannot be his work. It is now generally thought to have been an anonymous publication; and different critics have suggested Alcibiades, Critias, and even Thucydides as possible authors of the treatise.

§ 2. CYRUS AND THE GREEKS.

Cyrus, the younger and abler of the two surviving sons of Darius II King of Persia and his queen Parysatis, came into prominence in 408 B.C., when at the early age of seventeen he was appointed Satrap, or Viceroy, of Lydia, Phrygia and Cappadocia and Commander-in-chief of the royal troops in those parts. He was thus practically supreme in Asia Minor. In 404 B.C. Darius died before the Queen could obtain from him a declaration in favour of Cyrus on the ground that the elder son Artaxerxes was born before his father's accession,—an argument

which in old days Atossa had advanced on behalf of Xerxes.
Cyrus had hastened to his father's deathbed at Susa only to
find himself completely disappointed in his expectation of
succeeding to the throne, and to witness the accession of his
brother Artaxerxes II. Further, Cyrus nearly lost his life on a
charge of treason preferred against him by his enemy Tissaphernes, who had accompanied him to Susa. Tissaphernes was
Satrap of Caria and had rights of sovereignty over a number of
Greek towns in Ionia ; and Cyrus had provoked his hostility by
scheming to bring these under his own control. So now on the
evidence of a priest, the prince's spiritual director, Tissaphernes
accused Cyrus of conspiring to assassinate the King on the
occasion of his accession. Cyrus barely escaped death on the
intercession of his mother Parysatis, who threw herself between
the royal guards and her favourite son. Eventually he was
allowed to return with undiminished powers to his government
in Asia Minor ; Artaxerxes hoping to conquer his brother by
this generous treatment.

Meanwhile Cyrus, nursing the bitterest feelings of hatred
and revenge, conceived the brilliant idea of collecting a Greek
force, in addition to his large Asiatic army, to fight Artaxerxes
for the throne. The circumstances of the time were highly
favourable to this policy ; for at the end of the Peloponnesian
War began the rise of mercenary troops in the Hellenic world.
During the long years of that war many Greeks had become
professional soldiers, and, being unwilling to return to the quiet
life of citizens, were ready to hire themselves out as mercenaries.
The tyranny of the oligarchies established, under the Spartan
Empire, in the Greek cities had driven many from their homes ;
while the general demoralisation caused by a long period of
war and the dissolution of family ties hastened the decay
of patriotism and kindled the passion for a roving life of profit
and adventure.

Cyrus saw his opportunity ; despatching his agents in all
directions, he drew together to his court at Sardis many
Greeks of ruined fortunes. A born leader of men, he dazzled
the Greek imagination by his brilliant personality, his youthful

enthusiasm and his open-handed generosity. Hellenic patriotism was practically dead ; and here, apparently at the dawn of a new era, was a prince with a great future, having at his disposal 'the gold of Asia and the men of Hellas.' He demanded no sacrifices,—so ran his magnificent invitation to Sparta,— without ample rewards. The soldier who came on foot should receive a horse ; he who came on horseback, a chariot and pair. Owners of fields should be made masters of villages ; and masters of villages lords of cities. So successful was this policy that early in 401 B.C. Cyrus had concentrated at Sardis a force of 8000 men, whom his Greek officers had collected in the Peloponnese, Thessaly, Ionia and elsewhere.

§ 3   XENOPHON, PROXENUS AND CYRUS.

Among the Greek officers whom Cyrus had attracted to Sardis was the Theban Proxenus, an old friend of Xenophon, who in the Second Book gives a sympathetic account of his noble and ambitious nature. From his description of Proxenus as a disciple of the rhetorician Gorgias, and as one who recognised the importance of culture as an element of distinction in public life, we may infer that the bond which united the two friends was of a literary character. Moreover we are told elsewhere that Xenophon, who was a few years older than Proxenus, had acted as his tutor. Hence it appears probable that Cyrus wished to secure, through Proxenus, the services of Xenophon as a *civil* officer to aid him in his ambitious schemes. Xenophon expressly tells us that he joined the expedition *neither as general nor captain nor soldier.*

Early in 401 B.C. Xenophon, as he tells us at the beginning of the Third Book, received from Proxenus a letter, in which he undertook to introduce him to Cyrus, adding the cynical remark that he considered the friendship of such a patron was *worth more to himself than his native city*,—a striking illustration of the decay of patriotism during this period. He communicated the proposal of Proxenus to his master Socrates, who feared that his young friend might provoke the hostility of the democracy, if he threw in his lot with one who had been the bitter enemy of Athens and had actually furnished Sparta with the means of crushing her. He accordingly advised him to consult the oracle at Delphi. Thither Xenophon repaired. But, instead of asking the God, 'Shall I go to Sardis or shall I forbear?' he put the narrower question : 'Having a journey in view, to which of the gods must I offer prayers and sacrifices in order to make it propitious?' The oracle indicated to him the proper deities. Socrates, however, was displeased with his disciple because he had not submitted the question with perfect frankness. 'Nevertheless,' he added, 'since you have elected to put the question in your own way, you must act on the answer vouchsafed.' So Xenophon set sail after duly performing the necessary rites. Probably he was not sorry to leave his native city; for Athens under the restored democracy cannot have been an agreeable residence for a member of the Knights, the class which had been the chief support of the atrocious tyranny of the Thirty.

He reached Sardis in the spring of 401 B.C., and found Cyrus and Proxenus preparing to set out on an expedition directed, so it was alleged, against the Pisidians, a refractory robber tribe in a distant part of the prince's satrapy. They both expressed a strong wish that Xenophon should accompany them. He was deceived by their statements, for which, he adds, Proxenus was not responsible ; for neither Proxenus nor any other Greek officer except Clearchus, the intimate friend of Cyrus, had at present any suspicion that the expedition was really directed against the King of Persia.

§ 4. THE ANABASIS. CYRUS THE HERO OF BOOK I. HE MARCHES FROM SARDIS TO CUNAXA WHERE HE IS KILLED IN BATTLE.

The title Κύρου Ἀνάβασις can in strictness be applied to the First Book only, which describes the march *up country* from the west of Asia Minor into Babylonia. This occupied about six months. The Second Book begins the account of the Κατάβασις or the journey *down* to the Euxine Sea.

In March 401 B.C. Cyrus had completed his preparations. The 8000 Greek troops now concentrated at Sardis he placed under the command of his Spartan general Clearchus, an outlaw from his native city, having been condemned to death by the Lacedaemonian authorities for disobedience to their orders. The Asiatic troops of Cyrus, numbering 100,000, were commanded by his friend Ariaeus the Persian. Cyrus still told the Greeks that the object of his enterprise was merely to secure the frontiers of his province against the Pisidian free-booters ; and, in order to deceive Artaxerxes, he gave out that the Greek force which he had collected was designed for service against his jealous rival, Tissaphernes, Satrap of Caria. But Tissaphernes suspected the real designs of Cyrus, and, when he heard of the magnitude of the prince's army, started with all speed to inform the Great King, who at once began his preparations.

The route of Cyrus from Sardis to Cunaxa can be easily seen upon the Map. The chief events of the march may be briefly mentioned here. At Colossae Cyrus was overtaken by one of his Greek generals, Menon the Thessalian, at the head of 1500 troops. At Celaenae he halted for thirty days, waiting for further reinforcements which were brought by Clearchus and Sophaenetus. After their arrival a review was held, the Greek force now amounting to over 13,000 men. At Caystri Campus we have the interesting meeting of Cyrus with Epyaxa, wife of Syennesis, prince of Cilicia and a vassal of Persia. She pro-vided Cyrus with a large sum of money for the payment of his troops, and accompanied him for some way on his march. At Tyriaeum a grand review was held in her honour. The almost impregnable pass, called the Cilician Gates, was occupied by Syennesis ; but his resistance was a mere sham, and at Tarsus he furnished Cyrus with troops. It was at Tarsus that the diffi-culties of Cyrus with his Greeks first arose. Suspecting the real object of the expedition, they refused to advance. After much discussion they agreed to send to Cyrus a deputation including Clearchus, who was not known to be in the secrets of the prince. Cyrus replied that he was really marching against Abrocomas, Satrap of Syria, who was encamped on the Euphrates, and promised the Greeks additional pay. With these assurances they were satisfied.

At the port of Issus Cyrus received further reinforcements brought by his fleet, amongst them 700 Spartan hoplites under the command of Cheirisophus, sent, it was said, by the Lacedaemonian government. The number of his Greek force now reached 14,000. Abrocomas, who was in command of 300,000 men, seems to have been alarmed by the rapid progress of the invader and fled from the Syrian coast into the interior, abandoning three defensible positions in succession :—(1) the Syrian Gates, (2) the pass of Beilan over Mount Amanus, and (3) the passage of the Euphrates. At Thapsacus, just before crossing the Euphrates, Cyrus at last publicly informed the Greeks that he was leading them to Babylon to fight against the Great King. The announcement was received with loud murmurs ; but the soldiers were appeased by the promise of a liberal donation to be given to each man on arrival at Babylon. At Charmandé a serious dispute arose between Clearchus and Menon, in which the troops of the two generals joined. The intervention of Proxenus as peacemaker was unsuccessful ; and the gravity of the situation was only allayed by an appeal from Cyrus himself.

Hitherto Cyrus had been advancing with overweening self-confidence ; for he had been allowed to pass without resistance all the natural obstacles of which the Persians might have taken advantage to bar his progress, and now he seemed to think that victory would be his without a struggle. This feeling was only increased when, three days after leaving Pylae, he found quite undefended the great trench which Artaxerxes had caused to be dug across the plain for a length of 40 miles. It had been abandoned from some unaccountable panic. Cyrus now imagined that the Persians would never face him in the plains of Babylonia. And when one day early in September his troops were about to halt for their morning meal at the village of Cunaxa, it was announced that a vast Persian host of 900,000 men was approaching in order of battle over the open plain. Cyrus, quite taken by surprise, arranged his forces with all speed. The Greeks under Clearchus were on the right wing resting on the Euphrates; Ariaeus with his Asiatic troops was on the left; and Cyrus surrounded by a body-guard of 600 Persian cavalry was in the centre. So great was the superiority of Artaxerxes in numbers that his centre extended beyond the left wing of the Cyreians.

Just before the battle began, Cyrus ordered Clearchus to attack the Persian centre, because the King was there. But Clearchus, afraid of withdrawing his right from the river and exposing himself to an attack in flank and rear, simply answered that he was taking care that all should be well. He charged the Persian left and routed it almost without a blow; Tissaphernes alone, with his body of horse, not taking part in the general flight. Meanwhile the Persian centre under Artaxerxes began to surround the left wing of Cyrus. Then the reckless prince cried out, 'I see the man'; and rode forward with a mere handful of companions to attack the King who was protected by a body-guard of 6000 horse. Cyrus broke their ranks and hurling his javelin wounded his brother slightly in the breast; but he was immediately surrounded and slain. Next Ariaeus and all the Asiatic troops of Cyrus fled in confusion, and their camp was plundered by the enemy. The Persians were thus victorious both here and in the centre; and Artaxerxes drew up his troops to attack the Greeks, who were unaware of the death of Cyrus. Clearchus gained a second victory; for the Persians fled without awaiting his onset. Thus relieved of all enemies he remained on the field in hopes of hearing tidings of Cyrus. He then returned to his camp, which he found completely plundered. So the Greeks retired supperless to rest; most of them had had no morning meal owing to the early hour at which the battle had begun.

§ 5. THE ANABASIS CONTINUED. CLEARCHUS THE HERO
OF BOOK II. THE GREEKS BEGIN THEIR RETREAT.
THE TREACHEROUS SEIZURE OF THEIR GENERALS BY
TISSAPHERNES.

Early in the morning of the day after the battle of Cunaxa
Clearchus and the other Greek generals decided to march out
and meet Cyrus, whom they supposed to be still alive. On
learning the disastrous news the Greeks were deeply grieved.
Cyrus, the one hope of the expedition, was gone, and here they
were in the heart of the Persian empire entirely destitute of
resources and surrounded by treacherous foes. Still, with
splendid self-confidence, as conquerors in the battle of Cunaxa,
they proceeded to offer their prize of victory, the Persian
throne, to Ariaeus, who had commanded the Asiatic troops of
Cyrus. He politely declined their invitation ; probably he had
already made up his mind to seek the favour of Artaxerxes
and to betray his brothers in arms. Clearchus seems at first
to have placed a blind confidence in Ariaeus, who undertook
to conduct the Greeks to the sea by a route different from that
by which they had come. Accordingly it was resolved to begin
the retreat in his company.

' This strategy,' says Xenophon, ' was no better than running
away.' ' But Fortune,' he adds, ' proved a nobler strategist ' ;
for they had not proceeded far when they suddenly found
themselves close to the camp of the Persians, who at once
retreated in a panic. This led the Greeks to adopt a bolder
policy. The King, they saw, was evidently alarmed. On
the previous day he had claimed the victory on the ground
that Cyrus was dead, and he had demanded that the Greeks
should surrender their arms ; and now he sent envoys to
negotiate a truce. To overawe the Persians who came on this
mission Clearchus arranged a grand display of his forces. It
must be borne in mind that the two great difficulties of the
Greeks now were (1) lack of supplies and (2) ignorance of
routes. This will explain the course of the negotiations which
Xenophon describes.

Tissaphernes next appeared on the scene with another set of envoys. In three days a treaty was concluded, by which arrangements were made for provisioning the Greek force, and the Persians agreed to facilitate their progress with Tissaphernes as guide. Tissaphernes took his departure, the Greeks promising to await his return. Then ensued a fatal delay of twenty days, during which he was absent at the Persian court. Meanwhile, as we learn elsewhere, (1) the Great King had returned to Babylon to celebrate his supposed victory at Cunaxa ; (2) he gave to Tissaphernes his daughter's hand and the provinces previously held by Cyrus ; and (3) he received from the satrap a promise that the Greeks should be destroyed. At last Tissaphernes returned. The Greeks had already begun to suspect that Ariaeus was playing them false. When the retreat was resumed, there was great distrust between the Greeks and the Persian portion of the Cyreian army ; and they kept clear of one another both on the march and in their encampments. They soon approached the so-called 'Median Wall,' and marched on, keeping to the south of it. Then, after crossing two canals connected with the Tigris, they arrived at Sittacé, where the Greeks encamped. But the Persians crossed the river and attempted to alarm the Greeks by intimating that Tissaphernes intended to entrap them by breaking down the bridge. They were evidently afraid that the Greeks might conceive the idea of settling in Babylonia. The Greeks, however, crossed the Tigris and marching along the other bank reached the river Physcus and the town of Opis. Then they continued their march and, after plundering the villages of Queen Parysatis, they arrived at Caenae.

In a few days they reached a river called the Greater Zab. While encamping on its banks, Clearchus attempted to put an end to the constant jealousy and distrust between the Greek and Asiatic troops. Accordingly he consented to a conference with Tissaphernes, who promised that, if the Greek generals would come to his tent, he would give them the name of the treacherous person who was causing all the trouble. On the next day Clearchus went to Tissaphernes accompanied by four generals, twenty captains and two hundred soldiers. On their arrival the generals were seized and their companions massacred. Four of the generals, Clearchus, Proxenus, Agias and Socrates, were taken to the Persian court and soon afterwards beheaded. The other general Menon, who was the reputed traitor, was kept alive under torture for a year and then put to death. After the seizure of the generals, Ariaeus summoned the Greeks to surrender; but in an indignant and contemptuous message they declined.

§ 6. THE ANABASIS CONTINUED. XENOPHON THE HERO OF BOOKS III—VII. THE JOURNEY OF THE GREEKS TO TRAPEZUS. THEIR SUBSEQUENT TROUBLES.

Book III.

The situation of the Greeks now seemed more desperate than ever; Xenophon speaks of it in most pathetic language. Their spirits were however speedily revived by his own energetic action. During the night after the disaster he awoke from a remarkable dream and at once aroused the captains who had served under Proxenus. In a midnight council of war he urged them with simple and stirring eloquence to take measures for the common safety. They at once recognised his fitness for command and called upon him to fill the place of his friend. At Xenophon's suggestion, the captains of the other divisions were convened, and they nominated four other generals. At daybreak the new generals summoned the soldiers, who met after the fashion of a Greek Ecclesia and proceeded to discuss the future conduct of the expedition and to confirm the appointment of the generals proposed. They had soon risen from the paralysis of despair to a sense of their national greatness. The meetings of the Ten Thousand are an exact reproduction of the citizen-assemblies at home. The army is a wandering political community; and the national characteristics of the race are wonderfully brought out in the narrative of the Retreat.

It is very remarkable that an Athenian should have exercised a commanding influence over the Ten Thousand. For Athens was now unpopular in Greece, especially in the Peloponnese ; and a large majority of the soldiers were Peloponnesians, more than half being Arcadians or Achaeans. Xenophon was almost the only Athenian taking part in the expedition, and he had come 'neither as general nor captain nor soldier.' His extraordinary rise to power is doubtless due to the Athenian democratic training, which had given him flexibility and resource and, above all, persuasive eloquence. He displays throughout a marvellous faculty of tactful dealing with mixed multitudes and embarrassing circumstances ; and possesses in Athenian perfection the threefold power of thought and speech and action. 'The Athenian alone,' says Dr Curtius, 'possessed that superiority of culture which was necessary for giving order and self-control to the band of warriors barbarised by their selfish life, and for enabling him to serve them in the greatest variety of situations as spokesman, as general and as negotiator. And to him it was essentially due that, in spite of their unspeakable trials, through hostile tribes and desolate snow-ranges, 8000 Greeks in the end reached the coast.'

The Greeks began their march in a hollow square designed to protect the light-armed troops, camp-followers and baggage. They crossed the Great Zab River, strangely enough without any molestation from the enemy. Their route lay over the plain to the east of the Tigris, in a course, roughly speaking, parallel with that river. Soon they began to suffer severely from the attacks of the Persian cavalry under Mithradates, who continually harassed their rear. They next reached the ruins of two cities, called by Xenophon Larissa and Mespila, which Sir Austen Layard has identified as portions of the once colossal Nineveh. Tissaphernes now came up with a large army; and the Greeks suffered considerably in many skirmishes during their marches over the open plain. After this they reached hilly ground, where they found marching in a hollow square to be very inconvenient ; so they decided to give up this formation in favour of a new order of march. They soon arrived at some

villages near the modern town of Zakhu. Here they rested,
and then descended again into the plain. When Tissaphernes
proceeded to harass them once more, they halted and repelled
the Persian cavalry with ease. After this the Persians, who
had made a forced march by night, suddenly appeared in
advance of the Greeks on a mountain-spur commanding their
route. Then ensued a long and exciting engagement on the
hills, in which the Greeks gained the victory and Xenophon
shewed great prowess. After the battle the Greeks encamped
in some well-stocked villages on the bank of the Tigris; and
they suffered but little from the desultory attacks which the
enemy still continued to make upon them.

Book IV.

The Greeks, who were now in the neighbourhood of Jezireh,
had reached a very critical point in their journey. On their left
was the Tigris, which they had no means of crossing, especially
in face of a Persian army on the western bank; and in front
rose the Carduchian mountains, which, coming close down to
the river's edge, rendered further progress along the eastern
bank quite impracticable. The generals saw that their only
possible course was to enter the inhospitable region of northern
Kurdistan and to fight their way across the mountains into
Armenia. They found the first of the Carduchian mountain-
passes undefended. The mountaineers were completely taken
by surprise and left their well-stocked villages in the neighbourhood an easy prey to the Greeks; but immediately afterwards
they commenced a merciless guerilla warfare against the invaders. The Greek generals gave orders that all superfluous
baggage should be left behind, and then continued their march
for two days, the rear-guard under Xenophon being harassed
by repeated attacks. Meanwhile Cheirisophus, who commanded
the van, was pressing forward to anticipate the enemy in seizing
an important pass. On the other side of a deep ravine was
a steep road up to what Xenophon calls an ἔκβασις, i.e. an
'outlet' or pass which led on to the table-land beyond. In
spite of the efforts of Cheirisophus, this 'outlet' was occupied

by the enemy in great force. Xenophon discovered from a prisoner that, besides the road they saw before them, there was another way up to the pass,—a circuitous path, but practicable even for the baggage-train. A body of 2000 men, who volunteered for the purpose, was in the evening despatched by this path under the prisoner's guidance, in order to turn the Carduchian position next morning; and Xenophon was to make a feint attack along the direct road. At dawn the flank attack of the volunteers was entirely successful. This enabled Cheirisophus, who had followed the direct road, to occupy the 'outlet.' Then Xenophon, with the rear-guard and baggage-train, took the circuitous path, and, after several hazardous and exciting conflicts, joined the rest of the Greek army at the pass. The operations which he had planned had been a magnificent success. After two more days of harassing mountain-warfare the Greeks reached the Centrites, a tributary of the Eastern Tigris, the frontier river of Armenia. They bivouacked in some villages on the plateau above the river, glad enough to have ended their terrible week in Kurdistan.

But their troubles were by no means over. On the morrow they found a strong force of Armenians, Chaldaeans and others posted on the opposite bank of the Centrites, determined to dispute their passage of the ford; and their old enemies the Carduchians were ready to attack them in the rear. Next day by a fortunate discovery, which seemed to Xenophon to corroborate a favourable dream of the previous night, he became aware of the existence of another ford higher up the river at a point where the enemy's cavalry could not act. By this ford Cheirisophus crossed with his own division; while Xenophon first made a feint of crossing at the other place, and then by a rapid movement followed Cheirisophus over the upper ford. 'From this point,' says Mr Tozer (*History of Ancient Geography*, p. 116), 'the route by which they reached the high plateau of Armenia is clearly determined by the nature of the ground. Xenophon informs us that they passed the source of the Tigris, and, beyond that, came to a river of no great size, called the Teleboas, after which they forded the Euphrates, which was reported to rise not very far off. Now the pass

which crosses the Taurus range immediately above Bitlis
bifurcates at the point where the source of the Tigris lies,
one branch leading eastwards to the Lake of Van, which is
only a few miles distant though out of sight, the other west-
wards to the plain of Mush ; and, as no mention is made of
the lake, it is clear that the latter route is the one that they
followed. The Teleboas of Xenophon must be the Kara-su,
which rises at almost the same spot as the Tigris and runs in
the opposite direction to it, until it reaches the Murad-su, or
Eastern Euphrates, in the further part of the plain of Mush.'

It was now December, and in this plain of Mush, which
is a table-land more than 4000 feet above the sea, the Greeks
endured for some days terrible sufferings from the deep snow
and the intense cold of the Armenian winter. They were glad
to reach at last a group of villages on the southern slopes of
Bingheul-dagh, the ' mountain of a thousand springs.' Here
they rested for a week in luxurious quarters, and then started
again on their march taking with them the Armenian village
head-man as their guide. They proceeded for seven days
along the bank of the river which Xenophon calls the Phasis,
but which is better known as the Araxes. Then they left the
river and struck across a mountain-range, where a force of
Chalybes, Taochi and Phasiani presented themselves with the
view of obstructing a pass which led up to a plateau. Xenophon's side-march tactics were again brought into play and
again crowned with success. After passing through the terri-
tories of the Taochi and Chalybes, who did not offer any serious
opposition from their mountain fastnesses, the army reached
the river Harpasus, identified with the Tchoruk, which flows
into the Black Sea near Batoum.

They then passed into the territory of the Scythini, in some
of whose villages, rich in provisions, they rested for three days.
Four days' march brought them to the flourishing city of
Gymnias, which was probably not far from the modern town
of Baiburt on the banks of the Tchoruk. The chief man of
the city received them kindly and gave them a guide, who
undertook to bring them in five days to a hill from which
they would have a view of the sea. The promise was kept ;

on the fifth day they reached the top of a mountain called Theches, from which the Euxine was visible. The ecstatic enthusiasm of the army at the wished-for sight is vividly described by Xenophon. Mr Tozer, who knows the district well, has a striking passage on the subject:—'Though we cannot speak with confidence of the exact spot where the scene which Xenophon describes occurred, yet for a considerable distance along the mountain ridges in this part the impression would be the same. Here, from a height of between 7000 and 8000 feet above the sea, the eye which has been accustomed to the treeless uplands and monotonous plains of Armenia looks down upon forest-clad mountains and delicately cut ridges, separated from one another by ravines, and gradually descending towards Trebizond ; while, away to the northeast, cape after cape is seen extending into the Euxine, backed by ranges which run up to the snow-topped mountains of Lazistan, and the whole is completed and harmonized by the soft blue expanse of water. The entire view, from its delicacy and multiplicity of form, and its combination of sea and mountain, strikingly resembles the coasts of Greece. When suddenly presented to the eye of a Greek, it must have spoken to him of home in every line.'

From Mount Theches the Greeks reached the sea without great difficulty. They entered the land of the Macrones, who gave them a free passage and markets to buy provisions during a three days' march through their territory. The men of Colchis were not so compliant. They had occupied in great force the top of a mountain which formed their frontier. Their dislodgment by Xenophon was quite a brilliant operation. The Colchians fled, leaving the Greeks in possession of their camp and several well-stocked villages near at hand. Here they rested for several days. The story of the unwholesome honey, which this district still produces, is an interesting episode. After two days' march they reached the Greek city of Trapezus on the coast, the modern Trebizond. The inhabitants welcomed them with cordial hospitality. The Greeks took up their quarters in some Colchian villages near the city, where they rested for thirty days. But, in Greek fashion, they first discharged their vows, which they had made to the gods in the dread hour succeeding the seizure of the generals by Tissaphernes, by lavish sacrifices, high festival and games.

₊ The events narrated in Book IV. took place, according to Kühner's reckoning, from November 12th, 401 B.C. to February 8th, 400 (excluding the thirty days' rest at Trapezus).

Books V—VII.

The hopes which the Greeks had conceived of a speedy return home by sea were doomed to disappointment. Sparta was supreme in the Grecian world, and her officials on the Euxine refused to provide them with means for their voyage. After great difficulties they at last reached Byzantium. There, owing to their cruel treatment by the Spartan admiral Anaxibius, they resumed their profession of mercenaries, accepting the offer of the Theban Coeratidas, who promised them ample rewards if they would undertake a campaign in Thrace under his leadership. This agreement soon fell to the ground; and in 399 B.C. we find them in the service of the Thracian prince Seuthes, assisting him to subdue some rebel tribes. They fought for two months ; but met with cruel injustice as their reward.

Now, however, came a complete change in the policy of Sparta, which determined to support the Greek cities in Asia Minor against the satraps Tissaphernes and Pharnabazus. This meant war with Persia. Thimbron, the Spartan general, who was sent into Ionia, finding himself in want of reinforcements, invited to his aid Xenophon and the remnant of the Cyreians, whose numbers had now dwindled away to 6000. Smarting under the treatment they had just received from Seuthes, they obeyed the summons with alacrity. Xenophon crossed over into Asia and conducted his troops over Mount Ida to Pergamus. 'Then,' he says in the last words of the *Anabasis*, 'Thimbron took over the army and incorporated it with the rest of his Greek force, and fought against Tissaphernes and Pharnabazus.' So Tissaphernes, to quote again from Curtius, 'saw before him once more the hated men whom he had assumed on the day of Cunaxa to be doomed to perish hopelessly under the swords of the Carduchi or amid the snow-fields of Armenia.'

§ 7. LATER LIFE OF XENOPHON.

Before Xenophon handed over his troops to Thimbron in the spring of 399 B.C., he was, he tells us, *preparing* to return home ; for, he adds, the decree of banishment had *not yet* been passed against him at Athens. These words have an important bearing on the vexed question of the date of his banishment. They certainly support the view that the blow came *soon.* He seems to have expected such a disaster for some time past ; for he speaks of hoping for an asylum with Seuthes the Thracian prince, and his project of founding a colony of his own on the Euxine was probably due to the same fear. The decree of banishment was passed on the proposition of the orator Eubulus. His alleged offence is differently stated by two authorities. He was banished either (1) ' because he had taken part with Cyrus, the greatest enemy of the Athenian democracy, in an expedition against the Great King their well-wisher,' or (2) 'for Laconism,' *i.e.* for favouring Sparta. But these two statements may be looked upon as practically identical ; for taking part with Cyrus, who had shewn his friendship for Sparta by providing her with the 'sinews of war' against Athens, might well be looked upon as ' Laconism.' This view is strongly supported by the anxiety of Socrates on the subject (see above, § 3). Grote, however, owing to an apparent misunderstanding of a passage in the *Anabasis* (v. iii. 7), places Xenophon's banishment in 394 B.C. after the battle of Coroneia, when he actually fought for Sparta against his native city.

Xenophon was ' preparing to return.' Whether he actually did return to Greece in 399 B.C. is uncertain. The trial and death of his master Socrates took place in the summer of this year ; and the Athenians would not have been inclined to shew any tenderness to one of the Socratic brethren. The decree of banishment was probably passed very soon afterwards. Anyhow, in a few months we find him again in command of his old Cyreian troops in Asia Minor, serving first under Dercyllidas, who succeeded Thimbron in 398 B.C., and then under King Agesilaus, who went out in 396. For Agesilaus he entertained the warmest admiration and became his intimate friend. But the King was not allowed to remain long in Asia Minor; for, on the formation of the confederacy of Athens, Thebes and Corinth against Sparta, he wás summoned to fight for his country in Greece. Xenophon and his troops accompanied him into Boeotia and took part in his victory at Coroneia.

When Xenophon's service under Agesilaus was over, the Spartans gave him a house and grounds at Scillus, near Olympia. Soon after Xenophon had settled there he met Megabyzus, High-priest of the Ephesian Artemis, who chanced to have come to the Olympic Games. He paid over to Xenophon a sum of money, which represented a part of the tithe of plunder devoted by the Cyreian army to Artemis and deposited with her priest. With this money Xenophon purchased an estate near his own residence, which he consecrated to the goddess, and built thereon a chapel containing a statue, a copy in miniature of the great Ephesian temple. He appointed himself Conservator of the demesne of Artemis, which consisted largely of wild ground well stocked with game. He was an ardent sportsman; every year he held a hunting festival on a large scale, to which he invited his neighbours and entertained them lavishly at the expense of the Huntress Queen, who, he says, 'provided the fare.' At Scillus Xenophon was joined by his wife Philesia and his sons Gryllus and Diodorus; and there he lived a happy country life for twenty years, spending his time not only in sport, but in great literary labours, one of which was the composition of the *Anabasis*. From the fact that Xenophon is spoken of throughout the *Anabasis* in the third person, it has been thought by some that the writer was Themistogenes of Syracuse, whom Xenophon mentions elsewhere as the author of a history of the Retreat. Others hold that Xenophon published the *Anabasis* under the name of Themistogenes.

At Scillus he probably wrote the *Memorabilia* of his master

Socrates, 'whose loss,' he says, 'men even now continue to mourn'; and its appendix, the *Apology of Socrates*, if that work is really Xenophon's. The last five books of the *Hellenica* (see above, § 1), carrying the history of Greece down to the battle of Mantineia, 362 B.C., belong to a later time; so also does the *Cyropaedeia* or *Education of Cyrus the Great*, a political romance in eight books, 'not historically accurate nor a true picture of Persian thought and manners, but rather an encomium on Socratic principles and Spartan practice, in which Cyrus himself, drawn with some touches from the young Cyrus whom Xenophon had known, is half a Socrates and half an Agesilaus' (Jebb, *Primer of Greek Literature*, p. 113). Two Socratic dialogues by Xenophon are extant, the *Oeconomicus* and the *Symposium*; also another dialogue called *Hiero* and a treatise on the *Spartan Constitution*. The *Panegyric on Agesilaus*, ascribed to Xenophon, is probably a rhetorical exercise of later date. Three essays on horses and horsemanship are assigned to the time of his residence at Scillus:—(1) the *Cavalry Officer's Manual*, (2) *on Horsemanship*, in which he specially inculcates the duty of kindness to horses, (3) *on Hunting*, the work of a keen sportsman and lover of dogs, treating chiefly of hare-hunting. The hare, in the eyes of Xenophon, is a 'charming creature to hunt.'

In 371 B.C. after the battle of Leuctra, by which the power of Sparta was finally broken, the Eleians expelled Xenophon from Scillus. He then settled at Corinth. When Sparta became the ally of Athens against Thebes, his sentence of banishment was revoked on the motion of the same Eubulus who had proposed it. Xenophon's two sons, who had been educated at Sparta under the oversight of Agesilaus, fought on the Spartan side against Epameinondas at Mantineia, 362 B.C. The elder son, Gryllus, fell fighting with great bravery in the cavalry engagement at the gates just before the general battle began. From some passages in the essay *on the Athenian Revenues* (if it is Xenophon's work) it appears probable that towards the end of his life he spent some time at Athens. He died at Corinth. The date of his death is not known; but it cannot have been earlier than 355 B.C.

ΞΕΝΟΦΩΝΤΟΣ

ΚΥΡΟΥ ΑΝΑΒΑΣΙΣ.

Δ.

I.

The Greeks resolve to cross the Carduchian mountains.

Ὅσα μὲν δὴ ἐν τῇ ἀναβάσει ἐγένετο μέχρι τῆς 1
μάχης, καὶ ὅσα μετὰ τὴν μάχην ἐν ταῖς σπονδαῖς ἃς
βασιλεὺς καὶ οἱ σὺν Κύρῳ ἀναβάντες Ἕλληνες ἐποιήσαντο, καὶ ὅσα, παραβάντος τὰς σπονδὰς βασιλέως καὶ
Τισσαφέρνους, ἐπολεμήθη πρὸς τοὺς Ἕλληνας ἐπακο-
λουθοῦντος τοῦ Περσικοῦ στρατεύματος, ἐν τῷ πρόσθεν
λόγῳ δεδήλωται. ἐπεὶ δὲ ἀφίκοντο ἔνθα ὁ μὲν Τίγρης 2
ποταμὸς παντάπασιν ἄπορος ἦν διὰ τὸ βάθος καὶ
μέγεθος, πάροδος δὲ οὐκ ἦν, ἀλλὰ τὰ Καρδούχεια ὄρη
ἀπότομα ὑπὲρ αὐτοῦ τοῦ ποταμοῦ ἐκρέματο, ἐδόκει δὴ
τοῖς στρατιώταις διὰ τῶν ὀρέων πορευτέον εἶναι. ἤκουον 3
γὰρ τῶν ἁλισκομένων ὅτι, εἰ διέλθοιεν τὰ Καρδούχεια
ὄρη, ἐν τῇ Ἀρμενίᾳ τὰς πηγὰς τοῦ Τίγρητος ποταμοῦ,
ἢν μὲν βούλωνται, διαβήσονται, ἢν δὲ μὴ βούλωνται,

περιίασι. καὶ τοῦ Εὐφράτου δὲ τὰς πηγὰς ἐλέγετο οὐ
πρόσω τοῦ Τίγρητος εἶναι.

They enter the Carduchian territory.

4 τὴν δ' εἰς τοὺς Καρδούχους ἐμβολὴν ὧδε ποιοῦνται,
ἅμα μὲν λαθεῖν πειρώμενοι, ἅμα δὲ φθάσαι πρὶν τοὺς
5 πολεμίους καταλαβεῖν τὰ ἄκρα. ἡνίκα δ' ἦν ἀμφὶ τὴν
τελευταίαν φυλακὴν καὶ ἐλείπετο τῆς νυκτὸς ὅσον
σκοταίους διελθεῖν τὸ πεδίον, τηνικαῦτα ἀναστάντες
ἀπὸ παραγγέλσεως πορευόμενοι ἀφικνοῦνται ἅμα τῇ
6 ἡμέρᾳ πρὸς τὸ ὄρος. ἔνθα δὴ Χειρίσοφος μὲν ἡγεῖτο
τοῦ στρατεύματος λαβὼν τὸ ἀμφ' αὑτὸν καὶ τοὺς
γυμνῆτας πάντας, Ξενοφῶν δὲ σὺν τοῖς ὀπισθοφύλαξιν
ὁπλίταις εἵπετο οὐδένα ἔχων γυμνῆτα· οὐδεὶς γὰρ
κίνδυνος ἐδόκει εἶναι μή τις ἄνω πορευομένων ἐκ τοῦ
7 ὄπισθεν ἐπίσποιτο. καὶ ἐπὶ μὲν τὸ ἄκρον ἀναβαίνει
Χειρίσοφος, πρίν τινας αἰσθέσθαι τῶν πολεμίων· ἔπειτα
δ' ὑφηγεῖτο· ἐφείπετο δὲ ἀεὶ τὸ ὑπερβάλλον τοῦ
στρατεύματος εἰς τὰς κώμας τὰς ἐν τοῖς ἄγκεσί τε καὶ
8 μυχοῖς τῶν ὀρέων. ἔνθα δὴ οἱ μὲν Καρδοῦχοι ἐκλι-
πόντες τὰς οἰκίας ἔχοντες καὶ γυναῖκας καὶ παῖδας
ἔφευγον ἐπὶ τὰ ὄρη. τὰ δὲ ἐπιτήδεια πολλὰ ἦν λαμβάνειν, ἦσαν δὲ καὶ χαλκώμασι παμπόλλοις κατεσκευα-
σμέναι αἱ οἰκίαι, ὧν οὐδὲν ἔφερον οἱ Ἕλληνες, οὐδὲ τοὺς
ἀνθρώπους ἐδίωκον, ὑποφειδόμενοι, εἴ πως ἐθελήσειαν
οἱ Καρδοῦχοι διιέναι αὐτοὺς ὡς διὰ φιλίας τῆς χώρας,
9 ἐπείπερ βασιλεῖ πολέμιοι ἦσαν· τὰ μέντοι ἐπιτήδεια,
ὅτῳ τις ἐπιτυγχάνοι, ἐλάμβανον· ἀνάγκη γὰρ ἦν. οἱ
δὲ Καρδοῦχοι οὔτε καλούντων ὑπήκουον οὔτε ἄλλο
φιλικὸν οὐδὲν ἐποίουν.

They are harassed by the inhabitants.

ἐπεὶ δὲ οἱ τελευταῖοι τῶν Ἑλλήνων κατέβαινον εἰς 10 τὰς κώμας ἀπὸ τοῦ ἄκρου ἤδη σκοταῖοι—διὰ γὰρ τὸ στενὴν εἶναι τὴν ὁδὸν ὅλην τὴν ἡμέραν ἡ ἀνάβασις αὐτοῖς ἐγένετο καὶ κατάβασις—τότε δὴ συλλεγέντες τινὲς τῶν Καρδούχων τοῖς τελευταίοις ἐπετίθεντο, καὶ ἀπέκτεινάν τινας καὶ λίθοις καὶ τοξεύμασι κατέτρωσαν, ὀλίγοι τινὲς ὄντες· ἐξ ἀπροσδοκήτου γὰρ αὐτοῖς ἐπέπεσε τὸ Ἑλληνικόν. εἰ μέντοι τότε πλείους συνελέγησαν, 11 ἐκινδύνευσεν ἂν διαφθαρῆναι πολὺ τοῦ στρατεύματος. καὶ ταύτην μὲν τὴν νύκτα οὕτως ἐν ταῖς κώμαις ηὐλίσθησαν· οἱ δὲ Καρδοῦχοι πυρὰ πολλὰ ἔκαιον κύκλῳ ἐπὶ τῶν ὀρέων καὶ συνεώρων ἀλλήλους. ἅμα δὲ τῇ 12 ἡμέρᾳ συνελθοῦσι τοῖς στρατηγοῖς καὶ λοχαγοῖς τῶν Ἑλλήνων ἔδοξε τῶν τε ὑποζυγίων τὰ ἀναγκαῖα καὶ δυνατώτατα ἔχοντας πορεύεσθαι, καταλιπόντας τἆλλα, καὶ ὅσα ἦν νεωστὶ αἰχμάλωτα ἀνδράποδα ἐν τῇ στρατιᾷ πάντα ἀφεῖναι. σχολαίαν γὰρ ἐποίουν τὴν πορείαν 13 πολλὰ ὄντα τὰ ὑποζύγια καὶ τὰ αἰχμάλωτα, πολλοὶ δὲ οἱ ἐπὶ τούτοις ὄντες ἀπόμαχοι ἦσαν, διπλάσιά τε ἐπιτήδεια ἔδει πορίζεσθαι καὶ φέρεσθαι, πολλῶν τῶν ἀνθρώπων ὄντων. δόξαν δὲ ταῦτα, ἐκήρυξαν οὕτω ποιεῖν.

Renewed attacks.

ἐπεὶ δὲ ἀριστήσαντες ἐπορεύοντο, ὑποστήσαντες ἐν 14 τῷ στενῷ οἱ στρατηγοί, εἴ τι εὑρίσκοιεν τῶν εἰρημένων μὴ ἀφειμένον, ἀφῃροῦντο, οἱ δ᾽ ἐπείθοντο, πλὴν εἴ τίς τι ἔκλεψεν. καὶ ταύτην μὲν τὴν ἡμέραν οὕτως ἐπορεύθησαν, τὰ μέν τι μαχόμενοι, τὰ δὲ καὶ ἀναπαυόμενοι. εἰς δὲ τὴν ὑστεραίαν γίγνεται χειμὼν πολύς, ἀναγκαῖον 15

δ' ἦν πορεύεσθαι· οὐ γὰρ ἦν ἱκανὰ τἀπιτήδεια. καὶ
ἡγεῖτο μὲν Χειρίσοφος, ὠπισθοφυλάκει δὲ Ξενοφῶν.
16 καὶ οἱ πολέμιοι ἰσχυρῶς ἐπετίθεντο, καὶ στενῶν ὄντων
τῶν χωρίων ἐγγὺς προσιόντες ἐτόξευον καὶ ἐσφενδόνων·
ὥστε ἠναγκάζοντο οἱ Ἕλληνες ἐπιδιώκοντες καὶ πάλιν
ἀναχάζοντες σχολῇ πορεύεσθαι· καὶ θαμινὰ παρήγγελλεν ὁ Ξενοφῶν ὑπομένειν, ὅτε οἱ πολέμιοι ἰσχυρῶς
17 ἐπικέοιντο. ἐνταῦθα ὁ Χειρίσοφος ἄλλοτε μὲν ὅτε
παρεγγυῷτο ὑπέμενε, τότε δὲ οὐχ ὑπέμενεν, ἀλλ' ἦγε
ταχέως καὶ παρηγγύα ἕπεσθαι, ὥστε δῆλον ἦν ὅτι
πρᾶγμά τι εἴη· σχολὴ δ' οὐκ ἦν ἰδεῖν παρελθόντι τὸ
αἴτιον τῆς σπουδῆς· ὥστε ἡ πορεία ὁμοία φυγῇ ἐγίγνετο
18 τοῖς ὀπισθοφύλαξι. καὶ ἐνταῦθα ἀποθνήσκει ἀνὴρ
ἀγαθὸς Λακωνικὸς Κλεώνυμος τοξευθεὶς διὰ τῆς ἀσπίδος
καὶ τῆς σπολάδος εἰς τὰς πλευράς, καὶ Βασίας Ἀρκὰς
διαμπερὲς εἰς τὴν κεφαλήν.

Dispute between Xenophon and Cheirisophus.

19   ἐπεὶ δὲ ἀφίκοντο ἐπὶ σταθμόν, εὐθὺς ὥσπερ εἶχεν ὁ
Ξενοφῶν ἐλθὼν πρὸς τὸν Χειρίσοφον ᾐτιᾶτο αὐτὸν ὅτι
οὐχ ὑπέμενεν, ἀλλ' ἠναγκάζοντο φεύγοντες ἅμα μάχεσθαι. Καὶ νῦν, ἔφη, δύο καλώ τε καὶ ἀγαθὼ ἄνδρε
τέθνατον καὶ οὔτε ἀνελέσθαι οὔτε θάψαι ἐδυνάμεθα.
20 ἀποκρίνεται ὁ Χειρίσοφος, Βλέψον πρὸς τὰ ὄρη καὶ
ἰδὲ ὡς ἄβατα πάντα ἐστί· μία δ' αὕτη ὁδός, ἣν ὁρᾷς,
ὀρθία, καὶ ἐπὶ ταύτῃ ἀνθρώπων ὁρᾶν ἔξεστί σοι ὄχλον
τοσοῦτον, οἳ κατειληφότες φυλάττουσι τὴν ἔκβασιν.
21 ταῦτ' ἐγὼ ἔσπευδον καὶ διὰ τοῦτό σε οὐχ ὑπέμενον,
εἴ πως δυναίμην φθάσαι πρὶν κατειλῆφθαι τὴν ὑπερ-
βολήν· οἱ δ' ἡγεμόνες, οὓς ἔχομεν, οὔ φασιν εἶναι ἄλλην
22 ὁδόν. ὁ δὲ Ξενοφῶν λεγει, Ἀλλ' ἐγὼ ἔχω δύο ἄνδρας.

ἐπεὶ γὰρ ἡμῖν πράγματα παρεῖχον, ἐνηδρεύσαμεν, ὅπερ
καὶ ἡμᾶς ἀναπνεῦσαι ἐποίησε, καὶ ἀπεκτείναμέν τινας
αὐτῶν, καὶ ζῶντας προυθυμήθημεν λαβεῖν αὐτοῦ τούτου
ἕνεκα, ὅπως ἡγεμόσιν εἰδόσι τὴν χώραν χρησαίμεθα.

Examination of prisoners. Volunteers sent forward.

καὶ εὐθὺς ἀγαγόντες τοὺς ἀνθρώπους ἤλεγχον δια- 23
λαβόντες, εἴ τινα εἰδεῖεν ἄλλην ὁδὸν ἢ τὴν φανεράν.
ὁ μὲν οὖν ἕτερος οὐκ ἔφη μάλα πολλῶν φόβων προσ-
αγομένων· ἐπεὶ δὲ οὐδὲν ὠφέλιμον ἔλεγεν, ὁρῶντος
τοῦ ἑτέρου κατεσφάγη. ὁ δὲ λοιπὸς ἔλεξεν ὅτι οὗτος 24
μὲν οὐ φαίη διὰ ταῦτα εἰδέναι, ὅτι αὐτῷ ἐτύγχανε
θυγάτηρ ἐκεῖ παρ᾽ ἀνδρὶ ἐκδεδομένη· αὐτὸς δ᾽ ἔφη
ἡγήσεσθαι δυνατὴν καὶ ὑποζυγίοις πορεύεσθαι ὁδόν.
ἐρωτώμενος δ᾽ εἰ εἴη τι ἐν αὐτῇ δυσπάριτον χωρίον, 25
ἔφη εἶναι ἄκρον, ὃ εἰ μή τις προκαταλήψοιτο, ἀδύνατον
ἔσεσθαι παρελθεῖν. ἐνταῦθα δ᾽ ἐδόκει συγκαλέσαντας 26
λοχαγοὺς καὶ πελταστὰς καὶ τῶν ὁπλιτῶν λέγειν τε τὰ
παρόντα καὶ ἐρωτᾶν εἴ τις αὐτῶν ἔστιν ὅστις ἀνὴρ
ἀγαθὸς ἐθέλει γενέσθαι καὶ ὑποστὰς ἐθελοντὴς πορεύεσθαι. ὑφίσταται τῶν μὲν ὁπλιτῶν Ἀριστώνυμος 27
Μεθυδριεὺς Ἀρκὰς καὶ Ἀγασίας Στυμφάλιος Ἀρκάς,
ἀντιστασιάζων δὲ αὐτοῖς Καλλίμαχος Παρράσιος, Ἀρκὰς
καὶ οὗτος, ἔφη ἐθέλειν πορεύεσθαι προσλαβὼν ἐθελον-
τὰς ἐκ παντὸς τοῦ στρατεύματος. Ἐγὼ γὰρ, ἔφη, οἶδα
ὅτι ἕψονται πολλοὶ τῶν νέων ἐμοῦ ἡγουμένου. ἐκ 28
τούτου ἐρωτῶσιν εἴ τις καὶ τῶν γυμνήτων ταξιάρχων
ἐθέλοι συμπορεύεσθαι. ὑφίσταται Ἀριστέας Χῖος, ὃς
πολλαχοῦ πολλοῦ ἄξιος τῇ στρατιᾷ εἰς τὰ τοιαῦτα
ἐγένετο.

II.

The volunteers attack the enemy, while Xenophon deceives them by a feint.

1 Καὶ ἦν μὲν δείλη, οἱ δ' ἐκέλευον αὐτοὺς ἐμφαγόντας πορεύεσθαι. καὶ τὸν ἡγεμόνα δήσαντες παραδιδόασιν αὐτοῖς, καὶ συντίθενται τὴν μὲν νύκτα, ἢν λάβωσι τὸ ἄκρον, τὸ χωρίον φυλάττειν, ἅμα δὲ τῇ ἡμέρᾳ τῇ σάλπιγγι σημαίνειν· καὶ τοὺς μὲν ἄνω ὄντας ἰέναι ἐπὶ τοὺς κατέχοντας τὴν φανερὰν ἔκβασιν, αὐτοὶ δὲ συμ-
2 βοηθήσειν ἐκβαίνοντες ὡς ἂν δύνωνται τάχιστα. ταῦτα. συνθέμενοι οἱ μὲν ἐπορεύοντο πλῆθος ὡς δισχίλιοι· καὶ ὕδωρ πολὺ ἦν ἐξ οὐρανοῦ· Ξενοφῶν δὲ ἔχων τοὺς ὀπισθοφύλακας ἡγεῖτο πρὸς τὴν φανερὰν ἔκβασιν, ὅπως ταύτῃ τῇ ὁδῷ οἱ πολέμιοι προσέχοιεν τὸν νοῦν καὶ ὡς
3 μάλιστα λάθοιεν οἱ περιιόντες. ἐπεὶ δὲ ἦσαν ἐπὶ χαράδρᾳ οἱ ὀπισθοφύλακες, ἣν ἔδει διαβάντας πρὸς τὸ ὄρθιον ἐκβαίνειν, τηνικαῦτα ἐκύλινδον οἱ βάρβαροι ὁλοιτρόχους ἁμαξιαίους καὶ μείζους καὶ ἐλάττους, οἳ φερόμενοι πρὸς τὰς πέτρας παίοντες διεσφενδονῶντο· καὶ παντάπασιν οὐδὲ πελάσαι οἷόν τ' ἦν τῇ εἰσόδῳ.
4 ἔνιοι δὲ τῶν λοχαγῶν, εἰ μὴ ταύτῃ δύναιντο, ἄλλῃ ἐπειρῶντο· καὶ ταῦτα ἐποίουν μέχρι σκότος ἐγένετο· ἐπεὶ δὲ ᾤοντο ἀφανεῖς εἶναι ἀπιόντες, τότε ἀπῆλθον ἐπὶ τὸ δεῖπνον· ἐτύγχανον δὲ καὶ ἀνάριστοι ὄντες αὐτῶν οἱ ὀπισθοφυλακήσαντες. οἱ μέντοι πολέμιοι οὐδὲν ἐπαύσαντο δι' ὅλης τῆς νυκτὸς κυλίνδοντες τοὺς
5 λίθους· τεκμαίρεσθαι δ' ἦν τῷ ψόφῳ. οἱ δ' ἔχοντες τὸν ἡγεμόνα κύκλῳ περιιόντες καταλαμβάνουσι τοὺς φύλακας ἀμφὶ πῦρ καθημένους· καὶ τοὺς μὲν κατα-κανόντες τοὺς δὲ καταδιώξαντες αὐτοὶ ἐνταῦθ' ἔμενον

ὡς τὸ ἄκρον κατέχοντες. οἱ δ' οὐ κατεῖχον, ἀλλὰ 6
μαστὸς ἦν ὑπὲρ αὐτῶν, παρ' ὃν ἦν ἡ στενὴ αὕτη ὁδός,
ἐφ' ᾗ ἐκάθηντο οἱ φύλακες. ἔφοδος μέντοι αὐτόθεν ἐπὶ
τοὺς πολεμίους ἦν, οἳ ἐπὶ τῇ φανερᾷ ὁδῷ ἐκάθηντο.

The Greeks capture three positions in succession.

καὶ τὴν μὲν νύκτα ἐνταῦθα διήγαγον· ἐπεὶ δ' ἡμέρα 7
ὑπέφαινεν, ἐπορεύοντο σιγῇ συντεταγμένοι ἐπὶ τοὺς
πολεμίους· καὶ γὰρ ὁμίχλη ἐγένετο, ὥστ' ἔλαθον ἐγγὺς
προσελθόντες. ἐπεὶ δὲ εἶδον ἀλλήλους, ἥ τε σάλπιγξ
ἐφθέγξατο καὶ ἀλαλάξαντες ἵεντο ἐπὶ τοὺς ἀνθρώπους·
οἱ δὲ οὐκ ἐδέξαντο, ἀλλὰ λιπόντες τὴν ὁδὸν φεύγοντες
ὀλίγοι ἀπέθνῃσκον· εὔζωνοι γὰρ ἦσαν. οἱ δὲ ἀμφὶ 8
Χειρίσοφον ἀκούσαντες τῆς σάλπιγγος εὐθὺς ἵεντο ἄνω
κατὰ τὴν φανερὰν ὁδόν· ἄλλοι δὲ τῶν στρατηγῶν κατὰ
ἀτριβεῖς ὁδοὺς ἐπορεύοντο, ᾗ ἔτυχον ἕκαστοι ὄντες, καὶ
ἀναβάντες ὡς ἐδύναντο ἀνίμων ἀλλήλους τοῖς δόρασι.
καὶ οὗτοι πρῶτοι συνέμιξαν τοῖς προκαταλαβοῦσι τὸ 9
χωρίον. Ξενοφῶν δὲ ἔχων τῶν ὀπισθοφυλάκων τοὺς
ἡμίσεις ἐπορεύετο ᾗπερ οἱ τὸν ἡγεμόνα ἔχοντες· εὐοδω-
τάτη γὰρ ἦν τοῖς ὑποζυγίοις· τοὺς δὲ ἡμίσεις ὄπισθεν
τῶν ὑποζυγίων ἔταξε. πορευόμενοι δ' ἐντυγχάνουσι 10
λόφῳ ὑπὲρ τῆς ὁδοῦ κατειλημμένῳ ὑπὸ τῶν πολεμίων,
οὓς ἢ ἀποκόψαι ἦν ἀνάγκη ἢ διεζεῦχθαι ἀπὸ τῶν ἄλλων
Ἑλλήνων. καὶ αὐτοὶ μὲν ἂν ἐπορεύθησαν ᾗπερ οἱ
ἄλλοι, τὰ δὲ ὑποζύγια οὐκ ἦν ἄλλῃ ἢ ταύτῃ ἐκβῆναι.
ἔνθα δὴ παρακελευσάμενοι ἀλλήλοις προσβάλλουσι 11
πρὸς τὸν λόφον ὀρθίοις τοῖς λόχοις, οὐ κύκλῳ ἀλλὰ
καταλιπόντες ἄφοδον τοῖς πολεμίοις, εἰ βούλοιντο φεύγειν. καὶ τέως μὲν αὐτοὺς ἀναβαίνοντας, ὅπῃ ἐδύναντο 12
ἕκαστος, οἱ βάρβαροι ἐτόξευον καὶ ἔβαλλον, ἐγγὺς δ' οὐ

προσίεντο, ἀλλὰ φυγῇ λείπουσι τὸ χωρίον. καὶ τοῦτόν
τε παρεληλύθεσαν οἱ Ἕλληνες, καὶ ἕτερον ὁρῶσιν
ἔμπροσθεν λόφον κατεχόμενον ἐπὶ τοῦτον αὖθις ἐδόκει
13 πορεύεσθαι. ἐννοήσας δ' ὁ Ξενοφῶν μή, εἰ ἔρημον
καταλίποι τὸν ἡλωκότα λόφον, καὶ πάλιν λαβόντες οἱ
πολέμιοι ἐπιθοῖντο τοῖς ὑποζυγίοις παριοῦσιν—ἐπὶ πολὺ
δ' ἦν τὰ ὑποζύγια ἅτε διὰ στενῆς τῆς ὁδοῦ πορευόμενα—καταλείπει ἐπὶ τοῦ λόφου λοχαγοὺς Κηφισόδωρον
Κηφισοφῶντος Ἀθηναῖον καὶ Ἀμφικράτην Ἀμφιδήμου
Ἀθηναῖον καὶ Ἀρχαγόραν Ἀργεῖον φυγάδα, αὐτὸς δὲ
σὺν τοῖς λοιποῖς ἐπορεύετο ἐπὶ τὸν δεύτερον λόφον, καὶ
14 τῷ αὐτῷ τρόπῳ καὶ τοῦτον αἱροῦσιν. ἔτι δ' αὐτοῖς
τρίτος μαστὸς λοιπὸς ἦν πολὺ ὀρθιώτατος ὁ ὑπὲρ τῆς
ἐπὶ τῷ πυρὶ καταληφθείσης φυλακῆς τῆς νυκτὸς ὑπὸ
15 τῶν ἐθελοντῶν. ἐπεὶ δ' ἐγγὺς ἐγένοντο οἱ Ἕλληνες,
λείπουσιν οἱ βάρβαροι ἀμαχητὶ τὸν μαστόν, ὥστε θαυμαστὸν πᾶσι γενέσθαι καὶ ὑπώπτευον δείσαντας αὐτούς,
μὴ κυκλωθέντες πολιορκοῖντο, ἀπολιπεῖν. οἱ δ' ἄρα
ἀπὸ τοῦ ἄκρου καθορῶντες τὰ ὄπισθεν γιγνόμενα πάντες
16 ἐπὶ τοὺς ὀπισθοφύλακας ἐχώρουν. καὶ Ξειοφῶν μὲν
σὺν τοῖς νεωτάτοις ἀνέβαινεν ἐπὶ τὸ ἄκρον, τοὺς δὲ
ἄλλους ἐκέλευσεν ὑπάγειν, ὅπως οἱ τελευταῖοι λόχοι
προσμίξειαν, καὶ προελθόντας κατὰ τὴν ὁδὸν ἐν τῷ
17 ὁμαλῷ θέσθαι τὰ ὅπλα εἶπε. καὶ ἐν τούτῳ τῷ χρόνῳ
ἦλθεν Ἀρχαγόρας ὁ Ἀργεῖος πεφευγὼς καὶ λέγει ὡς
ἀπεκόπησαν ἀπὸ τοῦ λόφου καὶ ὅτι τεθνᾶσι Κηφισό-
δωρος καὶ Ἀμφικράτης καὶ ἄλλοι ὅσοι μὴ ἁλάμενοι
κατὰ τῆς πέτρας πρὸς τοὺς ὀπισθοφύλακας ἀφίκοντο.

*The Greeks are in great danger.   They encamp in a
well-stocked village.*

ταῦτα δὲ διαπραξάμενοι οἱ βάρβαροι ἧκον ἐπ' ἀντί- 18
πορον λόφον τῷ μαστῷ· καὶ Ξενοφῶν διελέγετο αὐτοῖς
δι' ἑρμηνέως περὶ σπονδῶν καὶ τοὺς νεκροὺς ἀπῄτει. οἱ 19
δὲ ἔφασαν ἀποδώσειν ἐφ' ᾧ μὴ καίειν τὰς οἰκίας.
συνωμολόγει ταῦτα ὁ Ξενοφῶν. ἐν ᾧ δὲ τὸ μὲν ἄλλο
στράτευμα παρῄει, οἱ δὲ ταῦτα διελέγοντο, πάντες οἱ ἐκ
τούτου τοῦ τόπου συνερρύησαν ἐνταῦθα πολέμιοι. καὶ 20
ἐπεὶ ἤρξαντο καταβαίνειν ἀπὸ τοῦ μαστοῦ πρὸς τοὺς
ἄλλους ἔνθα τὰ ὅπλα ἔκειντο, ἵεντο δὴ οἱ πολέμιοι
πολλῷ πλήθει καὶ θορύβῳ· καὶ ἐπεὶ ἐγένοντο ἐπὶ τῆς
κορυφῆς τοῦ μαστοῦ, ἀφ' οὗ Ξενοφῶν κατέβαινεν, ἐκύλινδον πέτρους· καὶ ἑνὸς μὲν κατέαξαν τὸ σκέλος,
Ξενοφῶντα δὲ ὁ ὑπασπιστὴς ἔχων τὴν ἀσπίδα ἀπέ-
λιπεν· Εὐρύλοχος δὲ Λουσιεὺς Ἀρκὰς προσέδραμεν 21
αὐτῷ ὁπλίτης, καὶ πρὸ ἀμφοῖν προβεβλημένος ἀπεχώρει,
καὶ οἱ ἄλλοι πρὸς τοὺς συντεταγμένους ἀπῆλθον. ἐκ 22
δὲ τούτου πᾶν ὁμοῦ ἐγένετο τὸ Ἑλληνικόν, καὶ ἐσκήνησαν αὐτοῦ ἐν πολλαῖς καὶ καλαῖς οἰκίαις καὶ ἐπιτηδείοις δαψιλέσι· καὶ γὰρ οἶνος πολὺς ἦν, ὥστε ἐν
λάκκοις κονιατοῖς εἶχον. Ξενοφῶν δὲ καὶ Χειρίσοφος 23
διεπράξαντο ὥστε λαβόντες τοὺς νεκροὺς ἀπέδοσαν τὸν
ἡγεμόνα· καὶ πάντα ἐποίησαν τοῖς ἀποθανοῦσιν ἐκ
τῶν δυνατῶν ὥσπερ νομίζεται ἀνδράσιν ἀγαθοῖς.

*They continue their march still harassed by the
mountaineers.*

τῇ δὲ ὑστεραίᾳ ἄνευ ἡγεμόνος ἐπορεύοντο· μαχόμενοι 24
δ' οἱ πολέμιοι καὶ ὅπῃ εἴη στενὸν χωρίου προκατα-
λαμβάνοντες ἐκώλυον τὰς παρόδους. ὁπότε μὲν οὖν 25

τοὺς πρώτους κωλύοιεν, Ξενοφῶν ὄπισθεν ἐκβαίνων
πρὸς τὰ ὄρη ἔλυε τὴν ἀπόφραξιν τῆς παρόδου τοῖς
πρώτοις ἀνωτέρω πειρώμενος γίγνεσθαι τῶν κωλυόντων·
26 ὁπότε δὲ τοῖς ὄπισθεν ἐπιθοῖντο, Χειρίσοφος ἐκβαίνων
καὶ πειρώμενος ἀνωτέρω γίγνεσθαι τῶν κωλυόντων ἔλυε
τὴν ἀπόφραξιν τῆς παρόδου τοῖς ὄπισθεν· καὶ ἀεὶ
οὕτως ἐβοήθουν ἀλλήλοις καὶ ἰσχυρῶς ἀλλήλων ἐπεμέ-
27 λοντο. ἦν δὲ καὶ ὁπότε αὐτοῖς τοῖς ἀναβᾶσι πολλὰ
πράγματα παρεῖχον οἱ βάρβαροι πάλιν καταβαίνουσιν·
ἐλαφροὶ γὰρ ἦσαν ὥστε καὶ ἐγγύθεν φεύγοντες ἀποφεύ-
γειν· οὐδὲν γὰρ εἶχον ἄλλο ἢ τόξα καὶ σφενδόνας.
28 ἄριστοι δὲ τοξόται ἦσαν· εἶχον δὲ τόξα ἐγγὺς τριπήχη,
τὰ δὲ τοξεύματα πλέον ἢ διπήχη· εἷλκον δὲ τὰς νευράς,
ὁπότε τοξεύοιεν, πρὸς τὸ κάτω τοῦ τόξου τῷ ἀριστερῷ
ποδὶ προσβαίνοντες. τὰ δὲ τοξεύματα ἐχώρει διὰ τῶν
ἀσπίδων καὶ διὰ τῶν θωράκων. ἐχρῶντο δὲ αὐτοῖς οἱ
Ἕλληνες, ἐπεὶ λάβοιεν, ἀκοντίοις ἐναγκυλῶντες. ἐν
τούτοις τοῖς χωρίοις οἱ Κρῆτες χρησιμώτατοι ἐγένοντο.
ἦρχε δὲ αὐτῶν Στρατοκλῆς Κρής.

III.

The Greeks reach the river Centrites.

1   Ταύτην δ' αὖ τὴν ἡμέραν ηὐλίσθησαν ἐν ταῖς κώμαις
ταῖς ὑπὲρ τοῦ πεδίου τοῦ παρὰ τὸν Κεντρίτην ποταμόν,
εὖρος ὡς δίπλεθρον, ὃς ὁρίζει τὴν Ἀρμενίαν καὶ τὴν
τῶν Καρδούχων χώραν. καὶ οἱ Ἕλληνες ἐνταῦθα
ἀνέπνευσαν ἄσμενοι ἰδόντες πεδίον· ἀπεῖχε δὲ τῶν
ὀρέων ὁ ποταμὸς ἓξ ἢ ἑπτὰ στάδια τῶν Καρδούχων.

τότε μὲν οὖν ηὐλίσθησαν μάλα ἡδέως καὶ τἀπιτήδεια 2
ἔχοντες καὶ πολλὰ τῶν παρεληλυθότων πόνων μνημο-
νεύοντες. ἑπτὰ γὰρ ἡμέρας, ὅσασπερ ἐπορεύθησαν διὰ
τῶν Καρδούχων, πάσας μαχόμενοι διετέλεσαν, καὶ
ἔπαθον κακὰ ὅσα οὐδὲ τὰ σύμπαντα ὑπὸ βασιλέως καὶ
Τισσαφέρνους. ὡς οὖν ἀπηλλαγμένοι τούτων ἡδέως
ἐκοιμήθησαν.

They are threatened by the hostile force on the opposite
bank and by the Carduchians in their rear.

ἅμα δὲ τῇ ἡμέρᾳ ὁρῶσιν ἱππέας που πέραν τοῦ 3
ποταμοῦ ἐξωπλισμένους ὡς κωλύσοντας διαβαίνειν,
πεζοὺς δ᾽ ἐπὶ ταῖς ὄχθαις παρατεταγμένους ἄνω τῶν
ἱππέων ὡς κωλύσοντας εἰς τὴν Ἀρμενίαν ἐκβαίνειν.
ἦσαν δ᾽ οὗτοι Ὀρόντα καὶ Ἀρτούχα, Ἀρμένιοι καὶ 4
Μάρδοι καὶ Χαλδαῖοι μισθοφόροι. ἐλέγοντο δὲ οἱ
Χαλδαῖοι ἐλεύθεροί τε καὶ ἄλκιμοι εἶναι· ὅπλα δ᾽ εἶχον
γέρρα μακρὰ καὶ λόγχας. αἱ δὲ ὄχθαι αὗται, ἐφ᾽ ὧν 5
παρατεταγμένοι οὗτοι ἦσαν, τρία ἢ τέτταρα πλέθρα
ἀπὸ τοῦ ποταμοῦ ἀπεῖχον· ὁδὸς δὲ μία ἡ ὁρωμένη ἦν
ἄγουσα ἄνω ὥσπερ χειροποίητος· ταύτῃ ἐπειρῶντο
διαβαίνειν οἱ Ἕλληνες. ἐπεὶ δὲ πειρωμένοις τό τε 6
ὕδωρ ὑπὲρ τῶν μαστῶν ἐφαίνετο, καὶ τραχὺς ἦν ὁ
ποταμὸς μεγάλοις λίθοις καὶ ὀλισθηροῖς, καὶ οὔτ᾽ ἐν τῷ
ὕδατι τὰ ὅπλα ἦν ἔχειν—εἰ δὲ μή, ἥρπαζεν ὁ ποταμός—
ἐπί τε τῆς κεφαλῆς τὰ ὅπλα εἴ τις φέροι, γυμνοὶ
ἐγίγνοντο πρὸς τὰ τοξεύματα καὶ τἆλλα βέλη, ἀνεχώ-
ρησαν καὶ αὐτοῦ ἐστρατοπεδεύσαντο παρὰ τὸν ποταμόν.
ἔνθα δὲ αὐτοὶ τὴν πρόσθεν νύκτα ἦσαν, ἐπὶ τοῦ ὄρους 7
ἑώρων τοὺς Καρδούχους πολλοὺς συνειλεγμένους ἐν

τοῖς ὅπλοις. ἐνταῦθα δὴ πολλὴ ἀθυμία ἦν τοῖς
Ἕλλησιν, ὁρῶσι μὲν τοῦ ποταμοῦ τὴν δυσπορίαν,
ὁρῶσι δὲ τοὺς διαβαίνειν κωλύσοντας, ὁρῶσι δὲ τοῖς
διαβαίνουσιν ἐπικεισομένους τοὺς Καρδούχους ὄπισθεν.

Xenophon's dream and its fulfilment.

8 ταύτην μὲν οὖν τὴν ἡμέραν καὶ νύκτα ἔμειναν ἐν
πολλῇ ἀπορίᾳ ὄντες. Ξενοφῶν δὲ ὄναρ εἶδεν· ἔδοξεν
ἐν πέδαις δεδέσθαι, αὗται δὲ αὐτῷ αὐτόμαται περιρρυῆναι, ὥστε λυθῆναι καὶ διαβαίνειν ὁπόσον ἐβούλετο.
ἐπεὶ δὲ ὄρθρος ἦν, ἔρχεται πρὸς τὸν Χειρίσοφον καὶ
λέγει ὅτι ἐλπίδας ἔχει καλῶς ἔσεσθαι, καὶ διηγεῖται
9 αὐτῷ τὸ ὄναρ. ὁ δὲ ἥδετό τε καί, ὡς τάχιστα ἕως
ὑπέφαινεν, ἐθύοντο πάντες παρόντες οἱ στρατηγοί· καὶ
τὰ ἱερὰ καλὰ ἦν εὐθὺς ἐπὶ τοῦ πρώτου. καὶ ἀπιόντες
ἀπὸ τῶν ἱερῶν οἱ στρατηγοὶ καὶ λοχαγοὶ παρήγγελλον
10 τῇ στρατιᾷ ἀριστοποιεῖσθαι. καὶ ἀριστῶντι τῷ Ξενοφῶντι προσέτρεχον δύο νεανίσκω· ᾔδεσαν γὰρ πάντες
ὅτι ἐξείη αὐτῷ καὶ ἀριστῶντι καὶ δειπνοῦντι προσελθεῖν
καί, εἰ καθεύδοι, ἐπεγείραντα εἰπεῖν, εἴ τίς τι ἔχοι τῶν
11 πρὸς τὸν πόλεμον. καὶ τότε ἔλεγον ὅτι τυγχάνοιεν
φρύγανα συλλέγοντες ὡς ἐπὶ πῦρ, κἄπειτα κατίδοιεν
ἐν τῷ πέραν ἐν πέτραις καθηκούσαις ἐπ' αὐτὸν τὸν
ποταμὸν γέροντά τε καὶ γυναῖκα καὶ παιδίσκας ὥσπερ
μαρσίπους ἱματίων κατατιθεμένους ἐν πέτρᾳ ἀντρώδει.
12 ἰδοῦσι δὲ σφίσι δόξαι ἀσφαλὲς εἶναι διαβῆναι· οὐδὲ
γὰρ τοῖς πολεμίοις ἱππεῦσι προσβατὸν εἶναι κατὰ
τοῦτο. ἐκδύντες δ' ἔφασαν ἔχοντες τὰ ἐγχειρίδια
γυμνοὶ ὡς νευσούμενοι διαβαίνειν· πορευόμενοι δὲ
πρόσθεν διαβῆναι πρὶν βρέξαι τὴν γαστέρα· καὶ
13 διαβάντες λαβόντες τὰ ἱμάτια πάλιν ἥκειν. εὐθὺς

οὖν ὁ Ξενοφῶν αὐτός τε ἔσπειδε καὶ τοῖς νεανίσκοις
ἐγχεῖν ἐκέλευε καὶ εὔχεσθαι τοῖς φήνασι θεοῖς τά τε
ὀνείρατα καὶ τὸν πόρον καὶ τὰ λοιπὰ ἀγαθὰ ἐπιτελέσαι.
σπείσας δ᾽ εὐθὺς ἦγε τοὺς νεανίσκους παρὰ τὸν Χειρίσοφον, καὶ διηγοῦνται ταῦτά. ἀκούσας δὲ καὶ ὁ Χειρίσοφος σπονδὰς ἐποίει.

Plan for crossing the river.

σπείσαντες δὲ τοῖς μὲν ἄλλοις παρήγγελλον συ- 14
σκευάζεσθαι, αὐτοὶ δὲ συγκαλέσαντες τοὺς στρατηγοὺς
ἐβουλεύοντο ὅπως ἂν κάλλιστα διαβαῖεν καὶ τούς τε
ἔμπροσθεν νικῷεν καὶ ὑπὸ τῶν ὄπισθεν μηδὲν πάσχοιεν
κακόν. καὶ ἔδοξεν αὐτοῖς Χειρίσοφον μὲν ἡγεῖσθαι καὶ 15
διαβαίνειν ἔχοντα τὸ ἥμισυ τοῦ στρατεύματος, τὸ δ᾽
ἥμισυ ἔτι ὑπομένειν σὺν Ξενοφῶντι, τὰ δὲ ὑποζύγια
καὶ τὸν ὄχλον ἐν μέσῳ τούτων διαβαίνειν. ἐπεὶ δὲ 16
ταῦτα καλῶς εἶχεν, ἐπορεύοντο· ἡγοῦντο δ᾽ οἱ νεανίσκοι
ἐν ἀριστερᾷ ἔχοντες τὸν ποταμόν· ὁδὸς δὲ ἦν ἐπὶ τὴν
διάβασιν ὡς τέτταρες στάδιοι. πορευομένων δ᾽ αὐτῶν 17
ἀντιπαρῇσαν αἱ τάξεις τῶν ἱππέων. ἐπειδὴ δὲ ἦσαν
κατὰ τὴν διάβασιν καὶ τὰς ὄχθας τοῦ ποταμοῦ, ἔθεντο
τὰ ὅπλα, καὶ αὐτὸς πρῶτος Χειρίσοφος στεφανωσάμενος
καὶ ἀποδὺς ἐλάμβανε τὰ ὅπλα καὶ τοῖς ἄλλοις πᾶσι
παρήγγελλε, καὶ τοὺς λοχαγοὺς ἐκέλευεν ἄγειν τοὺς
λόχους ὀρθίους, τοὺς μὲν ἐν ἀριστερᾷ, τοῖς δ᾽ ἐν δεξιᾷ
ἑαυτοῦ. καὶ οἱ μὲν μάντεις ἐσφαγιάζοντο εἰς τὸν 18
ποταμόν· οἱ δὲ πολέμιοι ἐτόξευον καὶ ἐσφενδόνων·
ἀλλ᾽ οὔπω ἐξικνοῦντο· ἐπεὶ δὲ καλὰ ἦν τὰ σφάγια, 19
ἐπαιάνιζον πάντες οἱ στρατιῶται καὶ ἀνηλάλαζον,
συνωλόλυζον δὲ καὶ αἱ γυναῖκες ἅπασαι· πολλαὶ γὰρ
ἦσαν ἐν τῷ στρατεύματι.

Xenophon deceives the enemy by a feint.

20　καὶ Χειρίσοφος μὲν ἐνέβαινε καὶ οἱ σὺν ἐκείνῳ· ὁ
δὲ Ξενοφῶν τῶν ὀπισθοφυλάκων λαβὼν τοὺς εὐζωνοτά-
τους ἔθει ἀνὰ κράτος πάλιν ἐπὶ τὸν πόρον τὸν κατὰ τὴν
ἔκβασιν τὴν εἰς τὰ τῶν Ἀρμενίων ὄρη, προσποιούμενος
ταύτῃ διαβὰς ἀποκλείσειν τοὺς παρὰ τὸν ποταμὸν
21 ἱππέας. οἱ δὲ πολέμιοι ὁρῶντες μὲν τοὺς ἀμφὶ Χειρίσοφον εὐπετῶς τὸ ὕδωρ περῶντας, ὁρῶντες δὲ τοὺς
ἀμφὶ Ξενοφῶντα θέοντας εἰς τοὔμπαλιν, δείσαντες μὴ
ἀποληφθείησαν, φεύγουσιν ἀνὰ κράτος ὡς πρὸς τὴν τοῦ
ποταμοῦ ἄνω ἔκβασιν. ἐπεὶ δὲ κατὰ τὴν ὁδὸν ἐγένοντο,
22 ἔτεινον ἄνω πρὸς τὸ ὄρος. Λύκιος δ' ὁ τὴν τάξιν ἔχων
τῶν ἱππέων καὶ Αἰσχίνης ὁ τὴν τάξιν τῶν πελταστῶν
τῶν ἀμφὶ Χειρίσοφον, ἐπεὶ ἑώρων ἀνὰ κράτος φεύγοντας,
εἵποντο· οἱ δὲ στρατιῶται ἐβόων μὴ ἀπολείπεσθαι,
23 ἀλλὰ συνεκβαίνειν ἐπὶ τὸ ὄρος. Χειρίσοφος δ' αὖ ἐπεὶ
διέβη, τοὺς μὲν ἱππέας οὐκ ἐδίωκεν, εὐθὺς δὲ κατὰ τὰς
προσηκούσας ὄχθας ἐπὶ τὸν ποταμὸν ἐξέβαινεν ἐπὶ
τοὺς ἄνω πολεμίους. οἱ δὲ ἄνω, ὁρῶντες μὲν τοὺς
ἑαυτῶν ἱππέας φεύγοντας, ὁρῶντες δ' ὁπλίτας σφίσιν
ἐπιόντας, ἐκλείπουσι τὰ ὑπὲρ τοῦ ποταμοῦ ἄκρα.
24 Ξενοφῶν δ' ἐπεὶ τὰ πέραν ἑώρα καλῶς γιγνόμενα,
ἀπεχώρει τὴν ταχίστην πρὸς τὸ διαβαῖνον στράτευμα·
καὶ γὰρ οἱ Καρδοῦχοι φανεροὶ ἤδη ἦσαν εἰς τὸ πεδίον
25 καταβαίνοντες ὡς ἐπιθησόμενοι τοῖς τελευταίοις. καὶ
Χειρίσοφος μὲν τὰ ἄνω κατεῖχε, Λύκιος δὲ σὺν ὀλίγοις
ἐπιχειρήσας ἐπιδιῶξαι ἔλαβε τῶν σκευοφόρων τὰ ὑπολειπόμενα καὶ μετὰ τούτων ἐσθῆτά τε καλὴν καὶ
26 ἐκπώματα. καὶ τὰ μὲν σκευοφόρα τῶν Ἑλλήνων καὶ
ὁ ὄχλος ἀκμὴν διέβαινε, Ξενοφῶν δὲ στρέψας πρὸς

τοὺς Καρδούχους ἀντία τὰ ὅπλα ἔθετο, καὶ παρήγγειλε
τοῖς λοχαγοῖς κατ' ἐνωμοτίας ποιήσασθαι ἕκαστον τὸν
ἑαυτοῦ λόχον, παρ' ἀσπίδα παραγαγόντας τὴν ἐνω-
μοτίαν ἐπὶ φάλαγγος· καὶ τοὺς μὲν λοχαγοὺς καὶ τοὺς
ἐνωμοτάρχους πρὸς τῶν Καρδούχων ἰέναι, οὐραγοὺς δὲ
καταστήσασθαι πρὸς τοῦ ποταμοῦ.

*The Greeks repel the Carduchians and succeed in crossing
the river.*

οἱ δὲ Καρδοῦχοι ὡς ἑώρων τοὺς ὀπισθοφύλακας τοῦ 27
ὄχλου ψιλουμένους καὶ ὀλίγους ἤδη φαινομένους, θᾶττον
δὴ ἐπῇσαν ᾠδάς τινας ᾄδοντες. ὁ δὲ Χειρίσοφος, ἐπεὶ
τὰ παρ' αὑτῷ ἀσφαλῶς εἶχε, πέμπει παρὰ Ξενοφῶντα
τοὺς πελταστὰς καὶ σφενδονήτας καὶ τοξότας καὶ
κελεύει ποιεῖν ὅ τι ἂν παραγγέλλῃ. ἰδὼν δ' αὐτοὺς 28
διαβαίνοντας ὁ Ξενοφῶν πέμψας ἄγγελον κελεύει αὐτοῦ
μεῖναι ἐπὶ τοῦ ποταμοῦ μὴ διαβάντας· ὅταν δ' ἄρξωνται αὐτοὶ διαβαίνειν, ἐναντίους ἔνθεν καὶ ἔνθεν σφῶν
ἐμβαίνειν ὡς διαβησομένους, διηγκυλωμένους τοὺς
ἀκοντιστὰς καὶ ἐπιβεβλημένους τοὺς τοξότας· μὴ πρόσω
δὲ τοῦ ποταμοῦ προβαίνειν. τοῖς δὲ παρ' ἑαυτῷ παρήγ- 29
γειλεν, ἐπειδὰν σφενδόνη ἐξικνῆται καὶ ἀσπὶς ψοφῇ,
παιανίσαντας θεῖν εἰς τοὺς πολεμίους· ἐπειδὰν δ' ἀνα-
στρέψωσιν οἱ πολέμιοι καὶ ἐκ τοῦ ποταμοῦ ὁ σαλπικτὴς
σημήνῃ τὸ πολεμικόν, ἀναστρέψαντας ἐπὶ δόρυ ἡγεῖσθαι
μὲν τοὺς οὐραγούς, θεῖν δὲ πάντας καὶ διαβαίνειν ὅτι
τάχιστα ᾗ ἕκαστος τὴν τάξιν εἶχεν, ὡς μὴ ἐμποδίζειν
ἀλλήλους· ὅτι οὗτος ἄριστος ἔσοιτο ὃς ἂν πρῶτος ἐν
τῷ πέραν γένηται. οἱ δὲ Καρδοῦχοι ὁρῶντες ὀλίγους 30
ἤδη τοὺς λοιπούς—πολλοὶ γὰρ καὶ τῶν μένειν τε-
ταγμένων ᾤχοντο ἐπιμελόμενοι οἱ μὲν ὑποζυγίων,

οἱ δὲ σκευῶν—ἐνταῦθα δὴ ἐπέκειντο θρασέως καὶ
31 ἤρχοντο σφενδονᾶν καὶ τοξεύειν. οἱ δὲ Ἕλληνες
παιανίσαντες ὥρμησαν δρόμῳ ἐπ᾽ αὐτούς· οἱ δὲ οὐκ
ἐδέξαντο· καὶ γὰρ ἦσαν ὡπλισμένοι, ὡς μὲν ἐν τοῖς
ὄρεσιν ἱκανῶς πρὸς τὸ ἐπιδραμεῖν καὶ φεύγειν, πρὸς
32 δὲ τὸ εἰς χεῖρας δέχεσθαι οὐχ ἱκανῶς. ἐν τούτῳ ση-
μαίνει ὁ σαλπικτής· καὶ οἱ μὲν πολέμιοι ἔφευγον πολὺ
ἔτι θᾶττον, οἱ δὲ Ἕλληνες τἀναντία στρέψαντες ἔφευγον
33 διὰ τοῦ ποταμοῦ ὅτι τάχιστα. τῶν δὲ πολεμίων οἱ
μέν τινες αἰσθόμενοι πάλιν ἔδραμον ἐπὶ τὸν ποταμὸν
καὶ τοξεύοντες ὀλίγους ἔτρωσαν, οἱ δὲ πολλοὶ καὶ πέραν
ὄντων τῶν Ἑλλήνων ἔτι φανεροὶ ἦσαν φεύγοντες. οἱ
δὲ ὑπαντήσαντες ἀνδριζόμενοι καὶ προσωτέρω τοῦ καιροῦ προϊόντες ὕστερον τῶν μετὰ Ξενοφῶντος διέβησαν
πάλιν· καὶ ἐτρώθησάν τινες καὶ τούτων.

IV.

The Greeks in Armenia.

1   Ἐπεὶ δὲ διέβησαν, συνταξάμενοι ἀμφὶ μέσον ἡμέρας
ἐπορεύθησαν διὰ τῆς Ἀρμενίας πεδίον ἅπαν καὶ λείους
γηλόφους οὐ μεῖον ἢ πέντε παρασάγγας· οὐ γὰρ ἦσαν
ἐγγὺς τοῦ ποταμοῦ κῶμαι διὰ τοὺς πολέμους τοὺς πρὸς
2 τοὺς Καρδούχους. εἰς δὲ ἣν ἀφίκοντο κώμην μεγάλη
τε ἦν καὶ βασίλειον εἶχε τῷ σατράπῃ καὶ ἐπὶ ταῖς
πλείσταις οἰκίαις τύρσεις ἐπῆσαν· ἐπιτήδεια δ᾽ ἦν
δαψιλῆ. ἐντεῦθεν δ᾽ ἐπορεύθησαν σταθμοὺς δύο, παρασάγγας δέκα, μέχρι ὑπερῆλθον τὰς πηγὰς τοῦ Τίγρητος
3 ποταμοῦ. ἐντεῦθεν δ᾽ ἐπορεύθησαν σταθμοὺς τρεῖς,

παρασάγγας πεντεκαίδεκα, ἐπὶ τὸν Τηλεβόαν ποταμόν.
οὗτος δ᾽ ἦν καλὸς μέν, μέγας δ᾽ οὔ· κῶμαι δὲ πολλαὶ
περὶ τὸν ποταμὸν ἦσαν. ὁ δὲ τόπος οὗτος Ἀρμενία 4
ἐκαλεῖτο ἡ πρὸς ἑσπέραν. ὕπαρχος δ᾽ ἦν αὐτῆς Τιρίβαζος, ὁ καὶ βασιλεῖ φίλος γενόμενος, καὶ ὁπότε παρείη,
οὐδεὶς ἄλλος βασιλέα ἐπὶ τὸν ἵππον ἀνέβαλλεν. οὗτος 5
προσήλασεν ἱππέας ἔχων, καὶ προπέμψας ἑρμηνέα
εἶπεν ὅτι βούλοιτο διαλεχθῆναι τοῖς ἄρχουσι. τοῖς δὲ
στρατηγοῖς ἔδοξεν ἀκοῦσαι· καὶ προσελθόντες εἰς ἐπήκοον ἠρώτων τί θέλοι. ὁ δὲ εἶπεν ὅτι σπείσασθαι 6
βούλοιτο ἐφ᾽ ᾧ μήτε αὐτὸς τοὺς Ἕλληνας ἀδικεῖν μήτε
ἐκείνους καίειν τὰς οἰκίας, λαμβάνειν τε τἀπιτήδεια
ὅσων δέοιντο. ἔδοξε ταῦτα τοῖς στρατηγοῖς καὶ ἐσπεί-
σαντο ἐπὶ τούτοις.

Winter sets in. Difficulties of the Greeks.

ἐντεῦθεν δ᾽ ἐπορεύθησαν σταθμοὺς τρεῖς διὰ πεδίου, 7
παρασάγγας πεντεκαίδεκα· καὶ Τιρίβαζος παρηκολούθει
ἔχων τὴν ἑαυτοῦ δύναμιν, ἀπέχων ὡς δέκα σταδίους·
καὶ ἀφίκοντο εἰς βασίλεια καὶ κώμας πέριξ πολλὰς
πολλῶν τῶν ἐπιτηδείων μεστάς. στρατοπεδευομένων 8
δ᾽ αὐτῶν γίγνεται τῆς νυκτὸς χιὼν πολλή· καὶ ἕωθεν
ἔδοξε διασκηνῆσαι τὰς τάξεις καὶ τοὺς στρατηγοὺς
κατὰ τὰς κώμας· οὐ γὰρ ἑώρων πολέμιον οὐδένα καὶ
ἀσφαλὲς ἐδόκει εἶναι διὰ τὸ πλῆθος τῆς χιόνος. ἐνταῦθα 9
εἶχον τὰ ἐπιτήδεια ὅσα ἐστὶν ἀγαθά, ἱερεῖα, σῖτον,
οἴνους παλαιοὺς εὐώδεις, ἀσταφίδας, ὄσπρια παντοδαπά.
τῶν δὲ ἀποσκεδαννυμένων τινὲς ἀπὸ τοῦ στρατοπέδου
ἔλεγον ὅτι κατίδοιεν νύκτωρ πολλὰ πυρὰ φαίνοντα.
ἐδόκει δὴ τοῖς στρατηγοῖς οὐκ ἀσφαλὲς εἶναι διασκηνοῦν, 10

ἀλλὰ συναγαγεῖν τὸ στράτευμα πάλιν. ἐντεῦθεν συν-
11 ῆλθον· καὶ γὰρ ἐδόκει διαιθριάζειν. νυκτερευόντων δ'
αὐτῶν ἐνταῦθα ἐπιπίπτει χιὼν ἄπλετος, ὥστε ἀπο-
κρύψαι καὶ τὰ ὅπλα καὶ τοὺς ἀνθρώπους κατακειμέ-
νους· καὶ τὰ ὑποζύγια συνεπόδισεν ἡ χιών· καὶ πολὺς
ὄκνος ἦν ἀνίστασθαι· κατακειμένων γὰρ ἀλεεινὸν ἦν
12 ἡ χιὼν ἐπιπεπτωκυῖα ὅτῳ μὴ παραρρυείη. ἐπεὶ δὲ
Ξενοφῶν ἐτόλμησε γυμνὸς ἀναστὰς σχίζειν ξύλα, τάχ'
ἀναστάς τις καὶ ἄλλος ἐκείνου ἀφελόμενος ἔσχιζεν. ἐκ
δὲ τούτου καὶ ἄλλοι ἀναστάντες πῦρ ἔκαιον καὶ ἐχρίοντο·
13 πολὺ γὰρ ἐνταῦθα εὑρίσκετο χρῖμα, ᾧ ἐχρῶντο ἀντ'
ἐλαίου, σύειον καὶ σησάμινον καὶ ἀμυγδάλινον ἐκ τῶν
πικρῶν καὶ τερμίνθινον. ἐκ δὲ τῶν αὐτῶν τούτων καὶ
μύρον εὑρίσκετο.

*The Greeks send out a reconnoitring party; after which
they attack and plunder the camp of Tiribazus.*

14   μετὰ ταῦτα ἐδόκει πάλιν διασκηνητέον εἶναι εἰς τὰς
κώμας εἰς στέγας. ἔνθα δὴ οἱ στρατιῶται σὺν πολλῇ
κραυγῇ καὶ ἡδονῇ ᾖσαν ἐπὶ τὰς στέγας καὶ τὰ ἐπι-
τήδεια· ὅσοι δέ, ὅτε τὸ πρότερον ἀπῆσαν, τὰς οἰκίας
ἐνέπρησαν ὑπὸ ἀτασθαλίας, δίκην ἐδίδοσαν κακῶς
15 σκηνοῦντες. ἐντεῦθεν ἔπεμψαν νυκτὸς Δημοκράτην
Τημνίτην ἄνδρας δόντες ἐπὶ τὰ ὄρη, ἔνθα ἔφασαν οἱ
ἀποσκεδαννύμενοι καθορᾶν τὰ πυρά· οὗτος γὰρ ἐδόκει
καὶ πρότερον πολλὰ ἤδη ἀληθεῦσαι τοιαῦτα, τὰ ὄντα
16 τε ὡς ὄντα καὶ τὰ μὴ ὄντα ὡς οὐκ ὄντα. πορευθεὶς
δὲ τὰ μὲν πυρὰ οὐκ ἔφη ἰδεῖν, ἄνδρα δὲ συλλαβὼν
ἧκεν ἄγων ἔχοντα τόξον Περσικὸν καὶ φαρέτραν καὶ

σάγαριν, οἷανπερ καὶ αἱ Ἀμαζόνες ἔχουσιν. ἐρωτώμενος 17
δὲ ποδαπὸς εἴη, Πέρσης μὲν ἔφη εἶναι, πορεύεσθαι δ'
ἀπὸ τοῦ Τιριβάζου στρατοπέδου, ὅπως ἐπιτήδεια λάβοι.
οἱ δὲ ἠρώτων αὐτὸν τὸ στράτευμα ὁπόσον τε εἴη καὶ
ἐπὶ τίνι συνειλεγμένον. ὁ δὲ εἶπεν ὅτι Τιρίβαζος εἴη 18
ἔχων τήν τε ἑαυτοῦ δύναμιν καὶ μισθοφόρους Χάλυβας
καὶ Ταόχους· παρεσκευάσθαι δὲ αὐτὸν ἔφη ὡς ἐπὶ τῇ
ὑπερβολῇ τοῦ ὄρους ἐν τοῖς στενοῖς, ᾗπερ μοναχῇ εἴη
πορεία, ἐνταῦθα ἐπιθησόμενον τοῖς Ἕλλησιν. ἀκού- 19
σασι τοῖς στρατηγοῖς ταῦτα ἔδοξε τὸ στράτευμα συνα-
γαγεῖν· καὶ εὐθὺς φύλακας καταλιπόντες καὶ στρατη-
γὸν ἐπὶ τοῖς μένουσι Σοφαίνετον Στυμφάλιον ἐπορεύοντο
ἔχοντες ἡγεμόνα τὸν ἁλόντα ἄνθρωπον. ἐπειδὴ δὲ 20
ὑπερέβαλλον τὰ ὄρη, οἱ πελτασταὶ προϊόντες καὶ
κατιδόντες τὸ στρατόπεδον οὐκ ἔμειναν τοὺς ὁπλίτας,
ἀλλ' ἀνακραγόντες ἔθεον ἐπὶ τὸ στρατόπεδον. οἱ δὲ 21
βάρβαροι ἀκούσαντες τὸν θόρυβον οὐχ ὑπέμειναν, ἀλλ'
ἔφευγον· ὅμως δὲ καὶ ἀπέθανόν τινες τῶν βαρβάρων
καὶ ἵπποι ἥλωσαν εἰς εἴκοσι καὶ ἡ σκηνὴ ἡ Τιριβάζου
ἑάλω καὶ ἐν αὐτῇ κλῖναι ἀργυρόποδες καὶ ἐκπώματα
καὶ οἱ ἀρτοκόποι καὶ οἱ οἰνοχόοι φάσκοντες εἶναι.
ἐπειδὴ δὲ ἐπύθοντο ταῦτα οἱ τῶν ὁπλιτῶν στρατηγοί, 22
ἐδόκει αὐτοῖς ἀπιέναι τὴν ταχίστην ἐπὶ τὸ στρατόπεδον,
μή τις ἐπίθεσις γένοιτο τοῖς καταλελειμμένοις. καὶ
εὐθὺς ἀνακαλεσάμενοι τῇ σάλπιγγι ἀπῇσαν, καὶ ἀφίκοντο αὐθημερὸν ἐπὶ τὸ στρατόπεδον.

V.

The Greeks cross the Eastern Euphrates. Their privations.

1   Τῇ δ' ὑστεραίᾳ ἐδόκει πορευτέον εἶναι ὅπῃ δύναιντο
τάχιστα, πρὶν συλλεγῆναι τὸ στράτευμα πάλιν καὶ
καταλαβεῖν τὰ στενά. συσκευασάμενοι δ' εὐθὺς ἐπορεύοντο διὰ χιόνος πολλῆς ἡγεμόνας ἔχοντες πολλούς·
καὶ αὐθημερὸν ὑπερβαλόντες τὸ ἄκρον, ἐφ' ᾧ ἔμελλεν
2 ἐπιτίθεσθαι Τιρίβαζος, κατεστρατοπεδεύσαντο. ἐντεῦθεν δ' ἐπορεύθησαν σταθμοὺς ἐρήμους τρεῖς, παρασάγγας
πεντεκαίδεκα, ἐπὶ τὸν Εὐφράτην ποταμόν, καὶ διέβαινον
αὐτὸν βρεχόμενοι πρὸς τὸν ὀμφαλόν. ἐλέγοντο δ' οὐδ'
3 αἱ πηγαὶ πρόσω εἶναι. ἐντεῦθεν ἐπορεύοντο διὰ χιόνος
πολλῆς καὶ πεδίου σταθμοὺς τρεῖς, παρασάγγας δέκα.
ὁ δὲ τρίτος ἐγένετο χαλεπὸς καὶ ἄνεμος βορρᾶς ἐναντίος
ἔπνει παντάπασιν ἀποκαίων πάντα καὶ πηγνὺς τοὺς
4 ἀνθρώπους. ἔνθα δὴ τῶν μάντεών τις εἶπε σφαγιά-
σασθαι τῷ ἀνέμῳ, καὶ σφαγιάζεται· καὶ πᾶσι δὴ
περιφανῶς ἔδοξεν ἀνεῖναι τὸ χαλεπὸν τοῦ πνεύματος. ἦν
δὲ τῆς χιόνος τὸ βάθος ὀργυιά· ὥστε καὶ τῶν ὑποζυγίων
καὶ τῶν ἀνδραπόδων πολλὰ ἀπώλετο καὶ τῶν στρατιω-
5 τῶν ὡς τριάκοντα. διεγένοντο δὲ τὴν νύκτα πῦρ καίοντες·
ξύλα δ' ἦν ἐν τῷ σταθμῷ πολλά· οἱ δὲ ὀψὲ προσιόντες
ξύλα οὐκ εἶχον. οἱ οὖν πάλαι ἥκοντες καὶ πῦρ καίοντες
οὐ προσίεσαν πρὸς τὸ πῦρ τοὺς ὀψίζοντας, εἰ μὴ
μεταδοῖεν αὐτοῖς πυροὺς ἢ ἄλλο τι εἴ τι ἔχοιεν βρωτόν.
6 ἔνθα δὴ μετεδίδοσαν ἀλλήλοις ὧν εἶχον ἕκαστοι. ἔνθα
δὲ τὸ πῦρ ἐκαίετο, διατηκομένης τῆς χιόνος βόθροι
ἐγίγνοντο μεγάλοι ἔστε ἐπὶ τὸ δάπεδον· οὗ δὴ παρῆν
7 μετρεῖν τὸ βάθος τῆς χιόνος. ἐντεῦθεν δὲ τὴν ἐπιοῦσαν

ἡμέραν ὅλην ἐπορεύοντο διὰ χιόνος, καὶ πολλοὶ τῶν
ἀνθρώπων ἐβουλιμίασαν. Ξενοφῶν δ' ὀπισθοφυλακῶν
καὶ καταλαμβάνων τοὺς πίπτοντας τῶν ἀνθρώπων
ἠγνόει ὅ τι τὸ πάθος εἴη. ἐπειδὴ δὲ εἶπέ τις αὐτῷ 8
τῶν ἐμπείρων ὅτι σαφῶς βουλιμιῶσι κἄν τι φάγωσιν
ἀναστήσονται, περιιὼν περὶ τὰ ὑποζύγια, εἴ πού τι
ὁρῴη βρωτόν, διεδίδου καὶ διέπεμπε διδόντας τοὺς
δυναμένους περιτρέχειν τοῖς βουλιμιῶσιν. ἐπειδὴ δέ τι
ἐμφάγοιεν, ἀνίσταντο καὶ ἐπορεύοντο.

Terrible sufferings of the Greeks.

πορευομένων δὲ Χειρίσοφος μὲν ἀμφὶ κνέφας πρὸς 9
κώμην ἀφικνεῖται, καὶ ὑδροφορούσας ἐκ τῆς κώμης
πρὸς τῇ κρήνῃ γυναῖκας καὶ κόρας καταλαμβάνει
ἔμπροσθεν τοῦ ἐρύματος. αὗται ἠρώτων αὐτοὺς τίνες 10
εἶεν. ὁ δ' ἑρμηνεὺς εἶπε περσιστὶ ὅτι παρὰ βασιλέως
πορεύονται πρὸς τὸν σατράπην. αἱ δὲ ἀπεκρίναντο ὅτι
οὐκ ἐνταῦθα εἴη, ἀλλ' ἀπέχει ὅσον παρασάγγην. οἱ
δ', ἐπεὶ ὀψὲ ἦν, πρὸς τὸν κωμάρχην συνεισέρχονται
εἰς τὸ ἔρυμα σὺν ταῖς ὑδροφόροις. Χειρίσοφος μὲν οὖν 11
καὶ ὅσοι ἐδυνήθησαν τοῦ στρατεύματος ἐνταῦθα ἐστρατοπεδεύσαντο, τῶν δ' ἄλλων στρατιωτῶν οἱ μὴ δυνάμενοι διατελέσαι τὴν ὁδὸν ἐνυκτέρευσαν ἄσιτοι καὶ
ἄνευ πυρός· καὶ ἐνταῦθά τινες ἀπώλοντο τῶν στρατιωτῶν. ἐφείποντο δὲ τῶν πολεμίων συνειλεγμένοι 12
τινὲς καὶ τὰ μὴ δυνάμενα τῶν ὑποζυγίων ἥρπαζον καὶ
ἀλλήλοις ἐμάχοντο περὶ αὐτῶν. ἐλείποντο δὲ τῶν
στρατιωτῶν οἵ τε διεφθαρμένοι ὑπὸ τῆς χιόνος τοὺς
ὀφθαλμοὺς οἵ τε ὑπὸ τοῦ ψύχους τοὺς δακτύλους τῶν
ποδῶν ἀποσεσηπότες. ἦν δὲ τοῖς μὲν ὀφθαλμοῖς 13
ἐπικούρημα τῆς χιόνος εἴ τις μέλαν τι ἔχων πρὸ τῶν

ὀφθαλμῶν ἐπορεύετο, τῶν δὲ ποδῶν εἴ τις κινοῖτο καὶ
μηδέποτε ἡσυχίαν ἔχοι καὶ εἰς τὴν νύκτα ὑπολύοιτο·
14 ὅσοι δὲ ὑποδεδεμένοι ἐκοιμῶντο, εἰσεδύοντο εἰς τοὺς
πόδας οἱ ἱμάντες καὶ τὰ ὑποδήματα περιεπήγνυντο·
καὶ γὰρ ἦσαν, ἐπειδὴ ἐπέλιπε τὰ ἀρχαῖα ὑποδήματα,
15 καρβάτιναι πεποιημέναι ἐκ τῶν νεοδάρτων βοῶν. διὰ
τὰς τοιαύτας οὖν ἀνάγκας ὑπελείποντό τινες τῶν
στρατιωτῶν· καὶ ἰδόντες μέλαν τι χωρίον διὰ τὸ
ἐκλελοιπέναι αὐτόθι τὴν χιόνα εἴκαζον τετηκέναι· καὶ
ἐτετήκει διὰ κρήνην τινά, ἣ πλησίον ἦν ἀτμίζουσα ἐν
νάπῃ. ἐνταῦθ' ἐκτραπόμενοι ἐκάθηντο καὶ οὐκ ἔφασαν
πορεύεσθαι.

Xenophon's efforts to save the troops.

16 ὁ δὲ Ξενοφῶν ἔχων ὀπισθοφύλακας ὡς ᾔσθετο,
ἐδεῖτο αὐτῶν πάσῃ τέχνῃ καὶ μηχανῇ μὴ ἀπολείπεσθαι,
λέγων ὅτι ἕπονται πολλοὶ πολέμιοι συνειλεγμένοι, καὶ
17 τελευτῶν ἐχαλέπαινεν. οἱ δὲ σφάττειν ἐκέλευον· οὐ
γὰρ ἂν δύνασθαι πορευθῆναι. ἐνταῦθα ἔδοξε κράτιστον
εἶναι τοὺς ἑπομένους πολεμίους φοβῆσαι, εἴ τις δύναιτο,
μὴ ἐπίοιεν τοῖς κάμνουσι. καὶ ἦν μὲν σκότος ἤδη, οἱ δὲ
προσῇσαν πολλῷ θορύβῳ ἀμφὶ ὧν εἶχον διαφερόμενοι.
18 ἔνθα δὴ οἱ ὀπισθοφύλακες, ἅτε ὑγιαίνοντες, ἐξανα-
στάντες ἔδραμον εἰς τοὺς πολεμίους· οἱ δὲ κάμνοντες
ἀνακραγόντες ὅσον ἐδύναντο μέγιστον τὰς ἀσπίδας
πρὸς τὰ δόρατα ἔκρουσαν. οἱ δὲ πολέμιοι δείσαντες
ἧκαν ἑαυτοὺς κατὰ τῆς χιόνος εἰς τὴν νάπην, καὶ
19 οὐδεὶς ἔτι οὐδαμοῦ ἐφθέγξατο. καὶ Ξενοφῶν μὲν καὶ
οἱ σὺν αὐτῷ εἰπόντες τοῖς ἀσθενοῦσιν ὅτι τῇ ὑστεραίᾳ
ἥξουσί τινες ἐπ' αὐτούς, πορευόμενοι, πρὶν τέτταρα

στάδια διελθεῖν, ἐντυγχάνουσιν ἐν τῇ ὁδῷ ἀναπαυομέ-
νοις ἐπὶ τῆς χιόνος τοῖς στρατιώταις ἐγκεκαλυμμένοις,
καὶ οὐδὲ φυλακὴ οὐδεμία καθειστήκει· καὶ ἀνίστασαν
αὐτούς. οἱ δ᾽ ἔλεγον ὅτι οἱ ἔμπροσθεν οὐχ ὑποχωροῖεν.
ὁ δὲ παριὼν καὶ παραπέμπων τῶν πελταστῶν τοὺς 20
ἰσχυροτάτους ἐκέλευε σκέψασθαι τί εἴη τὸ κωλῦον. οἱ
δὲ ἀπήγγελλον ὅτι ὅλον οὕτως ἀναπαύοιτο τὸ στράτευμα. ἐνταῦθα καὶ οἱ περὶ Ξενοφῶντα ηὐλίσθησαν 21
αὐτοῦ ἄνευ πυρὸς καὶ ἄδειπνοι, φυλακὰς οἵας ἐδύναντο
καταστησάμενοι. ἐπεὶ δὲ πρὸς ἡμέραν ἦν, ὁ μὲν
Ξενοφῶν πέμψας πρὸς τοὺς ἀσθενοῦντας τοὺς νεωτά-
τους ἀναστήσαντας ἐκέλευεν ἀναγκάζειν προϊέναι. ἐν 22
δὲ τούτῳ Χειρίσοφος πέμπει τῶν ἐκ τῆς κώμης σκεψομένους πῶς ἔχοιεν οἱ τελευταῖοι. οἱ δὲ ἄσμενοι
ἰδόντες τοὺς μὲν ἀσθενοῦντας τούτοις παρέδοσαν κομίζειν ἐπὶ τὸ στρατόπεδον, αὐτοὶ δὲ ἐπορεύοντο, καί, πρὶν
εἴκοσι στάδια διεληλυθέναι, ἦσαν πρὸς τῇ κώμῃ, ἔνθα
Χειρίσοφος ηὐλίζετο.

At last they reach comfortable quarters.

ἐπεὶ δὲ συνεγένοντο ἀλλήλοις, ἔδοξε κατὰ τὰς κώμας 23
ἀσφαλὲς εἶναι τὰς τάξεις σκηνοῦν. καὶ Χειρίσοφος
μὲν αὐτοῦ ἔμενεν, οἱ δὲ ἄλλοι διαλαχόντες ἃς ἑώρων
κώμας ἐπορεύοντο ἕκαστοι τοὺς ἑαυτῶν ἔχοντες. ἔνθα 24
δὴ Πολυκράτης Ἀθηναῖος λοχαγὸς ἐκέλευσεν ἀφιέναι
ἑαυτόν· καὶ λαβὼν τοὺς εὐζώνους, θέων ἐπὶ τὴν κώμην,
ἣν εἰλήχει Ξενοφῶν, καταλαμβάνει πάντας ἔνδον τοὺς
κωμήτας καὶ τὸν κωμάρχην, καὶ πώλους εἰς δασμὸν
βασιλεῖ τρεφομένους ἑπτακαίδεκα, καὶ τὴν θυγατέρα
τοῦ κωμάρχου ἐνάτην ἡμέραν γεγαμημένην· ὁ δ᾽ ἀνὴρ
αὐτῆς λαγὼς ᾤχετο θηράσων καὶ οὐχ ἥλω ἐν ταῖς

25 κώμαις. αἱ δ' οἰκίαι ἦσαν κατάγειοι, τὸ μὲν στόμα
ὥσπερ φρέατος, κάτω δ' εὐρεῖαι· αἱ δὲ εἴσοδοι τοῖς μὲν
ὑποζυγίοις ὀρυκταί, οἱ δὲ ἄνθρωποι κατέβαινον ἐπὶ
κλίμακος. ἐν δὲ ταῖς οἰκίαις ἦσαν αἶγες, οἶες, βόες,
ὄρνιθες, καὶ τὰ ἔκγονα τούτων· τὰ δὲ κτήνη πάντα
26 χιλῷ ἔνδον ἐτρέφοντο. ἦσαν δὲ καὶ πυροὶ καὶ κριθαὶ
καὶ ὄσπρια καὶ οἶνος κρίθινος ἐν κρατῆρσιν. ἐνῆσαν δὲ
καὶ αὐταὶ αἱ κριθαὶ ἰσοχειλεῖς, καὶ κάλαμοι ἐνέκειντο,
οἱ μὲν μείζους οἱ δὲ ἐλάττους, γόνατα οὐκ ἔχοντες·
27 τούτους ἔδει, ὁπότε τις διψῴη, λαβόντα εἰς τὸ στόμα
μύζειν. καὶ πάνυ ἄκρατος ἦν, εἰ μή τις ὕδωρ ἐπιχέοι·
28 καὶ πάνυ ἡδὺ συμμαθόντι τὸ πῶμα ἦν. ὁ δὲ Ξενοφῶν
τὸν ἄρχοντα τῆς κώμης ταύτης σύνδειπνον ἐποιήσατο
καὶ θαρρεῖν αὐτὸν ἐκέλευε λέγων ὅτι οὔτε τῶν τέκνων
στερήσοιτο τήν τε οἰκίαν αὐτοῦ ἀντεμπλήσαντες τῶν
ἐπιτηδείων ἀπίασιν, ἢν ἀγαθόν τι τῷ στρατεύματι
ἐξηγησάμενος φαίνηται, ἔστ' ἂν ἐν ἄλλῳ ἔθνει γένωνται.
29 ὁ δὲ ταῦτα ὑπισχνεῖτο, καὶ φιλοφρονούμενος οἶνον
ἔφρασεν ἔνθα ἦν κατορωρυγμένος. ταύτην μὲν οὖν
τὴν νύκτα διασκηνήσαντες οὕτως ἐκοιμήθησαν ἐν πᾶσιν
ἀφθόνοις πάντες οἱ στρατιῶται, ἐν φυλακῇ ἔχοντες τὸν
30 κωμάρχην καὶ τὰ τέκνα αὐτοῦ ὁμοῦ ἐν ὀφθαλμοῖς. τῇ
δ' ἐπιούσῃ ἡμέρᾳ Ξενοφῶν λαβὼν τὸν κωμάρχην πρὸς
Χειρίσοφον ἐπορεύετο· ὅπου δὲ παρίοι κώμην, ἐτρέπετο
πρὸς τοὺς ἐν ταῖς κώμαις καὶ κατελάμβανε πανταχοῦ
εὐωχουμένους καὶ εὐθυμουμένους, καὶ οὐδαμόθεν ἀφίεσαν
31 πρὶν παραθεῖναι αὐτοῖς ἄριστον· οὐκ ἦν δ' ὅπου οὐ
παρετίθεσαν ἐπὶ τὴν αὐτὴν τράπεζαν κρέα ἄρνεια,
ἐρίφεια, χοίρεια, μόσχεια, ὀρνίθεια, σὺν πολλοῖς ἄρτοις
32 τοῖς μὲν πυρίνοις τοῖς δὲ κριθίνοις. ὁπότε δέ τις φιλο-
φρονούμενός τῳ βούλοιτο προπιεῖν, εἷλκεν ἐπὶ τὸν

κρατῆρα, ἔνθεν ἐπικύψαντα ἔδει ῥοφοῦντα πινειν ὥσπερ
βοῦν. καὶ τῷ κωμάρχῃ ἐδίδοσαν λαμβάνειν ὅ τι βούλοιτο. ὁ δὲ ἄλλο μὲν οὐδὲν ἐδέχετο, ὅπου δέ τινα τῶν
συγγενῶν ἴδοι, πρὸς ἑαυτὸν ἀεὶ ἐλάμβανεν.

Interview with the village-chief.

ἐπεὶ δ᾽ ἦλθον πρὸς Χειρίσοφον, κατελάμβανον κἀ- 33
κείνους σκηνοῦντας ἐστεφανωμένους τοῦ ξηροῦ χιλοῦ
στεφάνοις, καὶ διακονοῦντας Ἀρμενίους παῖδας σὺν ταῖς
βαρβαρικαῖς στολαῖς· τοῖς δὲ παισὶν ἐδείκνυσαν ὥσπερ
ἐνεοῖς ὅ τι δέοι ποιεῖν. ἐπεὶ δ᾽ ἀλλήλους ἐφιλοφρονή- 34
σαντο Χειρίσοφος καὶ Ξενοφῶν, κοινῇ δὴ ἀνηρώτων
τὸν κωμάρχην διὰ τοῦ περσίζοντος ἑρμηνέως τίς εἴη ἡ
χώρα. ὁ δ᾽ ἔλεγεν ὅτι Ἀρμενία. καὶ πάλιν ἠρώτων
τίνι οἱ ἵπποι τρέφοιντο. ὁ δ᾽ ἔλεγεν ὅτι βασιλεῖ
δασμός· τὴν δὲ πλησίον χώραν ἔφη εἶναι Χάλυβας,
καὶ τὴν ὁδὸν ἔφραζεν ᾗ εἴη. καὶ αὐτὸν τότε μὲν ᾤχετο 35
ἄγων Ξενοφῶν πρὸς τοὺς ἑαυτοῦ οἰκέτας, καὶ ἵππον ὃν
εἰλήφει παλαίτερον δίδωσι τῷ κωμάρχῃ ἀναθρέψαντι
καταθῦσαι, ὅτι ἤκουεν αὐτὸν ἱερὸν εἶναι τοῦ Ἡλίου,
δεδιὼς μὴ ἀποθάνῃ· ἐκεκάκωτο γὰρ ὑπὸ τῆς πορείας·
αὐτὸς δὲ τῶν πώλων λαμβάνει, καὶ τῶν ἄλλων στρατηγῶν καὶ λοχαγῶν ἔδωκεν ἑκάστῳ πῶλον. ἦσαν δ᾽ οἱ 36
ταύτῃ ἵπποι μείονες μὲν τῶν Περσικῶν, θυμοειδέστεροι
δὲ πολύ. ἐνταῦθα δὴ καὶ διδάσκει ὁ κωμάρχης περὶ
τοὺς πόδας τῶν ἵππων καὶ τῶν ὑποζυγίων σακία
περιειλεῖν, ὅταν διὰ τῆς χιόνος ἄγωσιν· ἄνευ γὰρ τῶν
σακίων κατεδύοντο μέχρι τῆς γαστρός.

VI.

The Greeks resume their march.

1 Ἐπεὶ δ' ἡμέρα ἦν ὀγδόη, τὸν μὲν ἡγεμόνα παραδίδωσι Χειρισόφῳ, τοὺς δὲ οἰκέτας καταλείπει τῷ κωμάρχῃ, πλὴν τοῦ υἱοῦ τοῦ ἄρτι ἡβάσκοντος· τοῦτον δὲ Ἐπισθένει Ἀμφιπολίτῃ παραδίδωσι φυλάττειν, ὅπως, εἰ καλῶς ἡγήσοιτο, ἔχων καὶ τοῦτον ἀπίοι. καὶ εἰς τὴν οἰκίαν αὐτοῦ εἰσεφόρησαν ὡς ἐδύναντο πλεῖστα, 2 καὶ ἀναζεύξαντες ἐπορεύοντο. ἡγεῖτο δ' αὐτοῖς ὁ κωμάρχης λελυμένος διὰ χιόνος· καὶ ἤδη τε ἦν ἐν τῷ τρίτῳ σταθμῷ, καὶ Χειρίσοφος αὐτῷ ἐχαλεπάνθη ὅτι οὐκ εἰς κώμας ἤγαγεν. ὁ δ' ἔλεγεν ὅτι οὐκ εἶεν ἐν τῷ τόπῳ τούτῳ. ὁ δὲ Χειρίσοφος αὐτὸν ἔπαισε μέν, ἔδησε 3 δ' οὔ. ἐκ δὲ τούτου ἐκεῖνος τῆς νυκτὸς ἀποδρὰς ᾤχετο καταλιπὼν τὸν υἱόν. τοῦτό γε δὴ Χειρισόφῳ καὶ Ξενοφῶντι μόνον διάφορον ἐν τῇ πορείᾳ ἐγένετο, ἡ τοῦ ἡγεμόνος κάκωσις καὶ ἀμέλεια. Ἐπισθένης δὲ ἠράσθη τοῦ παιδὸς καὶ οἴκαδε κομίσας πιστοτάτῳ 4 ἐχρῆτο. μετὰ τοῦτο ἐπορεύθησαν ἑπτὰ σταθμοὺς ἀνὰ πέντε παρασάγγας τῆς ἡμέρας παρὰ τὸν Φᾶσιν ποταμόν, εὖρος πλεθριαῖον.

New enemies. A council of war. Altercation between Xenophon and Cheirisophus.

5 ἐντεῦθεν ἐπορεύθησαν σταθμοὺς δύο, παρασάγγας δέκα· ἐπὶ δὲ τῇ εἰς τὸ πεδίον ὑπερβολῇ ἀπήντησαν 6 αὐτοῖς Χάλυβες καὶ Τάοχοι καὶ Φασιανοί. Χειρίσοφος δ' ἐπεὶ κατεῖδε τοὺς πολεμίους ἐπὶ τῇ ὑπερβολῇ, ἐπαύσατο πορευόμενος, ἀπέχων εἰς τριάκοντα σταδίους, ἵνα

μὴ κατὰ κέρας ἄγων πλησιάσῃ τοῖς πολεμίοις· παρήγγειλε δὲ καὶ τοῖς ἄλλοις παράγειν τοὺς λόχους, ὅπως
ἐπὶ φάλαγγος γένοιτο τὸ στράτευμα. ἐπεὶ δὲ ἦλθον 7
οἱ ὀπισθοφύλακες, συνεκάλεσε τοὺς στρατηγοὺς καὶ
λοχαγούς, καὶ ἔλεξεν ὧδε· Οἱ μὲν πολέμιοι, ὡς ὁρᾶτε,
κατέχουσι τὰς ὑπερβολὰς τοῦ ὄρους· ὥρα δὲ βουλεύεσθαι ὅπως ὡς κάλλιστα ἀγωνιούμεθα. ἐμοὶ μὲν οὖν 8
δοκεῖ παραγγεῖλαι μὲν ἀριστοποιεῖσθαι τοῖς στρατιώταις, ἡμᾶς δὲ βουλεύεσθαι εἴτε τήμερον εἴτε αὔριον
δοκεῖ ὑπερβάλλειν τὸ ὄρος. Ἐμοὶ δέ γε, ἔφη ὁ Κλεάνωρ, 9
δοκεῖ, ἐπὰν τάχιστα ἀριστήσωμεν, ἐξοπλισαμένους ὡς
τάχιστα ἰέναι ἐπὶ τοὺς ἄνδρας. εἰ γὰρ διατρίψομεν
τὴν τήμερον ἡμέραν, οἵ τε νῦν ἡμᾶς ὁρῶντες πολέμιοι
θαρραλεώτεροι ἔσονται, καὶ ἄλλους εἰκὸς τούτων θαρ-
ρούντων πλείους προσγενέσθαι. μετὰ τοῦτον Ξενοφῶν 10
εἶπεν· Ἐγὼ δ' οὕτω γιγνώσκω· εἰ μὲν ἀνάγκη ἐστὶ
μάχεσθαι, τοῦτο δεῖ παρασκευάσασθαι ὅπως ὡς κράτιστα μαχούμεθα· εἰ δὲ βουλόμεθα ὡς ῥᾷστα ὑπερβάλλειν, τοῦτό μοι δοκεῖ σκεπτέον εἶναι ὅπως ὡς
ἐλάχιστα μὲν τραύματα λάβωμεν, ὡς ἐλάχιστα δὲ
σώματα ἀνδρῶν ἀποβάλωμεν. τὸ μὲν οὖν ὄρος ἐστὶ 11
τὸ ὁρώμενον πλέον ἢ ἐφ' ἑξήκοντα στάδια, ἄνδρες δ'
οὐδαμοῦ φυλάττοντες ἡμᾶς φανεροί εἰσιν ἀλλ' ἢ κατ'
αὐτὴν τὴν ὁδόν· πολὺ οὖν κρεῖττον τοῦ ἐρήμου ὄρους
καὶ κλέψαι τι πειρᾶσθαι λαθόντας καὶ ἁρπάσαι φθάσαντας, εἰ δυναίμεθα, μᾶλλον ἢ πρὸς ἰσχυρὰ χωρία
καὶ ἀνθρώπους παρεσκευασμένους μάχεσθαι. πολὺ 12
γὰρ ῥᾷον ὄρθιον ἀμαχεὶ ἰέναι ἢ ὁμαλὲς ἔνθεν καὶ ἔνθεν
πολεμίων ὄντων, καὶ νύκτωρ ἀμαχεὶ μᾶλλον ἂν τὰ
πρὸ ποδῶν ὁρῴη τις ἢ μεθ' ἡμέραν μαχόμενος, καὶ
ἡ τραχεῖα τοῖς ποσὶν ἀμαχεὶ ἰοῦσιν εὐμενεστέρα ἢ ἡ

13 ὁμαλῇ τὰς κεφαλὰς βαλλομένοις. καὶ κλέψαι δ' οὐκ ἀδύνατόν μοι δοκεῖ εἶναι, ἐξὸν μὲν νυκτὸς ἰέναι, ὡς μὴ ὁρᾶσθαι, ἐξὸν δ' ἀπελθεῖν τοσοῦτον ὡς μὴ αἴσθησιν παρέχειν. δοκοῦμεν δ' ἄν μοι ταύτῃ προσποιούμενοι προσβαλεῖν ἐρημοτέρῳ ἂν τῷ ὄρει χρῆσθαι· μένοιεν 14 γὰρ αὐτοῦ μᾶλλον ἁθρόοι οἱ πολέμιοι. ἀτὰρ τί ἐγὼ περὶ κλοπῆς συμβάλλομαι; ὑμᾶς γὰρ ἔγωγε, ὦ Χειρίσοφε, ἀκούω τοὺς Λακεδαιμονίους, ὅσοι ἐστὲ τῶν ὁμοίων, εὐθὺς ἐκ παίδων κλέπτειν μελετᾶν, καὶ οὐκ αἰσχρὸν 15 εἶναι ἀλλὰ καλὸν κλέπτειν ὅσα μὴ κωλύει νόμος. ὅπως δὲ ὡς κράτιστα κλέπτητε καὶ πειρᾶσθε λανθάνειν, νόμιμον παρ' ὑμῖν ἐστιν, ἐὰν ληφθῆτε κλέπτοντες, μαστιγοῦσθαι. νῦν οὖν μάλα σοι καιρός ἐστιν ἐπιδείξασθαι τὴν παιδείαν, καὶ φυλάξασθαι μὴ ληφθῶμεν 16 κλέπτοντες τοῦ ὄρους, ὡς μὴ πληγὰς λάβωμεν. Ἀλλὰ μέντοι, ἔφη ὁ Χειρίσοφος, κἀγὼ ὑμᾶς τοὺς Ἀθηναίους ἀκούω δεινοὺς εἶναι κλέπτειν τὰ δημόσια, καὶ μάλα ὄντος δεινοῦ τοῦ κινδύνου τῷ κλέπτοντι, καὶ τοὺς κρατίστους μέντοι μάλιστα, εἴπερ ὑμῖν οἱ κράτιστοι ἄρχειν ἀξιοῦνται· ὥστε ὥρα καὶ σοὶ ἐπιδείκνυσθαι τὴν παιδείαν.

Xenophon wishes to lead his proposed side-march.

17 Ἐγὼ μὲν τοίνυν, ἔφη ὁ Ξενοφῶν, ἕτοιμός εἰμι τοὺς ὀπισθοφύλακας ἔχων, ἐπειδὰν δειπνήσωμεν, ἰέναι καταληψόμενος τὸ ὄρος. ἔχω δὲ καὶ ἡγεμόνας· οἱ γὰρ γυμνῆτες τῶν ἑπομένων ἡμῖν κλωπῶν ἔλαβόν τινας ἐνεδρεύσαντες· τούτων καὶ πυνθάνομαι ὅτι οὐκ ἄβατόν ἐστι τὸ ὄρος, ἀλλὰ νέμεται αἰξὶ καὶ βουσίν· ὥστε, ἐάνπερ ἅπαξ λάβωμέν τι τοῦ ὄρους, βατὰ καὶ τοῖς 18 ὑποζυγίοις ἔσται. ἐλπίζω δὲ οὐδὲ τοὺς πολεμίους

μενεῖν ἔτι, ἐπειδὰν ἴδωσιν ἡμᾶς ἐν τῷ ὁμοίῳ ἐπὶ τῶν
ἄκρων· οὐδὲ γὰρ νῦν ἐθέλουσι καταβαίνειν εἰς τὸ ἴσον
ἡμῖν. ὁ δὲ Χειρίσοφος εἶπε, Καὶ τί δεῖ σὲ ἰέναι καὶ 19
λιπεῖν τὴν ὀπισθοφυλακίαν; ἀλλὰ ἄλλους πέμψον, ἂν
μή τινες ἐθέλοντες ἀγαθοὶ φαίνωνται. ἐκ τούτου 20
Ἀριστώνυμος Μεθυδριεὺς ἔρχεται ὁπλίτας ἔχων καὶ
Ἀριστέας Χῖος γυμνῆτας καὶ Νικόμαχος Οἰταῖος γυμ-
νῆτας· καὶ σύνθημα ἐποιήσαντο, ὁπότε ἔχοιεν τὰ ἄκρα,
πυρὰ καίειν πολλά. ταῦτα συνθέμενοι ἠρίστων· ἐκ δὲ 21
τοῦ ἀρίστου προήγαγεν ὁ Χειρίσοφος τὸ στράτευμα
πᾶν ὡς δέκα σταδίους πρὸς τοὺς πολεμίους, ὅπως ὡς
μάλιστα δοκοίη ταύτῃ προσάξειν.

Xenophon's success.

ἐπειδὴ δὲ ἐδείπνησαν καὶ νὺξ ἐγένετο, οἱ μὲν ταχ- 22
θέντες ᾤχοντο, καὶ καταλαμβάνουσι τὸ ὄρος, οἱ δὲ
ἄλλοι αὐτοῦ ἀνεπαύοντο. οἱ δὲ πολέμιοι, ἐπεὶ ᾔσθοντο
τὸ ὄρος ἐχόμενον, ἐγρηγόρεσαν καὶ ἔκαιον πυρὰ πολλὰ
διὰ νυκτός. ἐπειδὴ δὲ ἡμέρα ἐγένετο, Χειρίσοφος μὲν 23
θυσάμενος ἦγε κατὰ τὴν ὁδόν, οἱ δὲ τὸ ὄρος κατα-
λαβόντες κατὰ τὰ ἄκρα ἐπῇσαν. τῶν δ' αὖ πολεμίων 24
τὸ μὲν πολὺ ἔμενεν ἐπὶ τῇ ὑπερβολῇ τοῦ ὄρους, μέρος
δ' αὐτῶν ἀπήντα τοῖς κατὰ τὰ ἄκρα. πρὶν δὲ ὁμοῦ
εἶναι τοὺς πολλοὺς ἀλλήλοις, συμμιγνύασιν οἱ κατὰ
τὰ ἄκρα, καὶ νικῶσιν οἱ Ἕλληνες καὶ διώκουσιν. ἐν 25
τούτῳ δὲ καὶ οἱ ἐκ τοῦ πεδίου οἱ μὲν πελτασταὶ τῶν
Ἑλλήνων δρόμῳ ἔθεον πρὸς τοὺς παρατεταγμένους,
Χειρίσοφος δὲ βάδην ταχὺ ἐφείπετο σὺν τοῖς ὁπλίταις.
οἱ δὲ πολέμιοι οἱ ἐπὶ τῇ ὁδῷ ἐπειδὴ τὸ ἄνω ἑώρων 26
ἡττώμενον, φεύγουσι· καὶ ἀπέθανον μὲν οὐ πολλοὶ

αὐτῶν, γέρρα δὲ πάμπολλα ἐλήφθη· ἃ οἱ Ἕλληνες ταῖς
27 μαχαίραις κόπτοντες ἀχρεῖα ἐποίουν. ὡς δ' ἀνέβησαν,
θύσαντες καὶ τρόπαιον στησάμενοι κατέβησαν εἰς τὸ
πεδίον, καὶ εἰς κώμας πολλῶν κἀγαθῶν γεμούσας
ἦλθον.

VII.

The Greeks in the country of the Taochi.

1   Ἐκ δὲ τούτων ἐπορεύθησαν εἰς Τάοχους σταθμοὺς
πέντε, παρασάγγας τριάκοντα· καὶ τὰ ἐπιτήδεια ἐπέ-
λιπε· χωρία γὰρ ᾤκουν ἰσχυρὰ οἱ Τάοχοι, ἐν οἷς καὶ
2 τὰ ἐπιτήδεια πάντα εἶχον ἀνακεκομισμένοι. ἐπεὶ δ'
ἀφίκοντο πρὸς χωρίον, ὃ πόλιν μὲν οὐκ εἶχεν οὐδ'
οἰκίας—συνεληλυθότες δ' ἦσαν αὐτόσε καὶ ἄνδρες καὶ
γυναῖκες καὶ κτήνη πολλά—Χειρίσοφος μὲν οὖν πρὸς
τοῦτο προσέβαλλεν εὐθὺς ἥκων· ἐπειδὴ δὲ ἡ πρώτη
τάξις ἀπέκαμεν, ἄλλη προσῄει καὶ αὖθις ἄλλη· οὐ
γὰρ ἦν ἀθρόοις περιστῆναι, ἀλλὰ ποταμὸς ἦν κύκλῳ.
3 ἐπειδὴ δὲ Ξενοφῶν ἦλθε σὺν τοῖς ὀπισθοφύλαξι καὶ
πελτασταῖς καὶ ὁπλίταις, ἐνταῦθα δὴ λέγει Χειρίσοφος,
Εἰς καλὸν ἥκετε· τὸ γὰρ χωρίον αἱρετέον· τῇ γὰρ
στρατιᾷ οὐκ ἔστι τὰ ἐπιτήδεια, εἰ μὴ ληψόμεθα τὸ
4 χωρίον. ἐνταῦθα δὴ κοινῇ ἐβουλεύοντο· καὶ τοῦ
Ξενοφῶντος ἐρωτῶντος τί τὸ κωλῦον εἴη εἰσελθεῖν,
εἶπεν ὁ Χειρίσοφος, Μία αὕτη πάροδός ἐστιν ἣν ὁρᾷς·
ὅταν δέ τις ταύτῃ πειρᾶται παριέναι, κυλίνδουσι λίθους
ὑπὲρ ταύτης τῆς ὑπερεχούσης πέτρας· ὃς δ' ἂν κατα-
ληφθῇ, οὕτω διατίθεται. ἅμα δ' ἔδειξε συντετριμμένους

ἀνθρώπους καὶ σκέλη καὶ πλευράς. Ἦν δὲ τοὺς λίθους 5
ἀναλώσωσιν, ἔφη ὁ Ξενοφῶν, ἄλλο τι ἢ οὐδὲν κωλύει
παριέναι; οὐ γὰρ δὴ ἐκ τοῦ ἐναντίου ὁρῶμεν εἰ μὴ
ὀλίγους τούτους ἀνθρώπους, καὶ τούτων δύο ἢ τρεῖς
ὡπλισμένους. τὸ δὲ χωρίον, ὡς καὶ σὺ ὁρᾷς, σχεδὸν 6
τρία ἡμίπλεθρά ἐστιν ὃ δεῖ βαλλομένους διελθεῖν·
τούτου δὲ ὅσον πλέθρον δασὺ πίτυσι διαλειπούσαις
μεγάλαις, ἀνθ᾽ ὧν ἑστηκότες ἄνδρες τί ἂν πάσχοιεν
ἢ ὑπὸ τῶν φερομένων λίθων ἢ ὑπὸ τῶν κυλινδομένων;
τὸ λοιπὸν οὖν ἤδη γίγνεται ὡς ἡμίπλεθρον, ὃ δεῖ, ὅταν
λωφήσωσιν οἱ λίθοι, παραδραμεῖν. Ἀλλὰ εὐθύς, ἔφη 7
ὁ Χειρίσοφος, ἐπειδὰν ἀρξώμεθα εἰς τὸ δασὺ προσιέναι,
φέρονται οἱ λίθοι πολλοί. Αὐτὸ ἄν, ἔφη, τὸ δέον εἴη·
θᾶττον γὰρ ἀναλώσουσι τοὺς λίθους. ἀλλὰ πορευώμεθα
ἔνθεν ἡμῖν μικρόν τι παραδραμεῖν ἔσται, ἢν δυνώμεθα,
καὶ ἀπελθεῖν ῥᾴδιον, ἢν βουλώμεθα.

They take a stronghold of the Taochi.

ἐντεῦθεν ἐπορεύοντο Χειρίσοφος καὶ Ξενοφῶν καὶ 8
Καλλίμαχος Παρράσιος λοχαγός· τούτου γὰρ ἡ ἡγεμονία ἦν τῶν ὀπισθοφυλάκων λοχαγῶν ἐκείνῃ τῇ
ἡμέρᾳ· οἱ δὲ ἄλλοι λοχαγοὶ ἔμενον ἐν τῷ ἀσφαλεῖ.
μετὰ τοῦτο οὖν ἀπῆλθον ὑπὸ τὰ δένδρα ἄνθρωποι
ὡς ἑβδομήκοντα, οὐκ ἀθρόοι ἀλλὰ καθ᾽ ἕνα, ἕκαστος
φυλαττόμενος ὡς ἐδύνατο. Ἀγασίας δὲ ὁ Στυμφάλιος 9
καὶ Ἀριστώνυμος Μεθυδριεύς, καὶ οὗτοι τῶν ὀπισθοφυλάκων λοχαγοὶ ὄντες, καὶ ἄλλοι δὲ ἐφέστασαν ἔξω
τῶν δένδρων· οὐ γὰρ ἦν ἀσφαλὲς ἐν τοῖς δένδροις
ἑστάναι πλέον ἢ τὸν ἕνα λόχον. ἔνθα δὴ Καλλίμαχος 10
μηχανᾶταί τι· προύτρεχεν ἀπὸ τοῦ δένδρου, ὑφ᾽ ᾧ ἦν

αὐτός, δύο ἢ τρία βήματα· ἐπεὶ δὲ οἱ λίθοι φέροιντο,
ἀνέχαζεν εὐπετῶς· ἐφ' ἑκάστης δὲ προδρομῆς πλέον
11 ἢ δέκα ἅμαξαι πετρῶν ἀνηλίσκοντο. ὁ δὲ Ἀγασίας,
ὡς ὁρᾷ τὸν Καλλίμαχον ἃ ἐποίει, καὶ τὸ στράτευμα
πᾶν θεώμενον, δείσας μὴ οὐ πρῶτος παραδράμῃ εἰς
τὸ χωρίον, οὔτε τὸν Ἀριστώνυμον πλησίον ὄντα παρα-
καλέσας οὔτε Εὐρύλοχον τὸν Λουσιέα ἑταίρους ὄντας
οὔτε ἄλλον οὐδένα χωρεῖ αὐτός, καὶ παρέρχεται πάντας.
12 ὁ δὲ Καλλίμαχος, ὡς ὁρᾷ αὐτὸν παριόντα, ἐπιλαμβάνεται αὐτοῦ τῆς ἴτυος· ἐν δὲ τούτῳ παραθεῖ αὐτοὺς
Ἀριστώνυμος Μεθυδριεύς, καὶ μετὰ τοῦτον Εὐρύλοχος
Λουσιεύς· πάντες γὰρ οὗτοι ἀντεποιοῦντο ἀρετῆς καὶ
ἀντηγωνίζοντο πρὸς ἀλλήλους· καὶ οὕτως ἐρίζοντες
αἱροῦσι τὸ χωρίον. ὡς γὰρ ἅπαξ εἰσέδραμον, οὐδεὶς
13 πέτρος ἄνωθεν ἠνέχθη. ἐνταῦθα δὴ δεινὸν ἦν θέαμα.
αἱ γὰρ γυναῖκες ῥίπτουσαι τὰ παιδία εἶτα ἑαυτὰς ἐπι-
κατερρίπτουν, καὶ οἱ ἄνδρες ὡσαύτως. ἐνταῦθα δὴ καὶ
Αἰνείας Στυμφάλιος λοχαγὸς ἰδών τινα θέοντα ὡς
ῥίψοντα ἑαυτὸν στολὴν ἔχοντα καλὴν ἐπιλαμβάνεται
14 ὡς κωλύσων· ὁ δὲ αὐτὸν ἐπισπᾶται, καὶ ἀμφότεροι
ᾤχοντο κατὰ τῶν πετρῶν φερόμενοι καὶ ἀπέθανον.
ἐντεῦθεν ἄνθρωποι μὲν πάνυ ὀλίγοι ἐλήφθησαν, βόες
δὲ καὶ ὄνοι πολλοὶ καὶ πρόβατα.

The Chalybes.

15   ἐντεῦθεν ἐπορεύθησαν διὰ Χαλύβων σταθμοὺς ἑπτά,
παρασάγγας πεντήκοντα. οὗτοι ἦσαν ὧν διῆλθον
ἀλκιμώτατοι, καὶ εἰς χεῖρας ἦσαν. εἶχον δὲ θώρακας
λινοῦς μέχρι τοῦ ἤτρου, ἀντὶ δὲ τῶν πτερύγων σπάρτα
16 πυκνὰ ἐστραμμένα. εἶχον δὲ καὶ κνημῖδας καὶ κράνη
καὶ παρὰ τὴν ζώνην μαχαίριον ὅσον ξυήλην Λακωνικήν,

ᾧ ἔσφαττον ὧν κρατεῖν δύναιντο, καὶ ἀποτεμόντες ἂν
τὰς κεφαλὰς ἔχοντες ἐπορεύοντο, καὶ ᾖδον καὶ ἐχόρευον,
ὁπότε οἱ πολέμιοι αὐτοὺς ὄψεσθαι ἔμελλον. εἶχον δὲ
καὶ δόρυ ὡς πεντεκαίδεκα πήχεων μίαν λόγχην ἔχον.
οὗτοι ἐνέμενον ἐν τοῖς πολίσμασιν· ἐπεὶ δὲ παρέλθοιεν 17
οἱ Ἕλληνες, εἵποντο ἀεὶ μαχούμενοι. ᾤκουν δὲ ἐν τοῖς
ὀχυροῖς, καὶ τὰ ἐπιτήδεια ἐν τούτοις ἀνακεκομισμένοι
ἦσαν· ὥστε μηδὲν λαμβάνειν αὐτόθεν τοὺς Ἕλληνας,
ἀλλὰ διετράφησαν τοῖς κτήνεσιν ἃ ἐκ τῶν Ταόχων
ἔλαβον.

The city of Gymnias. Mount Theches.

ἐκ τούτου οἱ Ἕλληνες ἀφίκοντο ἐπὶ τὸν Ἅρπασον 18
ποταμόν, εὖρος τεττάρων πλέθρων. ἐντεῦθεν ἐπορεύθησαν διὰ Σκυθηνῶν σταθμοὺς τέτταρας, παρασάγγας
εἴκοσι διὰ πεδίου εἰς κώμας· ἐν αἷς ἔμειναν ἡμέρας
τρεῖς καὶ ἐπεσιτίσαντο. ἐντεῦθεν διῆλθον σταθμοὺς 19
τέτταρας, παρασάγγας εἴκοσι πρὸς πόλιν μεγάλην καὶ
εὐδαίμονα καὶ οἰκουμένην, ἣ ἐκαλεῖτο Γυμνιάς. ἐκ
ταύτης τῆς χώρας ὁ ἄρχων τοῖς Ἕλλησιν ἡγεμόνα
πέμπει, ὅπως διὰ τῆς ἑαυτῶν πολεμίας χώρας ἄγοι
αὐτούς. ἐλθὼν δ' ἐκεῖνος λέγει ὅτι ἄξει αὐτοὺς πέντε 20
ἡμερῶν εἰς χωρίον ὅθεν ὄψονται θάλατταν· εἰ δὲ μή,
τεθνάναι ἐπηγγείλατο. καὶ ἡγούμενος ἐπειδὴ ἐνέβαλλεν
εἰς τὴν ἑαυτοῦ πολεμίαν, παρεκελεύετο αἴθειν καὶ
φθείρειν τὴν χώραν· ᾧ καὶ δῆλον ἐγένετο ὅτι τούτου
ἕνεκεν συνέλθοι, οὐ τῆς τῶν Ἑλλήνων εὐνοίας. καὶ 21
ἀφικνοῦνται ἐπὶ τὸ ὄρος τῇ πέμπτῃ ἡμέρᾳ· ὄνομα δὲ
τῷ ὄρει ἦν Θήχης. ἐπεὶ δὲ οἱ πρῶτοι ἐγένοντο ἐπὶ τοῦ
ὄρους, κραυγὴ πολλὴ ἐγένετο. ἀκούσας δὲ ὁ Ξενοφῶν 22

καὶ οἱ ὀπισθοφύλακες ᾠήθησαν ἔμπροσθεν ἄλλους ἐπιτίθεσθαι πολεμίους· εἵποντο γὰρ ὄπισθεν οἱ ἐκ τῆς
καιομένης χώρας, καὶ αὐτῶν οἱ ὀπισθοφύλακες ἀπέκτεινάν τέ τινας καὶ ἐζώγρησαν ἐνέδραν ποιησάμενοι, καὶ
γέρρα ἔλαβον δασειῶν βοῶν ὠμοβόεια ἀμφὶ τὰ εἴκοσιν.

"The sea! The sea!"

23   ἐπειδὴ δ' ἡ βοὴ πλείων τε ἐγίγνετο καὶ ἐγγύτερον
καὶ οἱ ἀεὶ ἐπιόντες ἔθεον δρόμῳ ἐπὶ τοὺς ἀεὶ βοῶντας
καὶ πολλῷ μείζων ἐγίγνετο ἡ βοὴ ὅσῳ δὴ πλείους
24 ἐγίγνοντο, ἐδόκει δὴ μεῖζόν τι εἶναι τῷ Ξενοφῶντι, καὶ
ἀναβὰς ἐφ' ἵππον καὶ Λύκιον καὶ τοὺς ἱππέας ἀναλα-
βὼν παρεβοήθει· καὶ τάχα δὴ ἀκούουσι βοώντων τῶν
στρατιωτῶν Θάλαττα θάλαττα καὶ παρεγγυώντων. ἔνθα
δὴ ἔθεον πάντες καὶ οἱ ὀπισθοφύλακες, καὶ τὰ ὑποζύγια
25 ἠλαύνετο καὶ οἱ ἵπποι. ἐπεὶ δὲ ἀφίκοντο πάντες ἐπὶ
τὸ ἄκρον, ἐνταῦθα δὴ περιέβαλλον ἀλλήλους καὶ στρατηγοὺς καὶ λοχαγοὺς δακρύοντες. καὶ ἐξαπίνης, ὅτου
δὴ παρεγγυήσαντος, οἱ στρατιῶται φέρουσι λίθους καὶ
26 ποιοῦσι κολωνὸν μέγαν. ἐνταῦθα ἀνετίθεσαν δερμάτων
πλῆθος ὠμοβοείων καὶ βακτηρίας καὶ τὰ αἰχμάλωτα
γέρρα, καὶ ὁ ἡγεμὼν αὐτός τε κατέτεμνε τὰ γέρρα καὶ
27 τοῖς ἄλλοις διεκελεύετο. μετὰ ταῦτα τὸν ἡγεμόνα οἱ
Ἕλληνες ἀποπέμπουσι δῶρα δόντες ἀπὸ κοινοῦ ἵππον
καὶ φιάλην ἀργυρᾶν καὶ σκευὴν Περσικὴν καὶ δαρεικοὺς
δέκα· ᾔτει δὲ μάλιστα τοὺς δακτυλίους, καὶ ἔλαβε
πολλοὺς παρὰ τῶν στρατιωτῶν. κώμην δὲ δείξας αὐτοῖς οὗ σκηνήσουσι καὶ τὴν ὁδὸν ἣν πορεύσονται εἰς
Μάκρωνας, ἐπεὶ ἑσπέρα ἐγένετο, ᾤχετο τῆς νυκτὸς
ἀπιών.

VIII.

*The Greeks pass through the territory of the Macrones
and reach the Colchian frontier.*

Ἐντεῦθεν δ' ἐπορεύθησαν οἱ Ἕλληνες διὰ Μακρώ- 1
νων σταθμοὺς τρεῖς, παρασάγγας δέκα. τῇ πρώτῃ δὲ
ἡμέρᾳ ἀφίκοντο ἐπὶ τὸν ποταμόν, ὃς ὥριζε τὴν τῶν
Μακρώνων καὶ τὴν τῶν Σκυθηνῶν. εἶχον δ' ὑπὲρ 2
δεξιῶν χωρίον οἷον χαλεπώτατον καὶ ἐξ ἀριστερᾶς
ἄλλον ποταμόν, εἰς ὃν ἐνέβαλλεν ὁ ὁρίζων, δι' οὗ ἔδει
διαβῆναι. ἦν δὲ οὗτος δασὺς δένδρεσι παχέσι μὲν οὔ,
πυκνοῖς δέ. ταῦτ', ἐπεὶ προσῆλθον, οἱ Ἕλληνες ἔκοπτον,
σπεύδοντες ἐκ τοῦ χωρίου ὡς τάχιστα ἐξελθεῖν. οἱ δὲ 3
Μάκρωνες ἔχοντες γέρρα καὶ λόγχας καὶ τριχίνους
χιτῶνας κατ' ἀντιπέραν τῆς διαβάσεως παρατεταγμένοι
ἦσαν καὶ ἀλλήλοις διεκελεύοντο καὶ λίθους εἰς τὸν
ποταμὸν ἔρριπτον· ἐξικνοῦντο γὰρ οὐ οὐδ' ἔβλαπτον
οὐδέν. ἔνθα δὴ προσέρχεται Ξενοφῶντι τῶν πελτα- 4
στῶν ἀνὴρ Ἀθήνησι φάσκων δεδουλευκέναι, λέγων ὅτι
γιγνώσκοι τὴν φωνὴν τῶν ἀνθρώπων. Καὶ οἶμαι, ἔφη,
ἐμὴν ταύτην πατρίδα εἶναι· καὶ εἰ μή τι κωλύει, ἐθέλω
αὐτοῖς διαλεχθῆναι. Ἀλλ' οὐδὲν κωλύει, ἔφη, ἀλλὰ 5
διαλέγου καὶ μάθε πρῶτον τίνες εἰσίν. οἱ δ' εἶπον
ἐρωτήσαντος ὅτι Μάκρωνες. Ἐρώτα τοίνυν, ἔφη, αὐτοὺς
τί ἀντιτετάχαται καὶ χρῄζουσιν ἡμῖν πολέμιοι εἶναι.
οἱ δ' ἀπεκρίναντο, Ὅτι καὶ ὑμεῖς ἐπὶ τὴν ἡμετέραν 6
χώραν ἔρχεσθε. λέγειν ἐκέλευον οἱ στρατηγοὶ ὅτι οὐ
κακῶς γε ποιήσοντες, ἀλλὰ βασιλεῖ πολεμήσαντες

ἀπερχόμεθα εἰς τὴν Ἑλλάδα, καὶ ἐπὶ θάλατταν βου-
7 λόμεθα ἀφικέσθαι. ἠρώτων ἐκεῖνοι εἰ δοῖεν ἂν τούτων
τὰ πιστά. οἱ δ' ἔφασαν καὶ δοῦναι καὶ λαβεῖν ἐθέλειν.
ἐντεῦθεν διδόασιν οἱ Μάκρωνες βαρβαρικὴν λόγχην
τοῖς Ἕλλησιν, οἱ δὲ Ἕλληνες ἐκείνοις Ἑλληνικήν·
ταῦτα γὰρ ἔφασαν πιστὰ εἶναι· θεοὺς δ' ἐπεμαρτύ-
ραντο ἀμφότεροι.

The Colchians oppose the progress of the Greeks.
Xenophon's plan of attack.

8   μετὰ δὲ τὰ πιστὰ εὐθὺς οἱ Μάκρωνες τὰ δένδρα
συνεξέκοπτον τήν τε ὁδὸν ὡδοποίουν, ὡς διαβιβῶντες,
ἐν μέσοις ἀναμεμιγμένοι τοῖς Ἕλλησι, καὶ ἀγορὰν οἵαν
ἐδύναντο παρεῖχον, καὶ παρήγαγον ἐν τρισὶν ἡμέραις
ἕως ἐπὶ τὰ Κόλχων ὅρια κατέστησαν τοὺς Ἕλληνας.
9 ἐνταῦθα ἦν ὄρος μέγα προσβατὸν δέ· καὶ ἐπὶ τούτου
οἱ Κόλχοι παρατεταγμένοι ἦσαν. καὶ τὸ μὲν πρῶτον οἱ
Ἕλληνες ἀντιπαρετάξαντο φάλαγγα, ὡς οὕτως ἄξοντες
πρὸς τὸ ὄρος· ἔπειτα δὲ ἔδοξε τοῖς στρατηγοῖς βουλεύσασθαι συλλεγεῖσιν ὅπως ὡς κάλλιστα ἀγωνιοῦνται.
10 ἔλεξεν οὖν Ξενοφῶν ὅτι δοκοίη παύσαντας τὴν φάλαγγα
λόχους ὀρθίους ποιῆσαι· ἡ μὲν γὰρ φάλαγξ διασπασθή-
σεται εὐθύς· τῇ μὲν γὰρ ἄνοδον τῇ δὲ εὔοδον εὑρήσομεν
τὸ ὄρος· καὶ εὐθὺς τοῦτο ἀθυμίαν ποιήσει, ὅταν τεταγμένοι εἰς φάλαγγα ταύτην διεσπασμένην ὁρῶσιν.
11 ἔπειτα, ἢν μὲν ἐπὶ πολλοὺς τεταγμένοι προσάγωμεν,
περιττεύσουσιν ἡμῶν οἱ πολέμιοι καὶ τοῖς περιττοῖς
χρήσονται ὅ τι ἂν βούλωνται· ἐὰν δὲ ἐπ' ὀλίγων
τεταγμένοι ἴωμεν, οὐδὲν ἂν εἴη θαυμαστὸν εἰ διακοπείη
ἡμῶν ἡ φάλαγξ ὑπὸ ἀθρόων καὶ βελῶν καὶ ἀνθρώπων

ἐμπεσόντων· εἰ δέ πη τοῦτο ἔσται, τῇ ὅλῃ φάλαγγι
κακὸν ἔσται.   ἀλλά μοι δοκεῖ ὀρθίους τοὺς λόχους 12
ποιησαμένους τοσοῦτον χωρίον κατασχεῖν διαλιπόντας
τοῖς λόχοις ὅσον ἔξω τοὺς ἐσχάτους λόχους γενέσθαι
τῶν πολεμίων κεράτων· καὶ οὕτως ἐσόμεθα τῆς τε τῶν
πολεμίων φάλαγγος ἔξω οἱ ἔσχατοι λόχοι, καὶ ὀρθίους
ἄγοντες οἱ κράτιστοι ἡμῶν πρῶτον προσίασιν, ᾗ τε ἂν
εὔοδον ᾖ, ταύτῃ ἕκαστος ἄξει ὁ λόχος. καὶ εἴς τε τὸ 13
διαλεῖπον οὐ ῥᾴδιον ἔσται τοῖς πολεμίοις εἰσελθεῖν
ἔνθεν καὶ ἔνθεν λόχων ὄντων, διακόψαι τε οὐ ῥᾴδιον
ἔσται λόχον ὄρθιον προσιόντα. ἐάν τέ τις πιέζηται
τῶν λόχων, ὁ πλησίον βοηθήσει. ἤν τε εἴς πη δυνηθῇ
τῶν λόχων ἐπὶ τὸ ἄκρον ἀναβῆναι, οὐδεὶς μηκέτι μείνῃ
τῶν πολεμίων. ταῦτα ἔδοξε, καὶ ἐποίουν ὀρθίους τοὺς 14
λόχους. Ξενοφῶν δὲ ἀπιὼν ἐπὶ τὸ εὐώνυμον ἀπὸ τοῦ
δεξιοῦ ἔλεγε τοῖς στρατιώταις, Ἄνδρες, οὗτοί εἰσιν οὓς
ὁρᾶτε μόνοι ἔτι ἡμῖν ἐμποδὼν τὸ μὴ ἤδη εἶναι ἔνθα
πάλαι σπεύδομεν· τούτους, ἤν πως δυνώμεθα, καὶ
ὠμοὺς δεῖ καταφαγεῖν.

The Greeks dislodge the enemy and encamp in some
villages.

ἐπεὶ δ᾽ ἐν ταῖς χώραις ἕκαστοι ἐγένοντο καὶ τοὺς 15
λόχους ὀρθίους ἐποιήσαντο, ἐγένοντο μὲν λόχοι τῶν
ὁπλιτῶν ἀμφὶ τοὺς ὀγδοήκοντα, ὁ δὲ λόχος ἕκαστος
σχεδὸν εἰς τοὺς ἑκατόν· τοὺς δὲ πελταστὰς καὶ τοὺς
τοξότας τριχῇ ἐποιήσαντο, τοὺς μὲν τοῦ εὐωνύμου ἔξω,
τοὺς δὲ τοῦ δεξιοῦ, τοὺς δὲ κατὰ μέσον, σχεδὸν ἑξακο-
σίους ἑκάστους.   ἐκ τούτου παρηγγύησαν οἱ στρατηγοὶ 16
εὔχεσθαι· εὐξάμενοι δὲ καὶ παιανίσαντες ἐπορεύοντο.
καὶ Χειρίσοφος μὲν καὶ Ξενοφῶν καὶ οἱ σὺν αὐτοῖς

πελτασταὶ τῆς τῶν πολεμίων φάλαγγος ἔξω γενόμενοι
17 ἐπορεύοντο· οἱ δὲ πολέμιοι, ὡς εἶδον αὐτούς, ἀντιπαραθέοντες οἱ μὲν ἐπὶ τὸ δεξιὸν οἱ δὲ ἐπὶ τὸ εὐώνυμον
διεσπάσθησαν, καὶ πολὺ τῆς αὐτῶν φάλαγγος ἐν τῷ
18 μέσῳ κενὸν ἐποίησαν. οἱ δὲ κατὰ τὸ Ἀρκαδικὸν πελτασταί, ὧν ἦρχεν Αἰσχίνης ὁ Ἀκαρνάν, νομίσαντες
φεύγειν ἀνακραγόντες ἔθεον· καὶ οὗτοι πρῶτοι ἐπὶ τὸ
ὄρος ἀναβαίνουσι· συνεφείπετο δὲ αὐτοῖς καὶ τὸ Ἀρκα-
19 δικὸν ὁπλιτικόν, ὧν ἦρχε Κλεάνωρ ὁ Ὀρχομένιος. οἱ
δὲ πολέμιοι, ὡς ἤρξαντο θεῖν, οὐκέτι ἔστησαν, ἀλλὰ
φυγῇ ἄλλος ἄλλῃ ἐτράπετο. οἱ δὲ Ἕλληνες ἀναβάντες
ἐστρατοπεδεύοντο ἐν πολλαῖς κώμαις καὶ τἀπιτήδεια
20 πολλὰ ἐχούσαις. καὶ τὰ μὲν ἄλλα οὐδὲν ὅ τι καὶ
ἐθαύμασαν· τὰ δὲ σμήνη πολλὰ ἦν αὐτόθι, καὶ τῶν
κηρίων ὅσοι ἔφαγον τῶν στρατιωτῶν πάντες ἄφρονές
τε ἐγίγνοντο καὶ ἤμουν καὶ κάτω διεχώρει αὐτοῖς καὶ
ὀρθὸς οὐδεὶς ἐδύνατο ἵστασθαι, ἀλλ᾽ οἱ μὲν ὀλίγον
ἐδηδοκότες σφόδρα μεθύουσιν ἐῴκεσαν, οἱ δὲ πολὺ
21 μαινομένοις, οἱ δὲ καὶ ἀποθνήσκουσιν. ἔκειντο δὲ οὕτω
πολλοὶ ὥσπερ τροπῆς γεγενημένης, καὶ πολλὴ ἦν
ἀθυμία. τῇ δ᾽ ὑστεραίᾳ ἀπέθανε μὲν οὐδείς, ἀμφὶ δὲ
τὴν αὐτήν πως ὥραν ἀνεφρόνουν· τρίτῃ δὲ καὶ τετάρτῃ
ἀνίσταντο ὥσπερ ἐκ φαρμακοποσίας.

The Greeks reach Trapezus.   Sacrifices and games.

22   ἐντεῦθεν δ᾽ ἐπορεύθησαν δύο σταθμούς, παρασάγγας
ἑπτά, καὶ ἦλθον ἐπὶ θάλατταν εἰς Τραπεζοῦντα πόλιν
Ἑλληνίδα οἰκουμένην ἐν τῷ Εὐξείνῳ Πόντῳ, Σινωπέων
ἀποικίαν ἐν τῇ Κόλχων χώρᾳ. ἐνταῦθα ἔμειναν ἡμέρας
ἀμφὶ τὰς τριάκοντα ἐν ταῖς τῶν Κόλχων κώμαις·
23 κἀντεῦθεν ὁρμώμενοι ἐλήζοντο τὴν Κολχίδα. ἀγορὰν

δὲ παρεῖχον τῷ στρατοπέδῳ Τραπεζούντιοι, καὶ ἐδέ-
ξαντό τε τοὺς Ἕλληνας καὶ ξένια ἔδοσαν βοῦς καὶ
ἄλφιτα καὶ οἶνον. συνδιεπράττοντο δὲ καὶ ὑπὲρ τῶν 24
πλησίον Κόλχων τῶν ἐν τῷ πεδίῳ μάλιστα οἰκούν-
των, καὶ ξένια καὶ παρ' ἐκείνων ἦλθον βόες. μετὰ 25
δὲ τοῦτο τὴν θυσίαν, ἣν εὔξαντο, παρεσκευάζοντο·
ἦλθον δ' αὐτοῖς ἱκανοὶ βόες ἀποθῦσαι τῷ Διὶ σωτήρια
καὶ τῷ Ἡρακλεῖ ἡγεμόσυνα καὶ τοῖς ἄλλοις θεοῖς ἃ
εὔξαντο. ἐποίησαν δὲ καὶ ἀγῶνα γυμνικὸν ἐν τῷ ὄρει,
ἔνθαπερ ἐσκήνουν. εἵλοντο δὲ Δρακόντιον Σπαρτιάτην,
ὃς ἔφυγε παῖς ὢν οἴκοθεν, παῖδα ἄκων κατακανὼν
ξυήλῃ πατάξας, δρόμου τ' ἐπιμεληθῆναι καὶ τοῦ ἀγῶνος
προστατῆσαι. ἐπειδὴ δὲ ἡ θυσία ἐγένετο, τὰ δέρματα 26
παρέδοσαν τῷ Δρακοντίῳ, καὶ ἡγεῖσθαι ἐκέλευον ὅπου
τὸν δρόμον πεποιηκὼς εἴη. ὁ δὲ δείξας οὗπερ ἑστηκότες
ἐτύγχανον, Οὗτος ὁ λόφος, ἔφη, κάλλιστος τρέχειν ὅπου
ἄν τις βούληται. Πῶς οὖν, ἔφασαν, δυνήσονται πα-
λαίειν ἐν σκληρῷ καὶ δασεῖ οὕτως; ὁ δ' εἶπε, Μᾶλλόν
τι ἀνιάσεται ὁ καταπεσών. ἠγωνίζοντο δὲ παῖδες μὲν 27
στάδιον τῶν αἰχμαλώτων οἱ πλεῖστοι, δόλιχον δὲ
Κρῆτες πλείους ἢ ἑξήκοντα ἔθεον, πάλην δὲ καὶ πυγμὴν
καὶ παγκράτιον ἕτεροι· καὶ καλὴ θέα ἐγένετο· πολλοὶ
γὰρ κατέβησαν καί, ἅτε θεωμένων τῶν ἑταίρων, πολλὴ
φιλονεικία ἐγίγνετο. ἔθεον δὲ καὶ ἵπποι καὶ ἔδει αὐτοὺς 28
κατὰ τοῦ πρανοῦς ἐλάσαντας ἐν τῇ θαλάττῃ ὑποστρέ-
ψαντας πάλιν ἄνω πρὸς τὸν βωμὸν ἄγειν. καὶ κάτω
μὲν οἱ πολλοὶ ἐκαλινδοῦντο· ἄνω δὲ πρὸς τὸ ἰσχυρῶς
ὄρθιον μόλις βάδην ἐπορεύοντο οἱ ἵπποι· ἔνθα πολλὴ
κραυγὴ καὶ γέλως καὶ παρακέλευσις ἐγίγνετο.

41

NOTES.

I.

1. τῇ ἀναβάσει, the march *up country* from the west of Asia Minor to Babylonia.

τῆς μάχης, the battle of Cunaxa, in which Cyrus was killed; see Introduction, p. xvi.

ἐν ταῖς σπονδαῖς, 'as long as the truce lasted.'

βασιλεύς, Artaxerxes Mnemon, brother of Cyrus. Notice the omission of the article as usual when βασιλεύς denotes the 'Great King,' i.e. the King of Persia; cf. Ἰσθμός 'the well-known Isthmus,' i.e. of Corinth.

καὶ ὅσα—στρατεύματος, 'and all the warlike operations which (after the transgression of the treaty by the King and Tissaphernes) were conducted against the Greeks, while the Persian army was pursuing them.'

παραβάντος, i.e. by the treacherous seizure of the Greek generals in the camp of Tissaphernes. They were afterwards put to death. See Introduction, p. xix.

2. ἐπεὶ δὲ—ἔνθα, 'But when they arrived (at the point) where....'

πάροδος δὲ οὐκ ἦν. See Introduction, p. xxi.

τὰ Καρδούχεια—ἐκρέματο, 'the Carduchian mountains hung precipitous right over the river.' ἀπότομα is predicate.

αὐτοῦ τοῦ ποταμοῦ. For the force of αὐτός cf. Thuc. IV. 10 παρ' αὐτὴν τὴν ῥαχίαν '*just* by the breakers' edge.'

στρατιώταις. There is no occasion to read στρατηγοῖς as some do; for the Ten Thousand are often regarded as a democracy; see Introduction, p. xix.

3. ἁλισκομένων, imperfect participle:—'they were hearing from the prisoners whom they captured *from time to time.*'

Note the changes of mood in the *oratia obliqua* which follows:—

(*a*) εἰ διέλθοιεν, 'if they were to cross.'

(*b*) ἢν βούλωνται, 'if they wish' (more vivid).

(*c*) διαβήσονται, 'they will certainly be able to ford.'

The rules of *oratio obliqua* in Greek are much more elastic than in Latin. There is a good parallel to our passage in II. iii. 6 ἔλεγον ὅτι εἰκότα δοκοῖεν λέγειν βασιλεῖ, καὶ ἥκοιεν ἡγεμόνας ἔχοντες, οἱ αὐτούς, ἐὰν σπ‹ ›νδαὶ γένωνται, ἄξουσιν ἔνθεν ἕξουσι τὰ ἐπιτήδεια.

καὶ—δέ, 'Yes and...'; cf. vii. 9 καὶ ἄλλοι δὲ ἐφέστασαν.

οὐ πρόσω τοῦ Τίγρητος, 'not far from (those of) the Tigris,'—a condensed expression, cf. Hom. *Il.* XVII. 51 κόμαι Χαρίτεσσιν ὁμοῖαι 'hair like that of the Graces.'

[After Τίγρητος εἶναι several editors have the words καὶ ἔστιν οὕτως ἔχον 'and so it is,' an impossible reading, since we learn from Xenophon himself that the Greeks travelled nearly 150 miles from the sources of the Tigris before they came near the Euphrates; and the sources of that river are sixty miles higher up. The MSS. reading is καὶ ἔστιν οὕτω στενόν, which appears to be the marginal note of a scribe.]

4. ὧδε, as usual, refers to what follows, i.e. it is explained by the participial clause.

ποιοῦνται, historic present, less common in Greek than in Latin.

5. τὴν τελευταίαν φυλακήν, i.e. the third watch, according to the Greek reckoning.

ἐλείπετο—πεδίον, 'there was left of the night sufficient for them to pass over the plain in the dark.'

νυκτός, partitive genitive, with ὅσον. In full the sentence would run:—ἐλείπετο τοσοῦτο τῆς νυκτὸς ὅσον....

σκοταίους. Cf. § 10 κατέβαινον ἤδη σκοταῖοι. There is a similar predicative use of the adjective in Latin:—e.g. Virg. *Aen.* VIII. 465 *se matutinus agebat* 'was astir in the morning.'

διελθεῖν. 'The infinitive, after τοιοῦτος οἷος and τοσοῦτος ὅσος, depends on the idea of *ability, fitness,* or *sufficiency* which is expressed in these combinations. The antecedent may be omitted, leaving οἷος with the infinitive in the sense of *able, fit, likely,* and ὅσος in that of *sufficient*' (Goodwin, *Moods and Tenses,* § 759). Cf. II. iii. 13 οὐ γὰρ ἦν ὥρα οἵα τὸ πεδίον ἄρδειν 'it was not the proper season to irrigate the land.' Thuc. I. 2 νεμόμενοι τὰ αὐτῶν ὅσον ἀποζῆν 'cultivating their own land enough (*to an extent sufficient*) to live upon it.'

ἀπὸ παραγγέλσεως, 'by an order passed *along*, i.e. from man to man,' so as not to attract the attention of the enemy; cf. § 16 παρήγγελλεν ὁ Ξενοφῶν ὑπομένειν. For the idiomatic use of ἀπό cf. II. v. 32 ἀπὸ τοῦ αὐτοῦ σημείου.

6. ἡγεῖτο, 'led the van,' not 'commanded the army.' Cheirisophus was not commander-in-chief at this time, as some suppose. Matters of importance were as a rule settled by the board of generals in common. 'It seemed good to the generals' is a frequent phrase. Later on (VI. i. 32) Cheirisophus was elected sole commander; but the appointment was not a success, and he held office for only a week.

τὸ ἀμφ' αὐτόν, 'his own division.'

γυμνῆτας, a general term (opposed to ὁπλῖται, heavy infantry) including different kinds of light-armed troops recruited from peoples specially distinguished for the use of particular weapons, e.g. archers generally Cretans, and slingers generally Rhodians. Their common characteristic was the absence of all defensive armour.

ὀπισθοφύλαξιν, substantive used as an epithet,—'the heavy-armed *composing the rear-guard*'; cf. § 26.

οὐδεὶς—ἐπίσποιτο, 'For there seemed to be no danger of any one pursuing from behind while they (the Greeks) were moving upwards.' The construction οὐδεὶς κίνδυνος—μὴ ἐπίσποιτο is analogous to that after verbs of *fearing*; cf. ii. 13.

πορευομένων, genitive absolute with subject omitted; cf. § 9 καλούντων.

7. ἀναβαίνει. Cf. § 4 ποιοῦνται.

ἔπειτα δ'—κώμας, 'And then he led on slowly; and that portion of the army which happened to be mounting the crest from time to time followed on into the villages.'

ὑφηγεῖτο. For ὑπό in composition meaning 'slowly,' 'gently' cf. § 8 ὑποφειδόμενοι.

ἀεί, to be taken with ἐφείπετο, 'from time to time,' 'in succession'; cf. vii. 23 and Thuc. IV. 68 ὁ ἀεὶ ἐντὸς γενόμενος 'the man who from time to time got inside.'

ὑπερβάλλον. Mark the force of the imperfect participle; cf. § 3 ἁλισκομένων.

στρατεύματος, partitive genitive.

8. τὰ δὲ ἐπιτήδεια—λαμβάνειν, lit. 'provisions were in abundance to take.'

λαμβάνειν. The Greek infinitive was in its origin the dative of a noun; so λαμβάνειν means strictly '*for taking*.' Hence adjectives often take an infinitive, as here, to limit their meaning to a particular action ; e.g. Xen. *Memorabilia* III. xiii. 3 λούσασθαι ψυχρότερον 'colder (water) *for bathing*,' III. viii. 8 οἰκία ἡδίστη ἐνδιαιτᾶσθαι 'a house most pleasant *for living in*.' Cf. note on § 24 δυνατὴν πορεύεσθαι.

ὧν, partitive genitive depending on οὐδέν.

ἔφερον, 'plundered'; cf. Thuc. I. 7 ἔφερον ἀλλήλους, Eur. *Bacchae* 759 φερόμενοι Βαχχῶν ὕπο. Cf. the phrase ἄγειν καὶ φέρειν, Lat. *agere et ferre.*

οὐδὲ—χώρας, 'Nor did they pursue the natives either, sparing them a little, (to see) if perchance the Carduchians might be willing to let them pass through their country as a friendly one.'

ὑποφειδόμενοι, 'sparing them *somewhat*,' 'being *inclined* to spare them'; cf. § 7 ὑφηγεῖτο.

εἴ πως, Lat. *si forte*, often introduces what is virtually a final clause ; cf. § 21 εἴ πως δυναίμην.

ὡς διὰ φιλίας τῆς χώρας in full would be διὰ τῆς χώρας ὡς διὰ φιλίας χώρας.

βασιλεῖ πολέμιοι. These Kurds were a wild independent people, perpetually at war with the Great King their nominal suzerain.

9. τὰ μέντοι—ἐλάμβανον, 'However they seized provisions,— anything that anyone lighted on.'

ὅτῳ. For the singular after the plural ἐπιτήδεια cf. I. i. 5 ὅστις ἀφικνοῖτο—πάντας ἀπεπέμπετο.

ἐπιτυγχάνοι, optative of indefinite frequency.

καλούντων, 'when they called,' genitive absolute with omission of subject, 'the Greeks'; cf. § 6 πορευομένων.

ὑπήκουον, 'answered,' used especially of answering a knock at a door; so in Xen. *Symposium* i. 11 ὁ ὑπακούσας means the 'porter'; cf. Acts xii. 13 κρούσαντος δὲ αὐτοῦ τὴν θύραν τοῦ πυλῶνος προσῆλθε παιδίσκη ὑπακοῦσαι.

οὔτε—οὐδὲν ἐποίουν, 'nor did they do anything.' In Greek, as a rule, negatives do not neutralise but strengthen one another; cf. Eurip. *Cyclops* 120 ἀκούει δ' οὐδὲν οὐδεὶς οὐδενός 'no one obeys anybody in anything.'

10. σκοταῖοι. See note on § 5 σκοταίους διελθεῖν.

διὰ γὰρ—κατάβασις, 'For owing to the narrowness of the path their ascent and descent had occupied them the whole day.'

αὐτοῖς, dative of person concerned; cf. § 17 τοῖς ὀπισθοφύλαξι.

ὀλίγοι τινὲς ὄντες, '*though* they were only some few,' *concessive* use of the participle.

ἐξ ἀπροσδοκήτου, 'unexpectedly,' lit. '*starting from* the unexpected'; cf. ἐκ βίας 'by force,' ἐξ ἴσου 'equally,' ἐκ τοῦ αὐτομάτου 'by chance.' τὸ Ἑλληνικόν, 'the Greek force,' στράτευμα understood.

11. εἰ μέντοι—στρατεύματος, 'If however on this occasion (the enemy) had collected in greater force, a large part of the (Greek) army would have run the risk of being cut to pieces.'

νύκτα, accusative of duration of time ; cf. § 10 ὅλην τὴν ἡμέραν.

οὕτως, idiomatic, 'just as they were'; cf. Soph. *Phil.* 1067 ἀλλ' οὕτως ἄπει; 'will you go off just as you are (i.e. without a word more)?' S. John iv. 6 ὁ οὖν Ἰησοῦς κεκοπιακὼς ἐκ τῆς ὁδοιπορίας ἐκαθέζετο οὕτως ἐπὶ τῇ πηγῇ. Cf. also *sic temere* in Horace, '*just* at random.'

συνεώρων ἀλλήλους, 'they kept one another in view,' i.e. by means of their signals.

12. τῶν τε—ἐχοντας, 'taking with them those of the transport animals which were necessary and most competent.'

13. ἐποίουν, with τὰ ὑποζύγια καὶ τὰ αἰχμάλωτα as subject, is noteworthy. Xenophon does not keep the ordinary rule (of singular verb with neuter plural subject) as strictly as other Attic writers. Here there is a reason ; for τὰ αἰχμάλωτα 'captives' is personal. Cf. ii. 20 τὰ ὅπλα ἔκειντο.

πολλὰ ὄντα, 'on account of their number.' The participle has a *causal* force, as often.

οἱ ἐπὶ τούτοις, 'those set over these,' 'in charge of these' ; cf. *Hellenica* I. v. 11 ἐπὶ ταῖς ναυσὶν 'in charge of the ships,' *Cyropaedeia* VI. iii. 28 οἱ ἐπὶ ταῖς μηχαναῖς 'those in charge of the engines.'

διπλάσια, 'in double quantity,' a predicate.

13. δόξαν—ποιεῖν, 'When this was agreed upon, they proclaimed (to the troops) that so they should act.'

δόξαν, accusative absolute ; cf. Thuc. IV. 125 δοκοῦν ἀναχωρεῖν— ἐχώρουν ἐπ' οἴκου. The construction of ταῦτα is difficult. 'We may supply ποιεῖν, or δόξαν ταῦτα may represent ἔδοξε ταῦτα' (Goodwin, *Moods and Tenses*, § 855). In *Hellenica* III. ii. 19 Xenophon has δόξαντα δὲ ταῦτα—ἀπῆλθε, which is a simpler construction.

14. ὑποστήσαντες ἐν τῷ στενῷ, 'having secretly stationed in the defile (officers for the purpose),' i.e. to keep a look-out for things secreted by the soldiers. The omission of the object of ὑποστήσαντες is awkward ; but the meaning is clear from the parallel passage in *Hellenica* I. iv. 21 ἐπεὶ δὲ τὰ ληφθέντα χρήματα ἀπήγαγον, ὑποστήσας ταξιάρχους καὶ λοχαγοὺς ἀφείλετο πάντα.

εὑρίσκοιεν, optative of frequency; cf. § 9 ἐπιτυγχάνοι. This is a temporal, not a conditional clause; for εἰ here virtually means 'whenever.'

ἔκλεψεν, 'had smuggled.' κλέπτω sometimes means 'secrete,' 'spirit away' rather than 'steal.'

τι μαχόμενοι. τι 'somewhat,' 'a little,' cognate accusative used adverbially. This is also the explanation of τὰ μὲν—τὰ δέ 'partly— partly.'

15. εἰς τὴν ὑστεραίαν γίγνεται, lit. 'falls *on to* the morrow.' Cf. II. iii. 25 ἥκειν εἰς τὴν ὑστεραίαν.

16. ἐπικέοιντο, optative of frequency again; cf. ὅτε παρεγγνῷτο in the next section, 'whenever word was passed along to him.'

17. τότε δέ, 'but on one particular occasion.'

πρᾶγμά τι, 'some trouble'; cf. § 22 πράγματα παρεῖχον.

σχολὴ δ'—σπουδῆς, 'But there was no time (for any one) to pass forward and see the cause of his hurry.'

τοῖς ὀπισθοφύλαξι, dative of person concerned, 'for the rear-guard'; cf. § 10 αὐτοῖς.

18. σπολάδος, a leather cuirass or buff jerkin reaching over the hips and fringed with strips of leather, which formed a kind of kilt. The σπολάς was often covered wholly or partly with metal, especially in the form of scales. Cf. ii. 28.

διαμπερὲς εἰς τὴν κεφαλήν, 'right through into the head'; cf. Hom. *Il.* XVI. 640 διαμπερὲς ἐς πόδας.

19. ὥσπερ εἶχεν, 'just as he was,' 'without delay.'

ἅμα, to be taken with φεύγοντες, 'while fleeing.'

οὔτε ἀνελέσθαι οὔτε θάψαι, a most serious matter from the Greek point of view.

20. ἀποκρίνεται. Notice the *asyndeton* or absence of a connecting particle, which is rare in Greek; cf. § 27 ὑφίσταται.

μία—ὀρθία, 'And this is the only path, the one you see before you, a steep one.'

ἔκβασιν, 'outlet' on to higher ground; cf. ii. 1.

21. ταῦτ'—ἔσπευδον, 'I was making this haste'; cf. Homer *Il.* XIII. 235 ταῦτα δ' ἅμα χρὴ σπεύδειν.

εἰ πως δυναίμην. See note on § 8 εἰ πως ἐθελήσειαν.

22. πράγματα παρεῖχον, 'were giving trouble'; cf. § 17 πρᾶγμά τι.

αὐτοῦ τούτου—χρησαίμεθα, 'just with this object, viz. that we might use them as guides knowing the district.' For the force of αὐτοῦ cf. § 2 αὐτοῦ τοῦ ποταμοῦ.

23. ἤλεγχον—φανεράν, 'they took them separately and proceeded to examine them as to whether they knew of any other path than the visible one.'

μάλα—προσαγομένων, 'though very many threats were brought to bear upon him.' For the participial clause conveying a *concession* cf. § 10 ὀλίγοι τινὲς ὄντες.

24. ὅτι αὐτῷ—ἐκδεδομένη, 'because he happened to have a daughter living there with a man in marriage.'

αὐτὸς—ὁδόν, 'He said that he would conduct them himself along a path.' ὁδόν is accusative of *space over which*; cf. II. ii. 12 πορευτέον τοὺς πρώτους σταθμούς.

δυνατὴν καὶ ὑποζυγίοις πορεύεσθαι ὁδόν, 'a path practicable for the passage even of transport animals.' The infinitive here is to be explained on the same principle as λαμβάνειν in § 8; so that ὑποζυγίοις πορεύεσθαι is virtually a double dative,—'practicable *for animals for passing*.' An exact parallel is furnished by the well-known Homeric line:—αἰσχρὸν γὰρ τόδε γ' ἐστὶ καὶ ἐσσομένοισι πυθέσθαι 'this is shameful for the hearing even of future men,' on which Mr Monro remarks that this construction goes back to the time when the infinitive was still felt as a dative (*Homeric Grammar*, § 239).

25. ἔφη—παρελθεῖν, 'he stated that there was a height which, if it were not seized beforehand, would render a passage impossible.'

προκαταλήψοιτο. Note that the future optative can only be used in *oratio obliqua* (as here) or in virtual *oratio obliqua*; cf. iii. 29, v. 28, vi. 1.

26. ἐδόκει, 'it seemed good (to the generals).'

λοχαγοὺς καὶ πελταστὰς καὶ τῶν ὁπλιτῶν, 'captains,—both targeteer (captains) and (captains) of the heavy infantry.'

πελταστάς, substantive used as an epithet; cf. § 6 τοῖς ὀπισθοφύλαξιν ὁπλίταις.

λέγειν τὰ παρόντα, 'to explain the situation.'

εἴ τις—ἔστιν ὅστις—ἐθέλει. The verbs of the *oratio recta* are retained in the *obliqua*, as often in Greek.

καὶ ὑποστὰς—πορεύεσθαι, 'and, having offered himself, to go as a volunteer.'

27. ὑφίσταται. Notice (1) the *asyndeton*, cf. § 20 ἀποκρίνεται, and (2) the singular verb with the two subjects, Aristonymus and Agasias, cf. II. iv. 16 ἔπεμψέ με Ἀριαῖος καὶ Ἀρτάοζος.

τῶν ὁπλιτῶν, partitive genitive, 'from among the heavy infantry.'

28. ὃς πολλαχοῦ—ἐγένετο, 'who on many occasions proved of great value to the army for such enterprises.'

II.

1. καὶ ἦν μὲν—πορεύεσθαι, 'And it was afternoon when the generals ordered the volunteers to proceed after making a hurried meal.'

καὶ τὸν ἡγεμόνα—φυλάττειν, ' And they handed over to them the guide bound, and arranged with them that, if they seized the summit, they were to guard the position during the night and at daybreak give a signal by bugle.'

τὸ ἄκρον, marked a in the Plan on the opposite page.

καὶ τοὺς μὲν—τάχιστα, 'And (they arranged) that the volunteers when on the top should move against the enemy who held the visible outlet, and that they themselves (the generals) would sally out together to their assistance as quickly as possible.'

τὴν φανερὰν ἔκβασιν, the way out, or ordinary mountain road which they saw before them, as opposed to the circuitous path to be taken by the volunteers, who were led by a native guide. See Plan.

τοὺς μὲν—αὐτοὶ δέ, according to the rule exemplified in Thuc. IV. 28 οὐκ ἔφη αὐτὸς ἀλλ' ἐκεῖνον στρατηγεῖν.

2. ταῦτα συνθέμενοι—Ξενοφῶν δέ, ' They (i.e. the generals and the volunteers) having made these arrangements,—the volunteers departed...and Xenophon...,'—an instance of what is called *partitive apposition*; cf. § 12 and II. i. 15 οὗτοι μέν, ὦ Κλέαρχε, ἄλλος ἄλλα λέγει 'these men—one says one thing and one another.'

πλῆθος, 'in number,' accusative of respect; cf. iii. 1 εὖρος ὡς δίπλεθρον.

οἱ περιιόντες, i.e. the volunteers.

3. ἐπεὶ δὲ—ἐκβαίνειν, ' But when the rear-guard reached a ravine, which they had to cross before they could get out up the incline.'

χαράδρᾳ, marked χ in Plan.

οἱ ὀπισθοφύλακες, i.e. Xenophon's division.

διαβάντας—ἐκβαίνειν. The emphasis is on the participle, as often in Greek; cf. v. 28, viii. 6.

οἱ φερόμενοι—διεσφενδονῶντο, 'which, as they came down, struck against the rocks and were splintered into fragments (like stones from a sling).'

καὶ παντάπασιν—εἰσόδῳ, 'And it was utterly impossible even to approach the entrance.'

τῇ εἰσόδῳ, i.e. the beginning of the ascent (τὸ ὄρθιον § 3) on the other side of the ravine.

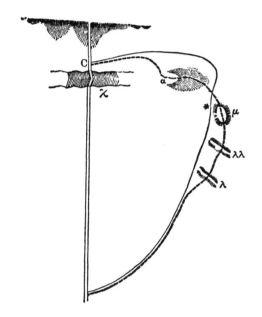

C position of Carduchian main body, stopping the road into the mountains which could be seen by the Greeks. This position was turned by the volunteers on the morning of the 2nd day, whilst Cheirisophus attacked it in front.

χ ravine, where the attack of Xenophon and the rear-guard was stopped on the 1st day.

* spot under the round hill where the volunteers defeated the outpost of the Carduchians on the 1st day and stayed the night.

λ 1st ridge
λλ 2nd ridge ⎱ where skirmishes took place on the 2nd day between Xenophon
μ round hill ⎰ and some Carduchians.
a height

═══ road leading to the mountains along which Xenophon's attack on the 1st day, and Cheirisophus' attack on the 2nd day, were made.

──── route of the volunteers [and of the baggage train on the 2nd day].

---- route of Xenophon and soldiers on the 2nd day.

4. εἰ μὴ ταύτῃ δύναιντο, '*in case* they could not do so this way'; cf. § 11 εἰ βούλοιντο φεύγειν.

ταῦτα ἐποίουν, 'continued these tactics,' i.e. to divert the attention of the enemy from the enterprise of the volunteers.

ἀφανεῖς εἶναι ἀπιόντες, 'they would get off without being noticed.' For the participial construction with ἀφανής cf. that with φαίνομαι, δῆλός εἰμι, and λανθάνω. See iii. 33, v. 28.

οὐδὲν ἐπαύσαντο. For οὐδέν 'not at all,' cognate accusative used adverbially, cf. i. 14 τὰ μέν τι μαχόμενοι.

τεκμαίρεσθαι δ᾽ ἦν, 'And it was possible to infer it'; cf. § 10 οὐκ ἦν ἐκβῆναι.

5. οἱ ἔχοντες τὸν ἡγεμόνα, i.e. the volunteers.

τοὺς φύλακας, i.e. the Carduchian outpost, marked * in Plan.

κατακανόντες, from κατακαίνω.

ὡς τὸ ἄκρον κατέχοντες, 'under the impression that they were holding the summit (which they had been instructed to occupy).'

6. παρ᾽ ὃν ἦν, 'along which ran...'; cf. iii. 6 παρὰ τὸν ποταμόν.

ἔφοδος—ἐπὶ τοὺς πολεμίους, 'a path from where they were to (the main body of) the enemy.' See Plan.

7. ὑπέφαινεν, 'was just beginning to break,' 'at the first glimpse of dawn.' For ὑπὸ in composition giving the meaning *gently* cf. i. 8 ὑποφειδόμενοι and § 16 ὑπάγειν.

οὐκ ἐδέξαντο, 'did not await (their onset).'

8. οἱ δὲ ἀμφὶ—ὁδόν, 'And Cheirisophus and his men when they heard the bugle—the signal agreed upon (§ 1)—at once charged up hill along the visible path.'

κατὰ τὴν—ὁδόν, '*along* the path.' Contrast § 17 κατὰ τῆς πέτρας '*down* the rock.'

ἕκαστοι. Note the plural 'each *party*,' i.e. 'the party with each general.' Contrast § 12 ἐδύναντο ἕκαστος.

9. τοῖς προκαταλαβοῦσι, i.e. the volunteers.

τοὺς δὲ ἡμίσεις—ἔταξε, i.e. the other half of the rear-guard.

10. πορευόμενοι—Ἑλλήνων, 'And as they went they came upon a crest occupied by the enemy, whom they must dislodge or else find themselves cut off from the rest of the Greeks.'

λόφῳ, marked λ in Plan.

διεξεῦχθαι. Mark the force of the perfect. There is an exact parallel in *Cyropaedeia* VII. v. 23 ὥστε ἀνάγκην εἶναι ἢ φεύγειν ἢ κατακεκαῦσθαι 'to be burnt *there and then*.'

καὶ αὐτοὶ—ἐκβῆναι, 'And though the men themselves could have taken the same route as the rest, yet it was impossible for the transport animals to mount up any other way than this.'

τὰ δὲ ὑποζύγια—ἐκβῆναι. This clause virtually furnishes the protasis to αὐτοὶ ἂν ἐπορεύθησαν, i.e. 'they would have gone, if it had not been impossible....'

οὐκ ἦν—ἐκβῆναι. Cf. § 4 τεκμαίρεσθαι δ' ἦν.

11. παρακελευσάμενοι. The middle has here a *reciprocal* force,—'having cheered on one another.'

ὀρθίοις τοῖς λόχοις, dative of instrument, 'with their companies in file,' 'in company columns,' Latin *rectis ordinibus*.

οὐ κύκλῳ—φεύγειν, 'Not however attacking all round, but leaving the enemy a way of escape in case they should prefer to flee,'—which was what the Greeks desired.

εἰ βούλοιντο. The apodosis is implied in ἄφοδον.

12. ὅπῃ ἐδύναντο ἕκαστος, 'by whatever way they could, each man of them.' For ἕκαστος in partitive apposition to a plural subject cf. Homer *Il.* XVIII. 496 αἱ δὲ γυναῖκες—θαύμαζον ἑκάστη. See note on § 2.

καὶ τοῦτον—πορεύεσθαι, 'And the Greeks had passed this ridge, when they found another in front of them occupied (by the enemy) and determined to attack this also.'

ἕτερον—λόφον, marked λλ in Plan.

ὁρῶσιν—ἐδόκει, literally 'it seemed good to them observing.'

13. ἐννοήσας—παριοῦσιν, 'But Xenophon struck with anxiety lest, if he left the ridge just taken unoccupied behind him, the enemy might seize it once more and then attack the transport animals as they went past.'

ἐννοήσας—μὴ—ἐπιθοῖντο. The construction is analogous to that after verbs of *fearing*, because Xenophon's thoughts were coloured by anxiety; cf. III. v. 3 ἐννοούμενοι μὴ—οὐκ ἔχοιεν. Cf. also i. 6.

καὶ πάλιν, emphatic, 'once again'; cf. καὶ τοῦτον below, 'this also.'

ἐπὶ πολὺ δ'—πορευόμενα, 'and the baggage train extended to a great length, since the path along which they had to go was narrow.'

στενῆς, predicate; cf. Soph. *Ajax* 1121 οὐ γὰρ βάναυσον τὴν τέχνην ἐκτησάμην 'The art I acquired is no sordid one.'

Κηφισοφῶντος—'Αμφιδήμου. The fathers' names are given in the case of two Athenians, according to Athenian custom.

14. μαστός, marked μ in Plan.

τῆς—φυλακῆς, 'the outpost which had been surprised over their fire.' Cf. § 5 τοὺς φύλακας ἀμφὶ πῦρ καθημένους.

15. ἄρα, 'as it turned out,' 'as the result proved'; cf. II. ii. 3 εἰκότως ἄρα οὐκ ἐγίγνετο.

16. τοὺς δὲ ἄλλους—προσμίξειαν, 'and gave orders to the rest to march on slowly in order to give time for the rear companies to come up.'

θέσθαι τὰ ὅπλα, 'to ground their arms,' 'to take up their position.' 'The Greek heavy-armed soldiers whenever they halted on a march immediately piled their spears and shields, and did not resume them till the halt was over. When they encamped anywhere, an open space within the camp was selected for piling the arms, and this naturally served also as a sort of parade for the soldiers. In a time of siege, when a large part of the population were on active military duty, their arms were kept constantly piled in some of the squares or open places of the town, that they might be ready on the first alarm. So inveterate was this practice of piling the spear and shield on every possible occasion, that in reviews the ordinary stand-at-ease of a Grecian soldier was to get rid of his long spear and shield'—ARNOLD on Thuc. II. 2.

17. τεθνᾶσι, 'are lying dead,' 'are dead men.' For the force of the perfect cf. i. 19 τέθνατον, and the use of *perii* in the comic poets, 'I'm a dead man.'

ὅσοι μὴ—ἀφίκοντο. From the speaker's point of view the number is *indefinite*; therefore μή, not οὐ, is used. Cf. iv. 11, v. 11.

ἀλάμενοι. ἡλάμην, not ἡλόμην, is the true form of the aorist of ἄλλομαι, though some editors read ἀλόμενοι here.

18. ἀντίπορον λόφον τῷ μαστῷ, 'a ridge opposite to the breast-like hill.'

19. οἱ δὲ ἔφασαν—οἰκίας, 'They undertook to restore the dead on condition that Xenophon did not burn their houses.'

ἐφ' ᾧ μὴ καίειν. ἐφ' ᾧ and ἐφ' ᾧτε take (1) the infinitive (like ὥστε in some of its senses); cf. iv. 6 ἐφ' ᾧ μήτε αὐτὸς ἀδικεῖν—or (2) the future indicative; cf. Thuc. I. 113 σπονδὰς ποιησάμενοι ἐφ' ᾧ τοὺς ἄνδρας κομιοῦνται.

συνωμολόγει. For the asyndeton cf. i. 27.

ἐν ᾧ, 'during the time when,' 'while.' For the temporal use of ἐν cf. i. 1 ἐν ταῖς σπονδαῖς.

πάντες οἱ ἐκ τούτου τοῦ τόπου συνερρύησαν, 'all the enemy in this neighbourhood had flocked together from it,'—a so-called *pregnant* construction; cf. Thuc. I. 8 οἱ ἐκ νήσων κακοῦργοι.

20. ἤρξαντο, i.e. the Greeks under Xenophon,—an awkward change of subject.

ἔνθα τὰ ὅπλα ἔκειντο, 'where the arms were piled'; cf. § 16 θέσθαι τὰ ὅπλα. Note that κεῖμαι is ordinarily used as perfect passive of τίθημι, e.g. Plato *leges* 793 B πάντων (i.e. νόμων) τῶν τεθέντων τε καὶ κειμένων καὶ τῶν ἔτι τεθησομένων.

ἔκειντο, plural verb with neuter plural subject, perhaps because the phrase really means 'where the hoplites were stationed'; for τὰ ὅπλα sometimes = οἱ ὁπλῖται, e.g. III. ii. 36, VI. ii. 8.   See note on i. 13 τὰ αἰχμάλωτα ἐποίουν.

ἵεντο δὴ—θορύβῳ, 'on rushed the foe, in full force, with hue and cry'—DAKYNS.

21. πρὸ ἀμφοῖν—ἀπεχώρει, 'having placed his shield so as to protect both Xenophon and himself, retreated (with him).'

προβεβλημένος, (supply τὴν ἀσπίδα) perfect passive used in a middle sense; cf. VII. iv. 17 ὄπισθεν περιβαλλόμενοι τὰς πέλτας and *Cyropaedeia* VI. iii. 24 προβεβλημένοι τοὺς θωρακοφόρους.

πρὸς τοὺς συντεταγμένους, 'to where the troops were massed,' i.e. ἔνθα τὰ ὅπλα ἔκειντο § 20.

22. ἐκ δὲ τούτου—αὑτοῦ, 'After this the whole Greek force united and they took up their quarters on the spot.'

ἐσκήνησαν, construction *according to the sense* after the noun of multitude τὸ Ἑλληνικόν. Cf. II. i. 6 τὸ στράτευμα ἐπορίζετο σῖτον, κόπτοντες τοὺς βοῦς καὶ ὄνους.

ἐν—οἰκίαις καὶ ἐπιτηδείοις δαψιλέσι, 'in many fine houses and (*amid*) luxurious provisions,'—an instance of *syllepsis* ('taking together'), a figure of speech by which one word is used in two different senses in the same sentence.   Here ἐν is used to denote (1) *locality* and (2) *circumstances*; for the latter cf. v. 29 ἐν πᾶσιν ἀφθόνοις.

πολὺς ἦν ὥστε—εἶχον, 'was so abundant that they kept it...'; cf. § 27 ἐλαφροὶ ἦσαν ὥστε....

23. διεπράξαντο—τὸν ἡγεμόνα, 'managed to recover the dead in exchange for the guide whom they gave up.'

τὸν ἡγεμόνα, the guide used by the volunteers.

πάντα—ἀγαθοῖς, 'they did everything for the dead to the best of their power, as is customary in the case of brave men.'

ἐκ τῶν δυνατῶν, literally '*starting from* their available means'; cf. Thuc. IV. 17 ὡς ἐκ τῶν παρόντων 'so far as present circumstances permit.'

ἀνδράσιν, like τοῖς ἀποθανοῦσιν above, is dative of person concerned.

24. εἴη, optative of frequency; cf. § 25 ὁπότε κωλύοιεν, § 28 ὁπότε τοξεύοιεν and ἐπεὶ λάβοιεν.

τὰς παρόδους, 'their passage time after time.'

25. ὁπότε—κωλυόντων, ' Whenever then they impeded the van, Xenophon from behind mounting the hills broke up for the vanguard the obstruction to their passage, by attempting to get above the enemy who impeded them,'—i.e. though he did not always succeed, the movement distracted the attention of the enemy.

τοῖς πρώτοις. Cf. § 23 ἀνδράσιν ἀγαθοῖς.

26. ἰσχυρῶς ἀλλήλων ἐπεμέλοντο, 'paid earnest heed to one another's requirements.'

27. ἦν δὲ—καταβαίνουσιν, 'And on occasion too the barbarians caused great annoyance to those who had mounted *in their turn* (αὐτοῖς), while they were descending.'

ἦν—ὁπότε. Cf. v. 31 οὐκ ἦν ὅπου οὐ, II. vi. 9 ἐσθ' ὅτε and Cicero *Tusc.* v. 23 *est ubi id valeat.*

πράγματα παρεῖχον. Cf. i. 22.

ἐλαφροὶ—ἀποφεύγειν, 'For they were so agile that even when fleeing with but a short start they could make good their escape.'

ἐγγύθεν, literally 'from near'; i.e. they could come up quite close to the Greeks and then turn and escape safely.

φεύγοντες, *concessive* use of the participle; cf. i. 10 ὀλίγοι ὄντες.

28. πρὸς τὸ κάτω—προσβαίνοντες, 'treading on the lower end of the bow.'

θωράκων. The θώραξ was a cuirass of metal, consisting of two separate pieces, one covering the chest, the other the back, joined by means of clasps or buckles. It was also fastened by a leather belt. The front plate was sometimes extended to cover the stomach. As a protection to the hips there were, as in the case of the στολάς—described in the note on i. 18—strips of leather or felt covered with metal plates, called πτέρυγες 'wings.'

ἀκοντίοις, predicate, ' *as* javelins.'

ἐναγκυλῶντες. The ἀγκύλη, or thong by which the javelin was hurled, must have been somewhat similar to the Latin *amentum*; cf. Cicero *Brutus* 271 *hastae amentatae* 'spears furnished with thongs.'

III.

1. τοῦ παρὰ—ποταμόν. For παρά denoting *extent along* cf. § 6 and ii. 6 παρ' ὃν ἦν ἡ στενὴ αὕτη ὁδός.

Κεντρίτην. 'This river, which is now called the River of Sert from the name of the chief town on its banks, is a tributary of the Eastern Tigris, which it joins between the head-waters of that stream near

Bitlis and its union with the western branch'—Tozer, *History of Ancient Geography*, p. 115.

εὖρος ὡς δίπλεθρον, 'about 200 feet in breadth.' εὖρος is accusative of respect; cf. ii. 2 πλῆθος ὡς δισχίλιοι.

στάδια, accusative of extent; cf. § 5 πλέθρα.

τῶν Καρδούχων, to be taken with τῶν ὀρέων.

2. πολλά, cognate accusative used adverbially,—'having many memories of...,' i.e. 'talking much of...'; cf. Herod. VI. 136 τῆς μάχης πολλὰ ἐπιμεμνημένοι.

ἑπτά—Τισσαφέρνους, 'For the seven days, during which they had passed through the Carduchian territory,—all of them they had spent in continuous fighting and they had endured greater hardships than even the whole of those inflicted by the Great King and Tissaphernes amounted to.'

ὅσα οὐδὲ τὰ σύμπαντα. Supply ἔπαθον from the previous clause. 'His expressions have a simple emphasis which marks how unfading was the recollection of what he had suffered in Carduchia'—Grote.

3. κωλύσοντας. The future participle is often used to denote a purpose, sometimes preceded by ὡς as here, but often without it, e.g. v. 22 πέμπει σκεψομένους, v. 24 ᾤχετο θηράσων. Homer *Iliad* I. 13 ἦλθε λυσόμενος θύγατρα 'he came to ransom his daughter.'

ἄνω τῶν ἱππέων, 'above the cavalry,' i.e. on rising ground behind them.

4. Ὀρόντα καὶ Ἀρτούχα, possessive genitives.

μισθοφόροι, to be taken with Χαλδαῖοι only.

ὅπλα—εἶχον, 'they had as arms.' For ὅπλα used predicatively cf. ii. 28 ἐχρῶντο—ἀκοντίοις.

5. ἦν ἄγουσα, 'was one leading'; cf. III. 3. 2 καὶ ἐνθάδε δ' εἰμὶ σὺν πολλῷ φόβῳ διάγων 'and here am I living in great fear.'

ὥσπερ χειροποίητος, 'apparently artificial,' perhaps part of the present road to Sert described by Ainsworth (*Travels in the Track of the Ten Thousand*), in which 'there is an artificial causeway carried up the face of the rock, partly by steps cut out of the rock itself and partly by a causeway carried circuitously up the hill-side and paved with large blocks of stone.'

6. καὶ οὔτ'—ποταμός, 'And it was impossible for them to hold their arms in the water—if they did, the stream carried them away—and if they tried to carry them over their heads, they became exposed....'

οὔτ', answered by τε, cf. iv. 6 μήτε—τε.

ἦν ἔχειν. Cf. ii. 4 τεκμαίρεσθαι ἦν and ii. 10 οὐκ ἦν ἐκβῆναι.

εἰ δὲ μή, not to be translated here 'but if not,' for it means 'otherwise,' i.e. '*if they did.*' The phrase has become quite stereotyped and is used even when the previous clause is negative, as here; cf. Aristoph. *Nubes* 1433 πρὸς ταῦτα μὴ τύπτ'· εἰ δὲ μή, σαυτόν ποτ' αἰτιάσει 'so don't beat me; else (i.e. *if you do*) you will only have yourself to blame.'

παρὰ τὸν ποταμόν, added to explain αὐτοῦ, 'where they were, along the river'; cf. § 28 αὐτοῦ ἐπὶ τοῦ ποταμοῦ. For παρά with the accusative cf. § 1.

7. πολλούς, predicate, 'in great numbers.'

ὁρῶσι μὲν—ὁρῶσι δὲ—ὁρῶσι δέ. Such a repetition is a favourite trick of style with Xenophon; cf. § 21 and § 23.

τοῖς διαβαίνουσιν ἐπικεισομένους, 'ready to attack any who should attempt to cross.'

8. αὗται—περιρρυῆναι, 'these seemed—ἔδοξαν supplied from ἔδοξεν in the previous clause—to fall off from him of their own accord.'

αὐτῷ, literally 'for him,' dative of person concerned.

περιρρυῆναι, from περιρρέω, cf. Thuc. IV. 12 ἡ ἀσπὶς περιερρύη ἐς τὴν θάλασσαν 'his shield slipped from round (his arm) into the sea.'

διαβαίνειν, 'to move his legs freely.' 'It is impossible to give the true sense and humour of the passage in English, depending as it does on the double meaning of διαβαίνειν, (1) to *cross* (a river), (2) to *stride*. The army is unable to *cross* the Centrites. Xenophon dreams that he is fettered; but the chains drop off his legs and he is able to *stride* as freely as ever. Next morning the two young men come to him with the story how they found themselves able to *walk across* the river. It is obvious to Xenophon that the dream is sent from heaven'—DAKYNS.

9. ὡς τάχιστα ἕως ὑπέφαινεν, 'at the very moment when dawn was just faintly glimmering.'

ὑπέφαινεν. Cf. ii. 7 ἡμέρα ὑπέφαινεν.

ἐθύοντο, 'had sacrifices offered,' *causal* force of the middle, a rare use except in the case of θύομαι, which is frequent in Xenophon. The example διδάσκομαι τὸν υἱόν 'I get my son taught' is a fiction of the grammars, due to a misunderstanding of Plato *Meno* 93 D, where διδάσκομαι means simply 'I teach *for myself.*'

ἐπὶ τοῦ πρώτου, 'in the case of the first (victim).'

10. προσέτρεχον, plural verb with dual subject, as often; for the Greeks seem to have disliked dual verbs, except when they wish to emphasise the *duality* of the subject.

ἐπεγείραντα—πόλεμον, 'it was allowable for any one to wake him and inform him of anything he had to tell of matters concerning the war.'

11. καὶ τότε, 'so now' in our idiom.

ὡς ἐπὶ πῦρ, 'with a view to lighting a fire.' **ἐπὶ** with the accusative is frequently used to denote a *purpose*; cf. Thuc. II. 83 ἔπλεον οὐχ ὡς ἐπὶ ναυμαχίαν.

ἐπ' αὐτὸν τὸν ποταμόν, 'right down to the edge of the river'; cf. i. 2 ὑπὲρ αὐτοῦ τοῦ ποταμοῦ.

ὥσπερ μαρσίπους ἱματίων, 'what seemed to be bags of clothes.'

12. δόξαι, continuation of the *oratio obliqua,* but with a change of construction, infinitive instead of ὅτι with optative. We find the reverse change in § 29 ὅτι ἔσοιτο.

κατὰ τοῦτο, 'at this point,' 'over this way'; cf. § 17 κατὰ τὴν διάβασιν and ii. 8 κατὰ τὴν φανερὰν ὁδόν.

ἐκδύντες—διαβαίνειν, 'And they said that they stript naked, thinking they would have to swim, and with their daggers in their hands began to cross.'

νευσούμενοι, from νέω. Some editors prefer the form νευσόμενοι. Cf. πλέω, future πλεύσομαι or πλευσοῦμαι.

καὶ διαβάντες, 'and, having crossed the river again, they recovered their clothes and had now come back.'

τὰ ἱμάτια, certainly 'their own clothes,' not 'the bundles of clothes' mentioned in § 11, as some take it.

13. τοῖς νεανίσκοις—ἐκέλευε, 'bade (his attendants) fill cups for the young men,'—so that they also might offer a libation.

καὶ εὔχεσθαι—ἐπιτελέσαι, 'and bade (the young men) pray to the gods, who had shewn the vision (to himself) and the ford (to them), to accomplish all other blessings also.'

σπονδὰς ἐποίει, 'proceeded to make libations.' Contrast i. 1 σπονδαῖς ἃς—ἐποιήσαντο.

14. αὐτοί, Xenophon and Cheirisophus.

τοὺς στρατηγούς, 'the other generals,' i.e. Cleanor the Arcadian, Philesius and Xanthicles the Achaeans, and Timasion of Dardanus in the Troad.

ὅπως ἂν—κακόν. In *oratio recta* the three clauses would run thus:—

    (1) πῶς ἂν κάλλιστα διαβαῖμεν ;

    (2) πῶς τοὺς ἔμπροσθεν νικῶμεν ;

    (3) πῶς ὑπὸ τῶν ὄπισθεν μηδὲν πάσχωμεν κακόν ;

Note (a) that **νικῶμεν** and **πάσχωμεν** are deliberative subjunctives,—'How are we to conquer?' 'How are we to suffer?'— (b) that **ἄν** goes with the first optative only, διαβαῖεν, (c) that **μή** is the negative used with the deliberative subjunctive, e.g. Plato πῶς μὴ φῶμεν; 'How are we not to say?' εἰσίω ἢ μή; 'Am I to go in or not?'

Translate:—'They took counsel how they would best cross the river and also how they were to overcome the Persians in front without suffering any damage from the Carduchians in the rear.'

15. τὸν ὄχλον, the mob of non-combatants, i.e. the camp-followers, porters, etc.

17. πορευομένων—ἱππέων, 'And as they marched (by the river), the squadrons of the cavalry kept pace with them on the opposite bank.'

ἀντιπαρῇσαν. The force of both prepositions must be brought out in translation,—(1) *opposite*, (2) *alongside*.

κατὰ τὴν διάβασιν, 'at the ford.' For this use of κατά with the accusative cf. § 12 κατὰ τοῦτο.

ἔθεντο τὰ ὅπλα. Cf. ii. 16 and 20.

στεφανωσάμενος, according to Spartan custom, probably with the reeds of the river bank (Taylor). Note that the word means 'having *wreathed* himself,' not '*crowned*'; for στέφανος is something *round* the head, not *on* it. Cf. v. 33.

ἀποδύς. Cf. § 12 ἐκδύντες.

τοῖς ἄλλοις—παρήγγελλε, 'passed an order along the ranks for all the rest (to do the same).'

ἄγειν τοὺς λόχους ὀρθίους. Cf. ii. 11 ὀρθίοις τοῖς λόχοις.

18. ἐσφαγιάζοντο εἰς τὸν ποταμόν, 'were cutting the throat of a victim over the river,' literally 'into the river.' The blood is let flow into the river; for to the river-god the offering is made. Cf. Herod. VII. 113 ἐς τὸν Στρύμονα σφάζοντες ἵππους λευκούς. And for the so-called *pregnant* construction cf. II. ii. 9 σφάξαντες εἰς ἀσπίδα. Arrian VI. iii ἔσπενδεν εἰς τὸν ποταμόν.

20. ἀνὰ κράτος, 'at full speed,' literally 'up to the full strength,' much the same as κατὰ κράτος.

κατὰ τὴν ἔκβασιν, 'at the outlet,' i.e. 'facing the outlet'; cf. § 12 κατὰ τοῦτο and § 21 κατὰ τὴν ὁδόν.

ἔκβασιν, again in the sense of an 'outlet' on to higher ground; cf. § 22 συνεκβαίνειν ἐπὶ τὸ ὄρος and § 23 ἐξέβαινεν.

προσποιούμενος—ἱππέας, 'making a feint of crossing here and cutting off the cavalry who were moving along the river bank.'

21. ὁρῶντες μὲν—ὁρῶντες δέ. Cf. § 7 and § 23.

ὡς πρὸς—ἔκβασιν, 'as if making for the pass which led up from the river.'

κατὰ τὴν ὁδὸν ἐγένοντο, 'when they found themselves at the path,' i.e. the ἔκβασις just mentioned.

ἔτεινον, intransitive ; cf. Eur. *Supplices* 720 ἔτεινον ἐς πύλας.

22. ἐβόων—ὄρος, 'shouted not to fall behind, but to follow them right up to the mountains'—DAKYNS.

23. κατὰ—ποταμόν, 'by the mounds which reached down to the river.'

24. τὴν ταχίστην, ὁδόν understood, cognate accusative used adverbially ; cf. μακρὰν 'a long way,' τὴν λοιπήν 'the rest of the way.'

φανεροὶ—ἦσαν—καταβαίνοντες. For the participial construction cf. § 33 φανεροὶ ἦσαν φεύγοντες and ii. 4 ἀφανεῖς εἶναι ἀπιόντες.

25. ἐπιχειρήσας—ὑπολειπόμενα, 'in an attempt to follow up the pursuit captured those of the baggage animals which were from time to time falling into the rear.'

ὑπολειπόμενα, imperfect participle ; cf. i. 3.

26. ὁ ὄχλος, i.e. of non-combatants ; cf. § 15.

ἀκμὴν διέβαινε, 'was just crossing.'

ἀκμήν, cognate accusative used adverbially; cf. § 24 τὴν ταχίστην. The word ἀκμή means literally 'point,' then 'highest point' or 'zenith,' then 'the right moment.' So with this adverbial use of ἀκμήν 'just at that moment' we may compare Soph. *Ajax* 34 καιρὸν δ' ἐφήκεις 'thou hast come at the right moment.'

Ξενοφῶν δὲ—ἔθετο, 'when Xenophon wheeled round and drew up his men to face the Carduchians.'

τὰ ὅπλα ἔθετο. Cf. ii. 16 θέσθαι τὰ ὅπλα and ii. 20 τὰ ὅπλα ἔκειντο.

κατ' ἐνωμοτίας—λόχον, 'that each should form his company into sections.'

παρ' ἀσπίδα—ἐπὶ φάλαγγος, 'bringing each section into line by deploying to the left.'

παρ' ἀσπίδα, 'towards the shield,' i.e. 'towards the left hand,' opposed to ἐπὶ δόρυ (§ 29) 'towards the spear,' i.e. the right. For παρὰ with accusative denoting *motion to* cf. § 27 πέμπει παρὰ Ξενοφῶντα.

παραγαγόντας. 'The παραγωγή is thus described by Xenophon in his treatise *de republica Lacedaemoniorum* xi. 8. The last section moves up to the left of the one before it, then the two together to the left of the one before that, and so on till the whole is in line with the first section. We do not know how the troops were marching on this occasion. If they were marching in parallel columns each λόχος in single file, the evolution would be very quickly performed. If, however, they were marching as was usual in two or three files, it would be a little more complicated, as the members of each section would have to get into single file '—TAYLOR.

ἐπὶ φάλαγγος, 'in line,' opposed to ἐπὶ κέρως 'in column.'

πρὸς τῶν Καρδούχων—πρὸς τοῦ ποταμοῦ, '*in the direction of* the Carduchians—*near* the river.' πρός with the genitive generally denotes '*from* or *on* the side of.' So there is nothing strange in καταστήσασθαι πρὸς τοῦ ποταμοῦ. But ἰέναι πρὸς τῶν Καρδούχων with the meaning given above seems curious. However, there are parallels, e.g. Herod. I. 84 χωρίον πρὸς τοῦ Τμώλου τετραμμένον 'facing Mount Tmolus.'

καταστήσασθαι, 'to keep their position.' But note that ἐστησάμην and its compounds are always active in sense, never deponent. So here καταστήσασθαι means to draw up (*their men* understood). Cf. Homer *Od.* IX. 54 στησάμενοι δ' ἐμάχοντο μάχην 'having set the battle in array they fought it.'

27. τοῦ ὄχλου ψιλουμένους, 'being stript of—i.e. abandoned by—the main body,' probably not 'separated from the mob of non-combatants,' though ὄχλος generally bears this sense in the *Anabasis*, e.g. § 26.

τοῦ ὄχλου, ablatival genitive of separation; cf. Herod. IV. 135 οἱ ὄνοι ἐρημωθέντες τοῦ ὁμίλου.

28. αὐτοῦ—ἐπὶ τοῦ ποταμοῦ. Cf. § 6 αὐτοῦ παρὰ τὸν ποταμόν.

ὅταν δ' ἄρξωνται—προβαίνειν, 'but, when he and his men began to cross, they were to enter the river facing them, some on one side of them and some on the other, as if intending to cross,—the javelin-men with their hands in the thong and the archers with their arrows on the string; but they were not to advance far into the river.'

αὐτοί, answering to ἡμεῖς αὐτοί of *oratio obliqua*.

διηγκυλωμένους. Cf. ii. 28 ἀκοντίοις ἐναγκυλῶντες. The perfect participle passive is here used in a middle sense, the object τὰ ἀκόντια being understood,—'holding their javelins by the thong.' Cf. ii. 21 προβεβλημένος with τὴν ἀσπίδα understood.

ἐπιβεβλημένους, perfect passive again in middle sense, the object τοὺς διστούς being understood, —'having their arrows fixed on the string.'

τοῦ ποταμοῦ, partitive genitive after πρόσω. Cf. *Hellenica* VII. ii. 19 πόρρω τῆς ἡμέρας. *Memorabilia* IV. viii. 1 πόρρω τῆς ἡλικίας.

29. ἐπειδὰν—ψοφῇ, i.e. when they were within range.

σημήνῃ τὸ πολεμικόν, (understand σημεῖον) 'sounds a war-note,' or 'the attack'; cf. Latin *bellicum canere*.

ἐπὶ δόρυ. See note on § 26 παρ' ἀσπίδα.

ἀναστρέψαντας—ἡγεῖσθαι μὲν τοὺς οὐραγούς, partitive apposition;
cf. § 28 ἐμβαίνειν—ἀκοντιστὰς—τοξότας. See also note on ii. 2.

ὡς μὴ ἐμποδίζειν. Xenophon often writes ὡς where other Attic
Prose writers would use ὥστε.

ὅτι—ἴσοιτο. Notice the change of construction from the accusative
and infinitive to ὅτι with optative. See note on § 12 δόξαι.

ἴσοιτο, answering to ἔσται of *oratio recta*. The future optative is
only used in *oratio obliqua* or virtual *oratio obliqua*; cf. i. 25.

ὃς ἂν—γένηται. For the change of mood cf. i. 3 διέλθοιεν—
βούλωνται.

31. ὡς μὲν—φεύγειν, 'adequately armed for mountain warfare with
a view to sudden attack and subsequent flight.'

ὡς ἐν τοῖς ὄρεσιν, ' as one might expect in the mountains'; cf. Thuc.
II. 65 πολλὰ ὡς ἐν μεγάλῃ πόλει ἡμαρτήθη.

εἰς χεῖρας δέχεσθαι, 'to withstand a hand to hand attack.'

32. τἀναντία, cognate accusative again, used adverbially, 'having
turned in the opposite direction'; cf. *Hellenica* III. iv. 12 τἀναντία
ἀποστρέψας.

33. καὶ πέραν ὄντων τῶν Ἑλλήνων, 'even when the Greeks had
crossed.'

34. οἱ δὲ ὑπαντήσαντες—πάλιν, 'But the party who came to meet
them (see § 27), making a display of their courage and advancing into
the river further than the occasion required, had to cross back again in
the rear of Xenophon's division.'

προσωτέρω τοῦ καιροῦ. Cf. *Hellenica* VII. v. 13 ἐδίωξαν πορρωτέρω
τοῦ καιροῦ.

IV.

1. πεδίον—γηλόφους, 'over one long plain broken only by smooth
hillocks,' accusatives of extent. This plain is the first Armenian table-
land, 2000 feet above the sea.

λείους, i.e. not rocky; cf. Hom. *Od.* V. 443 χῶρος λεῖος πετράων.

μεῖον—παρασάγγας, both accusatives of extent again; cf. § 3
ἐπορεύθησαν σταθμούς.

παρασάγγας. The *parasang* is an hour's journey, or roughly
speaking 3½ miles in these parts except in very wintry weather. Cf.
Layard, *Nineveh and Babylon*, p. 59 :—' The *parasang*, like its repre-
sentative the modern *farsang* or *farsakh* of Persia, was not a measure
of distance very accurately determined, but rather indicated a certain
amount of time employed in traversing a given space. Travellers are

well aware that the Persian *farsakh* varies considerably according to the nature of the country and the usual modes of conveyance adopted by its inhabitants. The *farsakh* and the hour are almost invariably used as expressing the same distance.'

2. εἰς δὲ ἦν ἀφίκοντο κώμην. For the attraction cf. Lysias XIX. 49 τὴν οὐσίαν ἣν κατέλιπεν οὐ πλείονος ἀξία ἐστίν 'The property which he left is not worth more,' and Virg. *Aen.* I. 573 *urbem quam statuo vestra est.*

κώμην, probably the modern Sert.

σατράπῃ, 'for the satrap (Orontas),' dative of person concerned.

σταθμοὺς δύο παρασάγγας δέκα, 'two days' march *consisting of* 10 parasangs.' For the apposition cf. III. v. 16 στρατιὰν δώδεκα μυριάδας 'an army consisting of 120,000.'

τὰς πηγάς, must be those 'of one of the most easterly of the tributaries of the Tigris. The main branch rises much to the west of the Greek route'—MACMICHAEL.

3. Τηλεβόαν, the modern Kara-su. See Map of Route and Introduction, p. xxiii. Another view is given by Layard, *Nineveh and Babylon*, p. 64, where he holds that the Teleboas is the river of Bitlis.

4. ὕπαρχος—Τιρίβαζος. 'Orontas was satrap of the entire province, while Tiribazus was his deputy in Western Armenia. This is better than to consider that they were both of them satraps, Orontas of Eastern and Tiribazus of Western Armenia'—PRETOR.

παρείη, optative of frequency.

5. εἰς ἐπήκοον, 'within ear-shot'; cf. *Cyropaedeia* I. iv. 23 εἰς τόξευμα 'within bow-shot.'

6. ἐφ' ᾧ—δέοιντο, 'on condition that he for his part did not injure the Greeks nor they burn his houses, merely taking such provisions as they required.'

ἐφ' ᾧ—ἀδικεῖν. See note on ii. 19 ἐφ' ᾧ μὴ καίειν.

αὐτὸς—ἐκείνους. Cf. ii. 1 τοὺς μὲν ἰέναι αὐτοὶ δὲ συμβοηθήσειν.

τε, after μήτε. Cf. iii. 6 οὔτ'—τε.

7. πεδίου, the second table-land of Armenia, the plateau of Mush, more than 4000 feet above the sea.

πολλῶν, predicative, 'in great abundance'; cf. iii. 7 τοὺς Καρδούχους πολλοὺς συνειλεγμένους.

8. ἕωθεν, literally 'starting from dawn.'

διασκηνῆσαι—κώμας, 'that the different divisions with their generals should be quartered separately throughout the villages.'

ἀσφαλές. They thought it would be safe to divide their forces, not expecting that any enemy would attack them in such wintry weather.

10. διασκηνοῦν, active verb, to be distinguished from διασκηνῆσαι § 8.

11. κατακειμένων, 'as they lay,' genitive absolute with subject omitted; cf. i. 6 πορευομένων.

ἀλεεινὸν ἦν ἡ χιών, 'the snow was a warm thing.' For the neuter adjective cf. II. v. 9 φοβερώτατόν (ἐστιν) ἐρημία. Virg. *Aen.* IV. 569 *varium et mutabile semper femina. Ecl.* III. 80 *triste lupus stabulis.*

ὅτῳ μὴ παραρρυείη, 'in the case of any from whom it had not slipped away.'

ὅτῳ, dative of person concerned; cf. iii. 8 αὐτῷ περιρρυῆναι, an exact parallel.

μή, not οὐ, because the antecedent is indefinite; cf. ii. 17 ὅσοι μή, also below § 15 τὰ μὴ ὄντα. This use of μή is usual where a class is described.

παραρρυείη, optative of frequency.

12. γυμνός, 'without his cloak' or, as we should say, 'in his shirt sleeves'; cf. Virg. *Georg.* I. 299 *nudus ara, sere nudus.* ' Doubtless he lay with his ἱμάτιον or cloak loosely wrapped round him. As he sprang to his feet, he would throw it off or it would fall off; and with the simple inner covering of the χιτών to protect him, and arms free, he fell to chopping the wood only half-clad '—DAKYNS.

ἀφελόμενος. The object, i.e. 'the axe,' is easily understood from the verb σχίζειν.

13. ἐκ τῶν πικρῶν, 'made out of the bitter (almonds),' ἀμυγδαλῶν understood out of ἀμυγδάλινον.

ἐκ τῶν αὐτῶν τούτων, 'made out of these same ingredients.'

14. διασκηνητέον—στέγας, 'that they must distribute their quarters in the villages under cover '; cf. § 8 διασκηνῆσαι κατὰ τὰς κώμας.

εἰς τὰς κώμας εἰς στέγας, *pregnant* construction; cf. Acts viii. 40 Φίλιππος εὑρέθη εἰς Ἄζωτον ' Philip was found at Azotus.'

κραυγῇ καὶ ἡδονῇ, *hendiadys*; cf. v. 3.

ὑπὸ ἀτασθαλίας, ' under the influence of recklessness.'

15. Τημνίτην. See Index of Proper Names.

τὰ μὴ ὄντα, ' such things as were not facts.' For μή cf. v. 12 τὰ μὴ δυνάμενα and see note on § 11. As Dakyns well renders, 'he had a happy gift to distinguish between fact and fiction.'

16. σάγαριν—Ἀμαζόνες ἔχουσιν, i.e. the axe seen in Greek sculptures of the Amazons. Cf. Horace, *Odes* IV. iv. 40 *Amazonia securi.*

17. ἠρώτων—εἴη, 'asked him about the army, how large it was.'

τὸ στράτευμα, *anticipatory* accusative ; cf. v. 29, 34, vii. 11. S. Luke iv. 34 οἶδά σε τίς εἶ.

ἐπὶ τίνι, 'on what ground,' i.e. 'with what object'; cf. *Memorabilia* I. ii. 56 ἐπὶ τῷ κέρδει 'with a view to the gain.'

18. ὁ δὲ εἶπεν—"Ἕλλησιν, ' He replied that it was Tiribazus with his own force and some mercenaries consisting of Chalybes and Taochi ; and he added that Tiribazus had completed his preparations with the view of attacking the Greeks on the pass over the mountains in the defiles, at which point only was there a passage for them.'

εἴη ἔχων. Cf. iii. 5 ἦν ἄγουσα.

ὡς, with ἐπιθησόμενον.

ᾗπερ—ἐνταῦθα. Note that the relative clause precedes the antecedent.

19. ἐπὶ τοῖς μένουσι, ' in command over those who remained (in camp)'; cf. i. 13 οἱ ἐπὶ τούτοις ὄντες.

21. ἥλωσαν—ἑάλω. The juxtaposition of the contracted and uncontracted forms is noteworthy. In v. 24 we have the contracted form ἦλω.

εἰς εἴκοσι, 'up to the number of 20.'

οἱ ἀρτοκόποι—εἶναι, ' those who called themselves bakers and those who called themselves butlers.'

22. τὴν ταχίστην. Cf. iii. 24.

τοῖς καταλελειμμένοις, dative after ἐπίθεσις γένοιτο, which here has the same construction as the verb ἐπιτίθεσθαι 'to attack.'

ἀνακαλεσάμενοι τῇ σάλπιγγι, Latin *cum receptui cecinissent.*

V.

2. παρασάγγας πεντεκαίδεκα. See note on iv. 1. 'The difficulties of winter in a district some 4000 feet above the sea-level would make the hour's march very short '—TAYLOR.

Εὐφράτην, the Eastern branch of the Euphrates, the modern Murad-su, 'which flows from the neighbourhood of Ararat and after skirting the northern foot of the Taurus range joins its brother stream before descending to the lowlands of Mesopotamia '—TOZER, *History of Ancient Geography*, p. 114.

3. χιόνος—καὶ πεδίου, *hendiadys*, 'a plain covered with deep snow '; cf. iv. 14 κραυγῇ καὶ ἡδονῇ.

ὁ δὲ τρίτος, i.e. σταθμός.

ἐναντίος, predicative, ' in their teeth '; cf. iii. 28 ἐναντίους ἐμβαίνειν.

ἀποκαίων πάντα, 'drying up everything'; cf. VII. iii. 4 ῥῖνες ἀπεκαίοντο 'noses were frost-bitten.' Virg. *Georgic* I. 92 *potentia solis acrior aut Boreae penetrabile frigus a.'urat.* Tacitus *Annals* XIII. 35 *ambusti multorum artus vi frigoris.*

4. εἶπε—σφαγιάζεται, 'bade them sacrifice to the wind—i.e. Boreas; and sacrifice was offered accordingly.' Note that σφαγιάζομαι is used both in a middle and a passive sense.

ἀνεῖναι, 'had dropped,' from ἀνίημι, cf. Herod. II. 113 οὐ γὰρ ἀνίει τὰ πνεύματα.

5. διεγένοντο—καίοντες, 'they continued burning.' For the participial construction cf. iii. 2 μαχόμενοι διετέλεσαν.

οὐ προσίεσαν—βρωτόν, 'would not admit the late-comers to their fire, unless they gave them a share of their corn or any other eatables they had with them.'

6. ὧν, partitive genitive, for ἐκείνων ἅ. Contrast this construction with μεταδοῖεν πυρούς in the previous sentence. The accusative is used of the *share* distributed, the partitive genitive of the *stock* from which the shares are taken.

ἕκαστοι, 'each party'; cf. ii. 8.

ἔνθα δέ, 'and where,'—awkward after the ἔνθα in the last sentence, which means 'thereupon.'

ἔστε ἐπὶ τὸ δάπεδον, 'right down to the soil,' Latin *usque ad solum.*

7. ἐβουλιμίασαν, 'were afflicted with βουλιμία or ravenous hunger (properly *hunger on the scale of an ox*).' For the prefix βου- cf. βού-βρωστις 'big appetite,' βουγάϊος 'big braggart,' βούπαις 'big boy,' βουκέφαλος 'big-headed.'

καταλαμβάνων—ἀνθρώπων, 'coming upon those of the men who were fainting.'

τῶν ἀνθρώπων, partitive genitive; cf. τῶν ἐμπείρων in the next section.

8. κἂν—ἀναστήσονται, 'and, if they have something to eat, they will revive.'

περιιών—βουλιμιῶσιν, 'he went round the baggage-train and any victuals (he saw) anywhere he distributed to the fainting, and those who had strength to run about he despatched in different directions ministering to them.'

διδόντας. Mark the tense, not δώσοντας, the ordinary future participle denoting purpose. They attend to the fainting at once, for it is a matter of life and death. Cf. iii. 30 ᾤχοντο ἐπιμελόμενοι, VI. i. 2 πέμπει πρέσβεις λέγοντας.

E. XEN. IV.   5

9. πορευομένων, genitive absolute with subject understood; cf. i. 6.

ἐκ τῆς κώμης, to be taken closely with γυναῖκας καὶ κόρας.

πρὸς τῇ κρήνῃ, 'close to the well.' Mark the article, 'the well which each village had'; cf. τοῦ ἐρύματος which follows.

10. περσιστί. Cf. S. John xix. 20 καὶ ἦν γεγραμμένον ἑβραϊστί, ῥωμαϊστί, ἑλληνιστί.

πορεύονται—εἴη—ἀπέχει. For the change of mood cf. ii. i. 3 ἔλεγεν ὅτι Κῦρος μὲν τέθνηκεν, Ἀριαῖος δὲ ἐν τῷ σταθμῷ εἴη.

ὅσον παρασάγγην, 'about a parasang,' literally 'as much as....'

11. τοῦ στρατεύματος, partitive genitive depending on ὅσοι. Cf. § 12 τῶν πολεμίων.

οἱ μὴ δυνάμενοι, 'such as were unable'; cf. iv. 15 τὰ μὴ ὄντα and τὰ μὴ δυνάμενα § 12.

12. ὀφθαλμοὺς—δακτύλους, accusatives of *respect* or *part affected*, 'ruined as to their eyes,' 'mortified as to their toes.'

13. χιόνος, objective genitive,—'protection *against* the snow'; cf. *Memorabilia* iv. iii. 7 τὸ πῦρ ἐπίκουρον ψύχους.

ποδῶν, objective genitive again,—'protection *for* the feet.'

εἰς τὴν νύκτα ὑπολύοιτο, 'took off his sandals for the night'; cf. i. 15 εἰς τὴν ὑστεραίαν.

14. τὰ ὑποδήματα περιεπήγνυντο. Cf. i. 13 τὰ αἰχμάλωτα ἐποίουν, ii. 20 τὰ ὅπλα ἔκειντο. But in our present passage there is no apparent reason for the plural verb as there is in the other two instances.

καὶ γὰρ—βοῶν, 'For in fact, after their old sandals failed, they had brogues of undressed leather made from newly-flayed ox-hides.'

15. ἦν ἀτμίζουσα. Cf. iii. 5 ἦν ἄγουσα. iv. 18 εἴη ἔχων.

ἀτμίζουσα, as was natural in a volcanic region.

ἐκτραπόμενοι, 'having turned aside from the path,' 'having fallen out.'

οὐκ ἔφασαν πορεύεσθαι, 'refused to proceed.'

πορεύεσθαι. Notice the present, marking the peremptory nature of their decision. They said 'we don't go on,' 'we stop here.' Cf. *Cyropaedeia* vi. ii. 39 προσαγαγὼν ἐγγυητὰς ἦ μὴν πορεύεσθαι 'having given securities that he *is* really *going* there and then.' So also in Latin, e.g. Livy XL. 7 '*quin imus?*'...*omnes ire se conclamarunt* '*Why don't we go?*'...All cried out together *We go.*' In our passage there is no need to read πορεύσεσθαι, as has been proposed.

17. οὐ γὰρ ἂν δύνασθαι, 'for they would not have strength,' for οὐ γὰρ ἂν δυναίμεθα of *oratio recta*.

ἀμφὶ ὧν εἶχον, 'about the booty which they had got'; cf. § 6 μετεδίδοσαν ὧν εἶχον.

18. μέγιστον, cognate accusative:—lit. 'as much as they could (shout) loudest.'

οὐδεὶς—ἐφθέγξατο, 'not one (of the enemy) uttered a sound any more anywhere,' i.e. they gave no more trouble.

οὐδεὶς—οὐδαμοῦ. Cf. § 19 οὐδὲ—οὐδεμία 'not even any guard,' and i. 9 οὔτε οὐδὲν ἐποίουν.

19. ἥξουσί τινες ἐπ' αὐτούς, 'some men will be there after them,' i.e. to rescue them.

ἐγκεκαλυμμένοις, i.e. in their cloaks.

ἀνίστασαν, imperfect of the attempt, 'tried to rouse them.'

οὐχ ὑποχωροῖεν, 'were not moving on,' i.e. were blocking the road.

20. παριὼν καὶ παραπέμπων, 'passing on himself and sending on....'

οὕτως, idiomatic, 'just as they were'; cf. i. 11 οὕτως ηὐλίσθησαν.

21. οἱ περὶ Ξενοφῶντα, 'Xenophon and his men'; cf. ii. 8 οἱ ἀμφὶ Χειρίσοφον.

πρὸς ἡμέραν, 'towards day.'

ἀναστήσαντας—ἀναγκάζειν, 'to rouse them up and compel them.'

22. πέμπει—οἱ τελευταῖοι, 'sent some of his men quartered in the village to enquire how those in the rear were faring.'

τῶν, partitive genitive depending on τινάς understood; cf. § 7 τοὺς πίπτοντας τῶν ἀνθρώπων.

τῶν ἐκ τῆς κώμης, pregnant construction,—'he sent those in the village from the village'; cf. ii. 19 οἱ ἐκ τούτου τοῦ τόπου συνερρύησαν.

κομίζειν, infinitive of purpose, properly 'for carrying'; see notes on i. 8 and 24.

πρὸς τῇ κώμῃ, 'close to the village'; cf. § 9 πρὸς τῇ κρήνῃ.

23. ἔδοξε—ἔχοντες, 'they agreed that it was safe for the divisions to billet themselves throughout the villages. Cheirisophus stayed in the village where he was; and the others, having drawn lots for the villages which they saw before them, marched off, each party of officers with their own detachments.'

ἕκαστοι, not 'each officer,' but 'each party of officers'; cf. § 6.

24. ἀφιέναι ἑαυτόν, 'to let him go,' i.e. he wished to have a free hand.

εἰς δασμόν, 'for tribute,' literally 'towards tribute'; cf. i. 28 εἰς τὰ τοιαῦτα.

βασιλεῖ, 'for the Great King,' dative of advantage; cf. § 25 τοῖς ὑποζυγίοις. iv. 2 βασίλειον εἶχε τῷ σατράπῃ.

ἐνάτην ἡμέραν, accusative of duration of time, 'now for the ninth day,' i.e. 'eight days ago'; cf. *Hellenica* II. iv. 13 οὒς ἡμέραν πέμπτην τρεψάμενοι ἐδιώξατε.

ἥλω. Cf. iv. 21.

25. αἱ δ' οἰκίαι ἦσαν κατάγειοι. 'These villages are still such as they were when Xenophon traversed Armenia. The low hovels, mere holes in the hill-side, and the common refuge of man, poultry, and cattle, cannot be seen from any distance, and they are purposely built away from the road to escape the unwelcome visits of travelling government officers and marching troops. It is not uncommon for a traveller to receive the first intimation of his approach to a village by finding his horse's fore feet down a chimney, and himself taking his place unexpectedly in the family circle through the roof'—LAYARD, *Nineveh and Babylon*, p. 14.

τὸ μὲν στόμα ὥσπερ φρέατος. 'It is usual to understand the participle ἔχουσαι with στόμα. But a far more simple explanation is admissible, viz. to supply the word στόμα itself with the genitive φρέατος,—*were as to their entrance like (the entrance to) a well*'—PRETOR.

στόμα, accusative of respect.

τὰ δὲ κτήνη πάντα—ἐτρέφοντο, neuter plural subject with plural verb; cf. i. 13 ἐποίουν πολλὰ ὄντα τὰ ὑποζύγια καὶ τὰ αἰχμάλωτα. Note that in both these passages the idea of *plurality* is emphasised. This may be the reason for the neglect of the ordinary rule here. But Xenophon occasionally breaks the rule without any apparent reason; e.g. § 14.

26. ἐνέκειντο, 'were placed in it.' For ἔγκειμαι used as perfect passive of ἐντίθημι cf. ii. 20 ἔκειντο.

27. συμμαθόντι, 'to one who has acquired the taste.'

28. οὔτε—τε. Cf. iii. 6 and iv. 6.

στερήσοιτο, passive in sense, 'he should be deprived.' For the future optative cf. i. 25, iii. 29, vi. 1.

ἀντεμπλήσαντες. The stress of the clause is on the participle, not on the finite verb; cf. ii. 3 διαβάντας ἐκβαίνειν. Translate:—'they would fill his house with necessaries in return (for what they took) before they went away.'

ἀπίασιν. For the change of mood, indicative after optative στερήσοιτο, cf. i. 3 and v. 10.

ἢν—γένωνται, 'if it should be proved that he had given useful information to the army, until they found themselves in another tribe.'

ἐξηγησάμενος φαίνηται. See note on ii. 4 ἀφανεῖς εἶναι ἀπιόντες.

29. οἶνον, *anticipatory* accusative; cf. iv. 17 ἠρώτων—τὸ στράτευμα ὁπόσον εἴη.

ἐν πᾶσιν ἀφθόνοις, 'in all abundance'; cf. III. ii. 25 ἐν ἀφθόνοις βιοτεύειν. Demosthenes p. 312 ἐν ἀφθόνοις τραφείς.

30. παρίοι, optative of frequency, 'wherever he approached a village.'

τοὺς ἐν ταῖς κώμαις, i.e. the Greek soldiers quartered there.

οὐδαμόθεν—ἄριστον, 'from no place did they (the merrymakers) suffer them to depart till they had set a breakfast before them.'

32. ὁπότε—βοῦν, 'And whenever any one in a friendly mood wished to drink another's health, he would draw him to the mixing-bowl, from which he had to drink stooping down and swilling like an ox.'

33. κἀκείνους, 'his party too.'

σκηνοῦντας, 'in comfortable quarters,' i.e. enjoying themselves.

ἐστεφανωμένους, as was usual at a Greek symposium; but in their present wintry abode they have to be content with wisps of hay instead of flowers. Cf. iii. 17.

χιλοῦ, genitive of material; cf. Plato *Symposium* 212 E ἐστεφανωμένον κιττοῦ στεφάνῳ καὶ ἴων 'wearing a wreath of ivy and violets.'

34. τὴν ὁδόν, *anticipatory* accusative again (cf. § 29),—'he pointed out the road, in what direction it lay.'

35. αὐτόν, emphatic, 'the village-chief himself.'

ἑαυτοῦ, which usually refers to the subject of the sentence, here refers to the object αὐτόν.

παλαίτερον, 'too old.'

ἀναθρέψαντι καταθῦσαι, 'to fatten up and sacrifice.'

αὐτὸν ἱερὸν εἶναι τοῦ Ἡλίου, 'that it was dedicated to the Sun'; cf. *Cyropaedeia* VIII. iii. 12 ἵπποι ἤγοντο θῦμα τῷ Ἡλίῳ.

τῶν πώλων, '(some) of the colts,' partitive genitive; cf. vi. 15 κλέπτοντες τοῦ ὄρους.

VI.

1. τὸν μὲν ἡγεμόνα—τῷ κωμάρχῃ, evidently one and the same person.

τὸν μὲν ἡγεμόνα, strictly 'him as guide.'

τῷ κωμάρχῃ, dative of advantage. Dakyns well renders:—'he left the headman's household safe behind in the village.' Cf. § 16 ὑμῖν οἱ κράτιστοι.

φυλάττειν. Cf. v. 22.

ἡγήσοιτο. The use of the future optative is justified, since it occurs in what is virtually *oratio obliqua*; cf. *Cyropaedeia* VIII. i. 43 ἐπεμελεῖτο ὅπως μήτε ἄσιτοι μήτε ἄποτοι ἔσοιντο, his thought being ὅπως μήτε— ἔσονται. See note on i. 25.

ἔχων καὶ τοῦτον ἀπίοι, 'he might take his son also when he departed.' The stress of the clause is on the participle; cf. v. 28 ἀντεμπλήσαντες ἀπίασιν.

2. ἦν, subject ὁ κωμάρχης.

καὶ Χειρίσοφος, '*when* Cheirisophus...' in our idiom.

οὐκ εἶεν, subject κῶμαι.

3. τοῦ ἡγεμόνος, objective genitive,—'maltreatment and neglect of precautions in regard to the guide.'

πιστοτάτῳ, predicate,—'found him most trustworthy'; cf. § 13 ἐρημοτέρῳ χρῆσθαι.

4. ἀνὰ πέντε, distributive use of ἀνά, 'at the rate of...'

τῆς ἡμέρας, genitive of time *within which*.

παρὰ τὸν Φᾶσιν, 'along the Phasis'; cf. ii. 6 and iii. 6.

Φᾶσιν. 'The next feature of the country which is mentioned after the Euphrates is the river Phasis, in the neighbourhood of which they met with a tribe called Phasiani. Now as the plain in which the Araxes (Aras) flows bears the name of Pasin at the present day, there is a presumption in favour of identifying that stream in this part of its course with the Phasis of Xenophon, especially as it lies to the north-westward of the valley of the Euphrates, and that would be the direction which the Greeks would naturally follow in endeavouring to reach their home'—TOZER, *History of Ancient Geography*, p. 116.

εὖρος, accusative of respect; cf. iii. 1 εὖρος ὡς δίπλεθρον.

πλεθριαῖον, in agreement with ποταμόν.

5. Χάλυβες—Τάοχοι—Φασιανοί. See Map of Route. On the Phasiani see also note on § 4 Φᾶσιν.

6. εἰς τριάκοντα. Cf. ἐς δραχμήν 'up to a drachma' and iv. 21.

κατὰ κέρας—ἐπὶ φάλαγγος. See note on iii. 26.

πλησιάσῃ, graphic use of the subjunctive after a past tense; cf. i. 3 and iii. 29.

7. ὥρα, understand ἐστί. Cf. § 9 εἰκός for εἰκός ἐστι.

βουλεύεσθαι—ἀγωνιούμεθα, 'to take counsel how we shall fight'; cf. the same construction in § 10.

9. ἐμοὶ δέ γε, 'yes and to me...'

εἰ διατρίψομεν, 'if we are going to waste,' 'if we mean to waste'; for εἰ with future indicative is not identical in meaning with ἐάν with subjunctive, as some say. A good example is Aristophanes *Birds* 759 αἶρε πλῆκτρον εἰ μαχεῖ 'up with spur *if you mean to fight,*' a sense which would not be given by ἐὰν μάχῃ.

προσγενέσθαι. After εἰκός the aorist infinitive with ἄν or the future infinitive are by no means necessary. The aorist alone 'denotes a *certain and instantaneous* result' (Pretor). Translate:—'It is probable that others join them *then and there* in greater numbers.' Cf. *Hellenica* III. v. 10 τοῦτο δὲ πῶς μᾶλλον εἰκὸς γενέσθαι; *Cyropaedeia* VI. i. 10 εἰκός ἐστι πόρον προσγενέσθαι. So also after words of *promising, hoping,* etc., e.g. *Anab.* I. ii. 2, II. i. 19. Teachers will find much valuable information on these constructions in Mr W. T. Lendrum's article in the *Classical Review,* vol. iv, p. 100 sqq.

10. οὕτω γιγνώσκω, 'I decide as follows,' 'I am of the following opinion.'

ὅπως—μαχούμεθα—ὅπως—λάβωμεν, (1) 'how we *shall* fight,' (2) 'how we *are to* receive.' The two uses are combined in the same sentence in *Memorabilia* II. ii. 10 ἐπιμελομένην ὅπως ὑγιαίνῃς τε καὶ ὅπως μηδενὸς ἐνδεὴς ἔσῃ.

11. τὸ μὲν οὖν—λαθόντας, 'Though the part of the mountain which is visible extends for more than 60 stadia, troops on the look-out for us are nowhere to be seen except along the road itself. It is far better then to attempt to steal a part of the deserted mountain unobserved.'

ὄρους, partitive genitive depending on τι.

καὶ ἁρπάσαι φθάσαντας, 'and before they know where we are secure the prize,' as Dakyns well translates.

λαθόντας—φθάσαντας. Cf. i. 4 ἅμα μὲν λαθεῖν πειρώμενοι ἅμα δὲ φθάσαι.

μᾶλλον, not superfluous after κρεῖττον as some say; rather it seems to justify κρεῖττον,—'*here* we shall be better able to defend ourselves.'

12. ὄρθιον—ὁμαλές, accusatives of *space traversed*; cf. iv. 1 ἐπορεύθησαν πεδίον ἅπαν.

τὰ πρὸ ποδῶν, 'what lies before one.'

μεθ' ἡμέραν, 'extending over day,' 'by day.'

καὶ ἡ τραχεῖα—βαλλομένοις, 'And a rough road is more pleasant to the feet when men go along it without fighting than a smooth road when missiles are flying at their heads.'

ἡ τραχεῖα—ἡ ὁμαλή. Cf. § 13 ταύτῃ and iii. 24 τὴν ταχίστην.

ἰοῦσιν—βαλλομένοις, datives of person concerned, 'to men going,' 'to men being hit.'

τὰς κεφαλάς, 'as to their heads,' accusatives of *respect*; cf. v. 12 διεφθαρμένοι τοὺς ὀφθαλμούς.

13. καὶ κλέψαι δ', ' *Yes and* to steal a march.' Cf. i. 3.

ἐξόν, accusative absolute; cf. i. 13 δόξαν.

ἐξὸν μὲν—ἐξὸν δέ. Cf. i. 4 and iii. 7.

ὡς μὴ ὁρᾶσθαι. Cf. iii. 29.

ἀπελθεῖν—παρέχειν, 'to retire so far as to prevent their noticing us.'

αἴσθησιν παρέχειν. Cf. Thuc. III. 22 ὅπως τὰ ὅπλα μὴ κρουόμενα πρὸς ἄλληλα αἴσθησιν παρέχοι.

δοκοῦμεν—πολέμιοι, 'And I think that if we make a feint of attacking by this path we shall find the mountain all the more deserted; for the enemy would be more likely to be waiting for us in a body where they now are.'

ἂν—ἂν—μένοιεν. Note that (1) ἂν is inserted early in order to show the character of the sentence; (2) it is repeated with the emphatic word ἐρημοτέρῳ; and (3) its force is carried on to μένοιεν (in the next sentence) which requires an ἄν. These three points are admirably illustrated by Aesch. *Agamemnon* 1031

 ἐντὸς δ' ἂν οὖσα μορσίμων ἀγρευμάτων

 πείθοι' ἄν, εἰ πείθοι'· ἀπειθοίης δ' ἴσως.

'And since thou art within the toils of fate thou shouldest obey, if it may be; but perhaps thou wouldest not.'

14. συμβάλλομαι, understand λόγους, Latin *confero* (*sermonem*); cf. *Cyropaedeia* II. ii. 21 συμβαλέσθαι περὶ τούτου λόγους.

τῶν ὁμοίων, partitive genitive, 'members of the Peers.' ' At Sparta full civic rights did not depend upon birth alone. Only those were full citizens (ὁμοῖοι) who had fulfilled all the exigencies of the Lycurgean discipline and continued to contribute and to belong to the συσσίτια (*public messes*). Those who neglected these two duties were probably excluded from the full civic rights; these are probably the ὑπομείονες (*inferiors*) mentioned by Xenophon, *Hellenica* III. iii. 6 '—J. B. MOYLE in *Dictionary of Antiquities*, vol. i, p. 447.

εὐθὺς ἐκ παίδων, ' from your earliest years,' Latin *usque a pueris*.

ὅσα μὴ κωλύει. He uses μή because the antecedent is general ; cf. ii. 17 ὅσοι μὴ ἀφίκοντο.

15. μάλα—καιρός, 'a good opportunity'; cf. *Hellenica* v. iv. 14 μάλα χειμῶνος ὄντος 'there being a violent storm.' For the ordinary use of μάλα see next section.

τοῦ ὄρους, partitive genitive, 'stealing part of the mountain'; cf. § 17 λάβωμέν τι τοῦ ὄρους.

16. ἀλλὰ μέντοι—παιδείαν, 'For all that, I too hear that you Athenians are clever at stealing public money even though the risk to the thief is very terrible; yes and that your best men do it most of all, if, that is, your best men are held worthy of office. So it is a good opportunity for you too, Xenophon, to make a display of your training.'

δεινοὺς κλέπτειν. For this use of the infinitive cf. note on i. 8 λαμβάνειν.

καὶ τοὺς κρατίστους μέντοι, literally 'and your best men notwithstanding (they are best).'

ὑμῖν, dative of advantage, almost a possessive, '*your* best man'; cf. § 1 τοὺς οἰκέτας καταλείπει τῷ κωμάρχῃ.

17. ἐπειδὰν δειπνήσωμεν, 'when we have *finished* supper.' For the force of the aorist subjunctive cf. ἐάνπερ ἅπαξ λάβωμεν below.

καταληψόμενος. Cf. note on iii. 3.

τῶν—κλωπῶν, 'the marauders hanging on our rear.'

τούτων, 'from these,' ablatival genitive.

νέμεται—βουσίν, properly 'is pasturage *for* goats and cattle,' dative of advantage, not 'is grazed *by*...'

βατὰ—ἔσται, literally '*things* will be passable even for our transport animals'; cf. III. iv. 49 ἐπεὶ δὲ ἄβατα ἦν. Thuc. I. 7 πλωϊμωτέρων ὄντων 'when things became more nautical.'

18. ἐν τῷ ὁμοίῳ, 'on equal terms with them'; cf. below εἰς τὸ ἴσον ἡμῖν 'on to an equal footing with us.' For the dative ἡμῖν cf. *Cyropaedeia* I. iv. 5 εἰς τὸ ἴσον ἀφίκετο τοῖς ἥλιξι.

ἄν, for ἐάν,—'unless some brave men come forward as volunteers.'

20. σύνθημα—πολλά, 'they made an agreement to kindle many watch-fires as soon as they occupied the heights.'

21. ἐκ τοῦ ἀρίστου, 'after their breakfast'; cf. § 20 ἐκ τούτου.

προσάξειν, object to be supplied 'his men'; cf. § 23 ἦγε.

22. ἐγρηγόρεσαν, 'kept awake.'

23. θυσάμενος. Cf. iii. 9. Contrast § 27 θύσαντες, which refers to an ordinary sacrifice, not to the taking of auspices.

κατὰ τὴν ὁδόν, 'along the path,' i.e. the one mentioned in § 11.

24. τοῖς κατὰ τὰ ἄκρα, 'those who were moving along the heights.'

τοὺς πολλούς, 'the main bodies' of both sides; cf. τῶν πολεμίων τὸ πολύ above.

25. οἱ ἐκ τοῦ πεδίου, broken up, by partitive apposition, into οἱ μὲν πελτασταί and Χειρίσοφος δέ. Cf. ii. 12.

βάδην ταχύ, 'at quick march,' opposed to δρόμῳ 'at a double.'

27. τρόπαιον, a memorial of a rout (τροπή), consisting of shields, helmets etc. of the defeated enemy, placed on the trunk of a tree.

VII.

1. Ταόχους, the modern Taikh, a district of Armenia. See Map of Route.

σταθμοὺς πέντε παρασάγγας τριάκοντα.   See note on iv. 2.

ἐν οἶς—ἀνακεκομισμένοι, 'in which they kept all their supplies also, having carried them up thither.'

ἀνακεκομισμένοι, perfect passive in middle sense; cf. ii. 21 προβεβλημένος.

2. συνεληλυθότες ἦσαν.   Cf. II. iii. 10 ἦσαν ἐκπεπτωκότες.

εὐθὺς ἥκων, 'immediately he had arrived.'

οὐ γὰρ ἦν ἀθρόοις περιστῆναι, ' For it was not possible to surround the place in a body.'

3. εἰς καλὸν ἥκετε, 'you have come at an opportune moment,' literally 'on to an opportune moment'; cf. i. 15 εἰς τὴν ὑστεραίαν γίγνεται χειμὼν πολύς.   Cyropaedeia III. i. 8 εἰς καιρὸν ἥκεις.

τῇ γὰρ στρατιᾷ—χωρίον, ' For the army has not got the necessary supplies, unless we mean to take the position.'

οὐκ ἔστι—εἰ μὴ ληψόμεθα.   For this form of conditional sentence cf. Eur. Hecuba 863 μ᾽ ἔχεις βραδὺν—Ἀχαιοῖς εἰ διαβληθήσομαι 'you have me as a slow helper if I am to fall into disfavour with the Achaeans.'   ' The future indicative with εἰ may be used in a present condition, if it expresses merely a *present* intention or necessity that something shall be done '—GOODWIN, *Moods and Tenses*, § 407.

4. τί τὸ κωλῦον εἴη εἰσελθεῖν, ' what was the hindrance to their entering.'

μία αὕτη πάροδός ἐστιν, 'This is the only passage.'   Cf. i. 20.

οὕτω διατίθεται, 'is treated just as you see.'

οὕτω, used δεικτικῶς, cf. τούτους in the next section.

σκέλη καὶ πλευράς, accusatives of *respect*; cf. v. 12 διεφθαρμένοι τοὺς ὀφθαλμούς.

5. ἄλλο τι ἤ, ' Is anything else the case than...?' i.e. 'Is it not the case that...?'   Cf. II. v. 10 ἄλλο τι ἢ ἂν ἢ ἀγωνιζοίμεθα 'Should we not be fighting?'

ὀλίγους τούτους ἀνθρώπους, not 'these few men,' which would require the insertion of the article, but 'a few men *here*,' 'a few men *as you see.'* Cf. III. v. 9 πολλὰ δ' ὁρῶ ταῦτα πρόβατα 'I see many sheep *here.'* Thuc. I. 51 νῆες ἐκεῖναι ἐπιπλέουσι 'there are ships *yonder* sailing up.'

6. βαλλομένους, 'under fire'; cf. vi. 12 τὰς κεφαλὰς βαλλομένοις.

τούτου—μεγάλαις, 'And of this distance about a hundred feet is covered with great pine-trees at intervals.'

ὅσον πλέθρον. Cf. § 16 ὅσον ξυήλην.

ἀνθ' ὦν, '*opposite to which* and therefore by inference from the context *behind which* '—PRETOR.

τὸ λοιπόν—παραδραμεῖν, 'The space left after that amounts only to about 50 feet, which we must run across, when the shower of stones has abated.'

ἤδη, 'when we have got so far,' i.e. after reaching the trees.

7. πολλοί, predicative, 'in showers.'

αὐτὸ ἄν—τὸ δέον εἴη, 'That is *just* what would be wanted.'

πορευώμεθα—βουλώμεθα, 'Let us go (to a point) from which we shall have only a short distance to run across, if we possibly can, and from which it will be easy to retire, if we wish.'

μικρόν—παραδραμεῖν, properly 'a short distance *for running across*'; see note on i. 8 πολλὰ λαμβάνειν.

8. τούτου, possessive genitive, 'to him *belonged* the lead.'

λοχαγῶν, partitive genitive, 'to him *among* the captains.'

ἀπῆλθον—ἕκαστος φυλαττόμενος, partitive apposition; cf. ii. 2.

9. καὶ οὗτοι, 'these also.'

καὶ ἄλλοι δέ, 'yes and others...' Cf. vi. 13 καὶ κλέψαι δέ.

ἐφέστασαν, pluperfect, 'were posted to support them.'

τὸν ἕνα λόχον, i.e. of Callimachus.

10. βήματα, cognate accusative after προὔτρεχεν.

ἐφ' ἑκάστης προδρομῆς, 'upon (*or* at) each of his runs forward'; cf. iii. 9 ἐπὶ τοῦ πρώτου.

11. Καλλίμαχον, *anticipatory* accusative; cf. v. 34 τὴν ὁδὸν ἔφραζεν ᾗ εἴη.

μὴ οὐ πρῶτος. The μή goes with παραδράμῃ; the οὐ with πρῶτος,— 'fearing *lest* (μή) he should *not* (οὐ) be the first to run past.' Cf. III. i. 12 ἐφοβεῖτο μὴ οὐ δύναιτο ἐξελθεῖν, 'he feared he might be *unable* (οὐ δύναιτο) to escape.'

12. ἀρετῆς, partitive genitive after a verb of *laying hold of*; cf. ἐπιλαμβάνεται τῆς ἴτυος above. Translate: 'laid claim to a reputation for valour.'

ἠνέχθη, 'came down'; cf. § 7 φέρονται οἱ λίθοι.

15. ἐντεῦθεν ἐπορεύθησαν. 'It is commonly supposed that the Greek troops followed the road to Kars which takes the same line as the modern route. The alternative theory assumes that they travelled in a north-easterly direction to the valley of the Tchoruk su'—PRETOR. See note on § 18 Ἅρπασον.

Χαλύβων. See Map of Route. The Chalybes were a people spread widely over the mountain regions of Armenia, Pontus and Paphlagonia. Those here mentioned are called *Armeno-Chalybes* by Pliny to distinguish them from the others.

ὧν διῆλθον, for ἐκείνων οὓς διῆλθον. Cf. v. 17 ἀμφὶ ὧν εἶχον.

πτερύγων, 'flaps' (literally 'wings'), forming a sort of kilt; see note on ii. 28, where the usual Greek θώραξ is described.

16. παρὰ τὴν ζώνην, 'at the belt.'

ὅσον ξυήλην, 'as large as a scimitar'; cf. § 6 ὅσον πλέθρον.

δύναιντο, optative of frequency.

ἀποτεμόντες. Notice that τέμνω has two forms for its second aorist, ἔταμον the older and ἔτεμον the later form.

ἂν—ἐπορεύοντο. The ἄν here is not *conditional*, but *frequentative*. It is thus used both with the imperfect and aorist indicative. Cf. II. iii. 3 ἔπαισεν ἄν 'he *would* give a blow.' III. iv. 22 ἂν ἐξεπίμπλασαν 'they *would* fill up.' Soph. *Philoctetes* 295 εἶτα πῦρ ἂν οὐ παρῆν 'then I *would* have no fire.'

κεφαλάς, object both of ἀποτεμόντες and ἔχοντες,—'they would cut off their heads and march off with them.'

ἔμελλον. The imperfect indicative is rare after ὁπότε, which is usually followed by the optative of frequency.

πήχεων, genitive of measure; cf. § 18 τεττάρων πλέθρων.

μίαν λόγχην, as opposed to the Greek spear, which had a spike at the butt end for fixing in the ground.

17. ἐν τούτοις, *pregnant* construction,—'they had carried up their supplies (and stored them) in these strongholds.' Cf. § 1 and *Hellenica* IV. v. 5 οἱ ἐν τῷ Ἡραίῳ καταπεφευγότες.

ὥστε μηδὲν λαμβάνειν, ἀλλὰ διετράφησαν. The infinitive denotes the *intended* consequence, the indicative the *actual* consequence.

κτήνεσιν, instrumental dative.

18. Ἅρπασον. See Map of Route. It is the river Apsarus mentioned by Pliny, the modern Tchoruk-su, 'a considerable river that flows to the south of the Balkhar Dagh, the great mountain-range of Eastern Pontus, and empties itself into the Black Sea by Batoum. There is no river, however, in this part of the country which is 400 feet broad. If the number is correct, they must have come to it at some point where the bed is flat and marshy, so that it overflows its banks in the winter season '—TAYLOR.

εὖρος, 'in breadth,' accusative of respect; cf. ii. 2 πλῆθος ὡς δισχίλιοι.

Σκυθηνῶν, probably the remnant of a body of Scythian invaders.

19. Γυμνιάς. See Map of Route. But the exact position of the town is entirely a matter of conjecture. Grote discusses the matter at length in the appendix to chapter LXX. of his History. But his identification of Gymnias with the modern Gumisch Khane, partly on the ground of similarity of name, is generally thought to be erroneous. Tozer thinks that it may have been near the modern town of Baiburt, which is situated on the banks of the Tchoruk.

τοῖς Ἕλλησιν, dative of advantage similar to τῷ κωμάρχῃ (vi. 1).

ἑαυτῶν πολεμίας, 'hostile to themselves,' i.e. to the man's own people; cf. *Hellenica* V. ii. 39 τὴν ἑαυτῶν συμμαχίδα.

ἄγοι. The optative is a perfectly justifiable sequence after the historic present πέμπει.

20. ἡμερῶν, genitive of time *within which*.

ὅθεν ὄψονται, 'from which they would see'; cf. § 27 οὗ σκηνήσουσι.

τεθνάναι. Mark the perfect,—'he offered himself for *instant death.*' Cf. Homer *Od.* XVI. 107 βουλοίμην κε τεθνάναι 'I would fain *lie dead.*' Aristophanes *Ranae* 1012 τί παθεῖν φήσεις ἄξιος εἶναι; Τεθνάναι. So also in Latin. e.g. Livy XL. 10 (*me*) *perisse expetunt* 'they wish to see me *lie dead.*' Cf. also ii. 17 τεθνᾶσι.

ἐνέβαλλεν, intransitive.

ᾦ, instrumental dative, 'by means of which thing.'

Ἑλλήνων, objective genitive, 'towards the Greeks'; cf. v. 13 τῆς χιόνος.

21. Θήχης, possibly the ridge now called Tekieh-Dagh. ' Unfortunately it seems impossible to verify the particular summit on which the interesting scene described by Xenophon took place. Mr Ainsworth presumes it to be the mountain Kop-Dagh; from whence, however, according to Koch, the sea cannot be discerned. D'Anville and some other geographers identify it with the ridge called Tekieh-Dagh to the east of Gumisch-Khane, nearer to the sea than that place. But modern travellers affirm that it is neither high enough nor near enough to the sea to permit any such view as that which Xenophon narrates. It stands at a distance of 35 miles from the sea, the view of which moreover seems intercepted by the still higher mountain-chain now called

Kolath-Dagh... However, the whole region is as yet very imperfectly known, and perhaps it is not impossible that there may be some particular locality even on Tekieh-Dagh, whence, through a gap in the intervening mountains, the sea might become visible'—GROTE. See Introduction, p. xxiv.

22. βοῶν, genitive of material,—'targets of shaggy untanned ox-hide.'

τὰ εἴκοσιν. This use of the article with numerals, when a round number is given, is idiomatic. It should be neglected in translation.

23. οἱ ἀεὶ ἐπιόντες, 'those who came up from time to time'; cf. i. 7. μεῖζόν τι, 'something more important (than usual).'

24. θάλαττα θάλαττα. Cf. Virg. *Aen.* III. 523 Italiam *primus conclamat Achates,* Italiam *socii laeto clamore salutant*; also Brachmann *Columbus* (quoted by Rehdantz) *Und Land! Land! rief es und donnert' es Land!*

παρεγγυώντων, 'passing on the cry (like a watchword to their friends behind)'; cf. i. 17.

25. ὅτου δή, 'some one whoever he was,' i.e. 'some one or other,' for τινὸς ὅστις δὴ παρηγγύησε.

παρεγγυήσαντος, 'having passed along the word (to do so).'

27. ἀπὸ κοινοῦ, 'from the common stock.'

ᾔτει—τοὺς δακτυλίους, 'he asked for *their* rings.'

μάλιστα, 'above all.'

Μάκρωνας. See Map of Route.

VIII.

2. ὑπὲρ δεξιῶν, χειρῶν understood, 'above on their right.'

οἷον χαλεπώτατον, literally 'such as is most difficult,' i.e. 'as difficult as could be.' Cf. VII. i. 24 χωρίον οἷον κάλλιστον.

ὁ ὁρίζων, 'the frontier river.'

δι' οὗ. The antecedent is ὁ ὁρίζων, not ἄλλον ποταμόν.

δένδρεσι. On this form see Vocabulary.

3. εἰς τὸν ποταμόν, instead of hitting the Greeks.

ἐξικνοῦντο γὰρ οὔ—οὐδέν, 'reach us they did not, nor did they do any harm either.'

4. ταύτην, subject, 'that this is my country'; hence the absence of the article. Cf. vii. 4 μία αὕτη πάροδός ἐστιν.

5. ἐρωτήσαντος, genitive absolute with subject omitted; cf. i. 6 πορευομένων.

ἀντιτετάχαται. See Vocabulary under ἀντιτάσσω.

6. καὶ ὑμεῖς, 'you too,' a retort.

οὐ κακῶς γε ποιήσοντες, 'Yes (we are coming, but) not with intent to do harm.'

7. εἰ δοῖεν ἄν—πιστά, 'whether they would give pledges for this.'

δοῖεν ἄν, for δοίητε ἄν of *oratio recta*, some condition being suppressed, e.g. '*if we were to ask*, would you give...?' 'An indicative or optative with ἄν retains its mood and tense (with ἄν) unchanged in indirect discourse and in indirect questions, after both primary and secondary tenses'—GOODWIN, *Moods and Tenses*, § 681. Cf. II. i. 10 ἀπεκρίνατο ὅτι πρόσθεν ἄν ἀποθάνοιεν (*oratio recta* ἄν ἀποθάνοιμεν).

τούτων, objective genitive.

ταῦτα πιστὰ εἶναι, 'that these were their pledges'; cf. § 4 ταύτην πατρίδα εἶναι.

8. ὡς διαβιβῶντες, 'with the view of helping them across (their territory).'

9. ὄρος μέγα, 'apparently the pass of Zigana across the Kolat-Dagh, the Colchians being posted at the summit of the pass '—TAYLOR.

Κόλχοι. See Map of Route.

ἄξοντες, intransitive; cf. § 12.

βουλεύσασθαι συλλεγείσιν, 'to collect and deliberate.'

ὅπως—ἀγωνιοῦνται. Cf. vi. 7.

10. λόχους ὀρθίους ποιῆσαι, 'to form companies in column '; cf. ii. 11 and iii. 17.

ὅταν—ὁρῶσιν, 'whenever (the soldiers) formed in line see this (line) thrown into disorder.'

11. ἐπὶ πολλούς, 'many deep,' the accusative implying motion into this formation; cf. § 10 τεταγμένοι εἰς φάλαγγα. Thuc. IV. 93 ἐπ᾽ ἀσπίδας εἴκοσι ἐτάξαντο. Contrast ἐπ᾽ ὀλίγων below.

προσάγωμεν, intransitive; cf. § 9 ἄξοντες.

ἡμῶν, genitive after the idea of *comparison* in περιττεύσουσιν 'they will be more numerous *than us*.'

ἴωμεν—διακοπείη—ἔσται. Notice the changes of mood (cf. note on i. 3):—(1) 'if we march in shallow order,' a supposed case distinctly stated; (2) 'if our line *were to be* cut through,' a more vague and uncertain statement; (3) 'if this *is to* happen anywhere,' a still stronger form of expression than the subjunctive. 'The future, as an emphatic form, is especially common when the condition contains a strong appeal to the feelings or a threat or warning'—GOODWIN, *Moods and Tenses*, § 447. Cf. vi. 9.

ἀθρόων, predicative, to be taken both with βελῶν and ἀνθρώπων.

12. ἀλλά μοι—κεράτων, 'No, my view is that we should form the companies in column and cover such an extent of ground with the companies, by leaving spaces between them, as to cause the extreme companies on each flank to be outside the enemy's wings.'

ὅσον—γενέσθαι. For this construction see note on **i.** 5 ὅσον σκοταίους διελθεῖν.

οἱ ἔσχατοι λόχοι, in apposition to 'we' the subject of ἐσόμεθα. Cf. note on **ii. 12.**

οἱ κράτιστοι, i.e. the λοχαγοί.

ᾗ ἂν εὔοδον ᾖ. Cf. **vi. 17** βατὰ ἔσται and *Cyropaedeia* **VI. iii. 2** ὅπου πέδινον εἴη.

ἄξει, intransitive; cf. § 9 ἄξοντες.

13. τὸ διαλεῖπον, 'the vacant space'; cf. **III. iv. 22** τὸ διέχον.

οὐδεὶς μηκέτι μείνῃ, 'not one of the enemy will any longer stand his ground.' This construction, which conveys a very strong negation, must be explained by an ellipse:—'no longer (*is there fear*) lest he stand his ground.' Cf. **II. ii. 12** οὐκέτι μὴ δύνηται. **VI. ii. 4** οὐ μὴ γένηται. Aesch. *Septem* 38 οὔ τι μὴ ληφθῶ δόλῳ 'I shall certainly never be caught by a trick.'

14. οὗτοί εἰσιν—σπεύδομεν, 'These men whom you see before you are the only remaining obstacle to our being now at once at the goal for which we have long been striving,'—i.e. the sea.

ἐμποδὼν τὸ μὴ εἶναι. For the redundant μή after a word of *hindering* cf. **III. iii. 6** εἴργειν ὥστε μὴ δύνασθαι.

πάλαι σπεύδομεν. Cf. Soph. *Ajax* 20 κεῖνον ἰχνεύω πάλαι and the Latin *iamdudum cupio*.

καὶ ὠμούς, 'even raw'; cf. *Hellenica* **III. iii. 6** ἡδέως ἂν καὶ ὠμῶν ἐσθίειν αὐτῶν (partitive genitive). Hom. *Iliad* **IV. 35** ὠμὸν βεβρώθοις Πρίαμον.

15. ἐν ταῖς χώραις, 'at their posts'; cf. **III. iv. 33** ἐκ χώρας ὁρμῶντας. Aesch. *Agam.* 78 Ἄρης οὐκ ἐνὶ χώρᾳ 'Ares is not at his post.'

ἕκαστοι, 'each division'; cf. **ii. 8** and **v. 23.**

τοὺς ὀγδοήκοντα. For the article with round numbers cf. **vii. 22** τὰ εἴκοσιν.

16. εὐξάμενοι, 'having made vows'; cf. § 25.

17. ἀντιπαραθέοντες, 'running along on either flank to confront them.'

18. οἱ κατὰ τὸ Ἀρκαδικὸν πελτασταί, 'the targeteers stationed with the Arcadian contingent.' For this use of κατά with the accusative cf. Thuc. VII. 78 τοῖς καθ' ἑαυτόν.

τὸ—ὁπλιτικὸν ὤν, construction *according to the sense*; cf. ii. 22 and VI. iv. 20 πᾶσα ἡ στρατιὰ—ἐκυκλοῦντο.

19. ἤρξαντο, subject οἱ πελτασταί.

20. τὰ μὲν ἄλλα—ἐθαύμασαν, 'in other respects there was nothing which really excited surprise.'

τὰ ἄλλα, 'for the rest,' accusative of respect used adverbially; cf. *Hellenica* III. ii. 2 τὰ μὲν ἄλλα ὁ Δερκυλίδας φέρων καὶ ἄγων τὴν Βιθυνίδα.

τῶν κηρίων, partitive genitive after ἔφαγον. Cf. v. 35 τῶν πώλων λαμβάνει.

τῶν στρατιωτῶν, partitive genitive after ὅσοι.

ἤμουν—αὐτοῖς, 'were attacked with sickness and violent purgings.'

ἀποθνῄσκουσιν, participle, 'to men in their death agony.'

'This is now known to have been due to the moisture that distils from the flowers of the *Azalea pontica*, which grows in profusion in the valleys at the back of Trebizond; this is poisonous and affects the honey of the bees that feed upon it. A similar circumstance is related by Strabo with regard to Pompey's forces during his campaign in these parts; only in that case the honey seems to have been obtained immediately from the trees'—TOZER, *History of Ancient Geography*, p. 118.

22. Τραπεζοῦντα. See Index of Proper Names.

ἐντεῦθεν ὁρμώμενοι, 'making this their base of operations.'

24. μάλιστα, 'for the most part,' to be taken with ἐν τῷ πεδίῳ.

25. εὔξαντο. Cf. § 16.

αὐτοῖς, dative of advantage.

ἱκανοὶ—ἀποθῦσαι. Cf. § 26 κάλλιστος τρέχειν and see notes on i. 5 and 8.

σωτήρια, i.e. sacrifices to Zeus in his capacity of Σωτήρ.

ἡγεμόσυννα, i.e. sacrifices to Heracles in his capacity of Ἡγεμών. Cf. VI. ii. 15 θυομένῳ αὐτῷ τῷ ἡγεμόνι Ἡρακλεῖ.

ἐπιμεληθῆναι—προστατῆσαι, infinitives of purpose.

26. τὰ δέρματα, i.e. as prizes for the victors.

πεποιηκὼς εἴη. Cf. vii. 2 συνεληλυθότες ἦσαν.

27. στάδιον, cognate accusative; so also the four accusatives which follow.

κατέβησαν, i.e. into the arena ; cf. Horace *Odes* III. i. 11 *descendat in campum petitor*.

28. ἔδει—ἄγειν, 'they had to ride down the steep and turn in the sea, and then make their way up again to the altar.' It was one of the conditions of the race that they must actually ride *into* the sea before they turned.

VOCABULARY.

ABBREVIATIONS.

accus.	accusative.	nom.	nominative.
adj.	adjective.	opt.	optative.
adv.	adverb.	partic.	participle.
aor.	aorist.	pass.	passive.
comp.	comparative.	pers.	personal.
conj.	conjunction.	pf.	perfect.
contr.	contracted.	plup.	pluperfect.
dat.	dative.	plur.	plural.
demonstr.	demonstrative.	prep.	preposition.
fut.	future.	pres.	present.
gen.	genitive.	pron.	pronoun.
imp.	imperfect.	subj.	subjunctive.
imper.	imperative.	subs.	substantive.
indecl.	indeclinable.	superl.	superlative.
indic.	indicative.	v. a.	verb active.
infin.	infinitive.	v. d.	„ deponent.
intrans.	intransitive.	v. impers.	„ impersonal.
mid.	middle.	v. mid.	„ middle.
neg.	negative.	v. n.	„ neuter.
neut.	neuter.	v. subst.	„ substantive.

*** For the principal parts of some of the compound verbs reference must be made to the simple verbs.

ἄ-βατος, ον, *impassable*, vi. 17.

ἀγαθός, ή, όν (borrowed comp. ἀμείνων, βελτίων or λώων, superl. ἄριστος, βέλτιστος or λῷστος), *good; noble, brave*, i. 18, vi. 19; subst. ἀγαθόν τό, *good thing, advantage*, i. 17, iv. 9, v. 28, vi. 27.

ἀγγέλλω, v. a., fut. ἀγγελῶ, aor. ἤγγειλα, pf. ἤγγελκα, *report, announce.*

ἄγγελος, ὁ, *messenger.*

ἀγείρω, v.a., fut. ἀγερῶ, aor. ἤγειρα, *collect, gather.*

ἄγκος τό, -εος, *glen, valley*, i. 7.

ἀγνοέω, v. a. *be ignorant of*, v. 7.

ἀγορά ἡ, *market-place, market.* ἀγορὰν παρέχω, *provide a market*, viii. 8, 23.

ἄγω, v.a., fut. ἄξω, aor. ἤγαγον, *lead, bring;* absolute, of a general, *march* (*troops* understood), vi. 23; of troops, *march*, viii. 9; of a road, *lead*, iii. 5.

ἀγών ὁ, -ῶνος, *contest*, viii. 25.

ἀγωνίζομαι, v.d. *strive, contend*, vi. 7.

ἄ-δειπνος, ον, *without supper*, v. 21.

ἀδελφός ὁ, *brother.*
ἀ-δικέω, (1) v. n. *be unjust.*
　　(2) v. a. *injure,* iv. 6.
ἀ-δύνατος, ον, (1) of persons, *unable;*
　　(2) of things, *impossible.*
ἀεί, adv. *always; from time to time,*
　　i. 7, vii. 23.
ἀείδω, contr. ᾄδω, fut. ᾄσομαι, v.a.
　　sing, viii. 16.
ἀθρόος, α, ον, *all together, in crowds,* vi. 13, vii. 2, viii. 11.
ἀ-θυμία ἡ, *want of spirit, despondency,* viii. 10.
αἴθω, v. a. and n. *burn,* vii. 20.
αἴξ ὁ, ἡ, αἰγός, *goat,* v. 25, vi. 17.
αἱρετέος, α, ον, verbal adj. of αἱρέω, *to be taken,* vii. 3.
αἱρέω, v.a., fut. αἱρήσω, aor. εἷλον, pf. ᾕρηκα, *take, seize;* mid. *choose.*
αἰσθάνομαι, v.d., fut. αἰσθήσομαι, aor. ᾐσθόμην, pf. ᾔσθημαι, *perceive, be aware of.*
αἴσθησις ἡ, -εως, *sensation, observation,* vi. 13.
αἰσχρός, ά, όν, *shameful, disgraceful.* αἰσχρῶς, adv. *shamefully.*
αἰτέω, v.a. *ask; ask for;* mid. *ask for oneself.*
αἰτιάομαι, v.d. *accuse, blame,* i. 19.
αἴτιος, α, ον, *causing, guilty* (with gen.); αἴτιον, *cause,* i. 17.
αἰχμ-άλωτος, ον, *taken by the spear, taken captive,* i. 12; subst. *captive,* viii. 27.
ἀκμήν, adv. (properly accus. of ἀκμή, *point*) *just,* iii. 26.
ἀκόντιον τό, *javelin,* ii. 28.
ἀκοντιστής ὁ, -οῦ, *javelin-man,* iii. 28.
ἀκούω, v.a., fut. ἀκούσομαι, aor. ἤκουσα, pf. ἀκήκοα, *hear; obey* (with gen. of person).

ἄκρατος, ον, *unmixed, strong,* v. 27.
ἄκρος, α, ον, *pointed, high;* subst. ἄκρον τό, *summit,* i. 7, 25.
ἄκων, ουσα, ον, *unwilling.*
ἀλαλάζω, v.n. *shout,* ii. 7.
ἀλεεινός, ή, όν, *warm,* iv. 11.
ἀληθεύω, v.n. *speak the truth,* iv. 15, vii. 15.
ἀληθής, ές, *true.*
ἁλίσκομαι, v.d., fut. ἁλώσομαι, aor. ἑάλων, contr. ἥλων, pf. ἑάλωκα, contr. ἥλωκα, *be captured,* i. 3.
ἄλκιμος, ον, *strong, brave,* iii. 4.
ἀλλά, conj. *but, yet; well.* ἀλλ' ἤ, *except,* vi. 10.
ἀλλήλω, α, ω, reciprocal pron. *one another.*
ἄλλομαι, v.d., aor. 1 ἡλάμην, *leap,* ii. 17.
ἄλλος, η, ο, *another, other.* οἱ ἄλλοι, *the rest.* ἄλλη (ὁδῷ), *by another way, elsewhere,* ii. 4. ἄλλο τι ἤ, Latin *nonne,* vii. 5.
ἄλλοτε, adv. *at one time,* i. 17; *at another time.*
ἄλλως, adv. *otherwise.*
ἄλφιτον τό, *barley meal;* plur., viii. 23.
ἅμα, (1) adv. *at the same time;* with participle, *while,* i. 19.
　　(2) prep. *together with* (with dat.), i. 5, 12.
ἅμαξα ἡ, *waggon.*
ἁμαξιαῖος, α, ον, *sufficient to fill a waggon,* i.e. *huge,* ii. 3.
ἁμαρτάνω, v.n., fut. ἁμαρτήσομαι, aor. ἥμαρτον, pf. ἡμάρτηκα, *err, make a mistake; miss a mark.*
ἀ-μαχεί, adv. *without fighting,* vi. 12.
ἀ-μαχητί, adv. *without fighting,* ii. 15.

ἀμείνων. See ἀγαθός.

ἀ-μέλεια ἡ, *carelessness*, vi. 3.

ἀμυγδάλινος, η, ον, *made of almonds*, iv. 13.

ἀμύνω, v.a. *ward off*; with dat.
protect; mid. *defend oneself*;
revenge oneself on, punish (with
accus.).

ἀμφί, prep. (1) with accus.
(i) *around*, i. 6, ii. 5, iii. 21.
(ii) *about* (of time or number),
i. 5, iv. 1, v. 9, vii. 22.
(2) with gen. *concerning*, v.
17.

ἀμφότερος, α, ον, *both*.

ἀμφοτέρωθεν, adv. *from both sides;
on both sides of* (with gen.).

ἄμφω -οῖν, *both*.

ἄν (ἄ), particle,
(1) conditional, with indic. or
opt. in the apodosis of a conditional sentence.
(2) potential, with infin., v.
16, vi. 13.
(3) frequentative, with imp.
or aor. indic., vii. 16.
(4) indefinite, with relative or
relative particle with subj., iii.
27, 28.
See note on vi. 13.

ἄν (ᾱ) = ἐάν, vi. 19.

ἀνά, prep. (with accus.).
(1) *up along; up to*, iii. 20.
(2) distributive use, vi. 4.

ἀνα-βαίνω, v. n. *go up* (esp. up
country from the sea); *mount*.

ἀνα-βάλλω, v. a. *put up, help to
mount* (*a horse*), iv. 4.

ἀνάβασις ἡ, -εως, *going up*, i. 10;
march up country, i. 1.

ἀναγκάζω, v.a. *compel*.

ἀναγκαῖος, α, ον, *necessary*.

ἀνάγκη ἡ, *necessity*.

ἀν-άγω, v. a. *lead up*.

ἀνα-ζεύγνυμι, v. a. *yoke again;
break up a camp*, vi. 1.

ἀν-αιρέω, v.a. *take up*; mid. i. 19.

ἀνα-καλέω, v. a. *call up, summon;*
mid. *recall*, iv. 22.

ἀνα-κομίζω, v.a. *carry up;* mid.
carry up for oneself, vii. 1.

ἀνα-κράζω, v.n. *cry out*, iv. 20.

ἀν-αλαλάζω, v. n. *shout out*, iii.
19.

ἀνα-λαμβάνω, v.a. *take up*, vii. 23.

ἀν-αλίσκω, v.a., fut. ἀναλώσω, *use
up*, vii. 5.

ἀνα-μίγνυμι, v.a. *mix up*.

ἀνα-παύω, v.a. *make to rest;* mid.
rest, v. 19.

ἀνα-πηδάω, v. n. *leap up*.

ἀνα-πνέω, v.n. *take breath, recover*,
i. 22, iii. 1.

ἀν-άριστος, ον, *without breakfast*,
ii. 4.

ἀνα-στρέφω, v.a. *turn round*; abs.
wheel round, iii. 29, v. 35.

ἀνα-τίθημι, v.a. *place upon; set
up, dedicate*, vii. 26; mid. *pack
up, load*.

ἀνα-τρέφω, v. a. *feed up, rear*.

ἀνα-φρονέω, v.n. *recover one's
senses*, viii. 21.

ἀνα-χάζω, v.n. *retire*, i. 16, vii. 10.

ἀνα-χωρέω, v. n. *retreat*.

ἀνδράποδον τό, *slave*, i. 12.

ἀνδρίζομαι, v.d. *play the man*, iii.
34.

ἀν-εκ-πίμπλημι, v.a. *fill up in
return*, v. 28.

ἄνεμος ὁ, *wind*.

ἀν-ερωτάω, v.a. *ask repeatedly*.

ἄνευ, prep. *without* (with gen.).

ἀνήρ ὁ, ἀνδρός, *man*.

ἄνθρωπος ὁ, *human being, man*.

ἀνιάω, v.a. *annoy*, viii. 26.

ἀν-ίημι, v.a. *relax*; abs. *abate*,
v. 4.

ἀν-ιμάω, v.a. *haul up*, ii. 8.

ἀν-ίστημι, v.a. *raise up*, v. 19, 21; mid. (and pf. and 2 aor. act.) *rise up, start*, i. 5.

ἄν-οδος, ον, *pathless*, viii. 10.

ἀντ-αγωνίζομαι, v.d. *contend against*, vii. 12.

ἀντ-εμ-πίμπλημι, v.a. *fill up in return*, v. 28.

ἀντί, prep. (1) *opposite to*, vii. 6. (2) *instead of*, iv. 13, vii. 15.

ἀντίος, α, ον, *opposite, opposed*, iii. 26.

ἀντι-παρα-θέω, v.n. *run along opposite*, viii. 17.

ἀντι-παρα-τάττω, v.a. *draw up opposite*, viii. 9.

ἀντι-πάρ-ειμι, v.n. *march along opposite*, iii. 17.

ἀντι-πέραν, adv.; κατ' ἀντιπέραν, *over against*, viii. 3.

ἀντι-ποιῶ, v.a. *do in return, retaliate*; mid. *lay claim to against* (with gen. of thing), vii. 12.

ἀντί-πορος, ον, *over against*, ii. 18.

ἀντι-στασιάζω, v.n. *belong to an opposite faction*, i. 27.

ἀντι-τάττω, v. a. *range against*. ἀντι-τετάχαται, 3rd plur. pf. pass., viii. 5.

ἀντρώδης, ες, *cave-like*, iii. 11.

ἄνω, adv. *upwards, above*, iii. 3; comp. ἀνωτέρω, superl. ἀνωτάτω.

ἄνωθεν, adv. *from above*, vii. 12.

ἄξιος, α, ον, *worthy, befitting;* with gen. *worth*, i. 28.

ἀξιόω, v.a. *think worthy* (with infin.), vi. 16.

ἀπ-αγγέλλω, v.a. *bring back tidings*.

ἀπ-αιτέω, v.a. *demand*.

ἀπ-αλλάττω, v.a. *set free*, iii. 2.

ἀπ-αντάω, v.n. *meet*, vi. 5.

ἅπαξ, adv. *once, once for all*.

ἅπας, ασα, αν, *all together*.

ἄπ-ειμι, v.n. *be absent* (εἰμί).

ἄπ-ειμι, v. n. *go away* (εἶμι), often with fut. signification.

ἀπ-έρχομαι, v.d. *go away*.

ἀπ-έχω, v.a. *keep away;* intrans. *keep away, be distant* (with gen.), v. 10, vi. 6.

ἄ-πλετος, ον, *immense*, iv. 11.

ἀπό, prep. with gen. (1) place, *away from; from*, vii. 27. (2) time, *from*. (3) means, *from*.

ἀπο-βαίνω, v.n. *depart; happen*.

ἀπο-βάλλω, v.a. *throw away; lose*, vi. 10.

ἀπο-βλέπω, v. n. *look away at*.

ἀπο-διδράσκω, v.n., fut. -δράσω, aor. 2 -έδραν, *run away*, vi. 3.

ἀπο-δίδωμι, v.a. *give back*.

ἀπο-δύω, v. a. *strip off;* mid. (and aor. 2 act.) *strip, undress*, iii. 17.

ἀπο-θνήσκω, v. n. *die, be killed*.

ἀπο-θύω, v.a. *sacrifice as a due*, viii. 25.

ἀπ-οικία ἡ, *colony*, viii. 22.

ἀπο-καίω, v.a. *burn up; parch up*, v. 3.

ἀπο-κάμνω, v. n. *be exhausted*.

ἀπο-κλείω, v.a. *shut out from*.

ἀπο-κόπτω, v.a. *cut off, dislodge*. ii. 10, 17.

ἀπο-κρίνομαι, v.d. *answer*.

ἀπο-κρύπτω, v.a. *hide away*.

ἀπο-κτείνω, v. a. *kill*.

ἀπο-λαμβάνω, v. a. *cut off*, iii. 21.

ἀπο-λείπω, v.a. *leave behind;* mid. *fall behind*, iii. 22, v. 16.

ἀπ-όλλυμι, v.a., fut. ἀπολῶ, aor. ἀπώλεσα, pf. ἀπολώλεκα, 2 pf. ἀπόλωλα (intrans.), aor. mid. ἀπωλόμην, *kill, destroy; lose;* mid. *die, perish*.

ἀπό-μαχος, ον, *unfit for fighting, disabled*, i. 13.

ἀπο-πέμπω, v.a. *send away.*

ἀ-πορία ἡ, *want, resourcelessness, perplexity.*

ἄ-πορος, ον, (1) of persons, *helpless, resourceless.*

(2) of things, *impracticable; impassable*, i. 2.

ἀπο-σήπομαι, v. mid., pf. ἀποσέσηπα, *rot off*, v. 12.

ἀπο-σκεδάννυμι, v.a. *scatter*, iv. 9.

ἀπο-τέμνω, v. a. *cut off*, vii. 16.

ἀπό-τομος, ον, *precipitous*, i. 2.

ἀπο-φεύγω, v. n. *escape*, ii. 27.

ἀπό-φραξις ἡ, -εως, *fencing off*, ii. 25.

ἀπο-χωρέω, v.n. *go away, retire.*

ἀ-προσ-δόκητος, ον, *unexpected.* ἐξ ἀπροσδοκήτου, *unexpectedly*, i. 10.

ἄρα, particle, *then, as it seems, after all*, ii. 15.

ἆρα, interrogative particle, *then.*

ἀργύριον τό, *silver, money.*

ἀργυρό-πους, -ποδος, *with silver feet*, iv. 21.

ἀργυροῦς, ᾶ, οῦν, *of silver*, vii. 27.

ἀρετή ἡ, *virtue, bravery.*

ἄριστα, adv. superl. *best.*

ἀριστάω, v. n. *take the morning meal*, i. 14, iii. 10.

ἀριστερός, ά, όν, *left.* ἡ ἀριστερά (χείρ), *the left hand.*

ἄριστον τό, *morning meal, breakfast*, v. 30.

ἀριστοποιέομαι, v. mid. *take the morning meal*, iii. 9.

ἄριστος, η, ον. See ἀγαθός.

ἄρνειος, α, ον, *of lamb*, v. 31.

ἁρπάζω, v. a. *seize, plunder*, v. 12; of a river, *carry away*, iii. 6.

ἄρτι, adv. *lately, just now.*

ἀρτο-κόπος ὁ, *baker*, vi. 21.

ἄρτος ὁ, *loaf.*

ἀρχαῖος, α, ον, *ancient, old.*

ἄρχω, v.a., fut. ἄρξω, *rule* (with gen. or absolute), ii. 28; act. and mid. *begin* (with gen.), iii. 28. Subst. ὁ ἄρχων, *commander, ruler*, vii. 19.

ἀ-σθενέω, v.n. *to be weak, to be ill.*

ἄ-σιτος, ον, *without food*, v. 11.

ἄσμενος, η, ον, *well-pleased, glad;* with verbs, *gladly*, v. 22.

ἀσπίς ἡ, -ίδος, *shield*, the large oval shield of the hoplite. See note on iii. 26.

ἀσταφίς ἡ, -ίδος, *raisin*, iv. 9.

ἀ-σφαλής, ές, *safe*, comp. ἀσφαλέστερος, superl. ἀσφαλέστατος. ἀσφαλῶς, adv. *safely.*

ἀτασθαλία ἡ, *wanton folly*, iv. 14.

ἅτε, particle, *inasmuch as*, v. 18.

ἀτμίζω, v. n. *steam*, v. 15.

ἀ-τριβής, ές, *untrodden, pathless*, ii. 8.

αὐθήμερον, adv. *on the same day*, iv. 22, v. 1.

αὖθις, adv. *again.*

αὐλίζομαι, v. d. *bivouack*, v. 21.

αὔριον, adv. *on the morrow.*

αὐτίκα, adv. *immediately.*

αὐτόθεν, adv. *from the very spot; on the spot*, ii. 6.

αὐτόθι, adv. *on the spot.*

αὐτό-ματος, η, ον, *of one's own accord*, iii. 18.

αὐτός, ή, ό, demonstr. pron., *self; in person;* in oblique cases, *he, she, it*, etc. ὁ αὐτός, *the same.*

αὐτόσε, adv. *to the very spot, thither*, vii. 2.

αὐτοῦ, adv. *at the very place, on the spot*, v. 21.

ἀφ-αιρέω, v.a. *take away;* mid. *take away for oneself, for one's own interest*, i. 14, iv. 12.

ἀ-φανής, ές, *unseen;* with partic., ii. 4.

ἄ-φθονος, ον, *ungrudging, plentiful.* ἐν ἀφθόνοις, *in plenty,* v. 29.

ἀφ-ίημι, v.a., fut. ἀφήσω, aor. ἀφῆκα, pf. ἀφεῖκα, *send away, let go,* i. 12, v. 24, 30; *leave,* i. 14.

ἀφ-ικνέομαι, v.d., fut. ἀφίξομαι, aor. ἀφικόμην, *arrive.*

ἄφ-οδος ἡ, *way of escape,* ii. 11.

ἄ-φρων, ον, *senseless, mad,* viii. 20.

ἀ-χρεῖος, ον, *useless.*

βάδην, adv. *at a walk,* vi. 26, viii. 28.

βάθος τό, *depth.*

βαίνω, v.n., fut. βήσομαι, aor. ἔβην, pf. βέβηκα, *go, march.*

βακτηρία ἡ, *staff,* vii. 26.

βάλλω, v.a., fut. βαλῶ, aor. ἔβαλον, pf. βέβληκα, *throw, shoot; pelt* (with accus. or absolute), vi. 12.

βαρβαρικός, ή, όν, *barbarous, foreign.*

βάρβαρος, ον, *barbarous, foreign, not Greek.*

βασίλειος, α, ον, *royal;* subst. βασίλειον τό, *castle,* iv. 2, 7.

βασιλεύς ὁ, *king.* Without article, *the Great King,* i.e. the King of Persia, i. i.

βατός, ή, όν, *passable,* vi. 17.

βέλος τό, *missile, dart.*

βελτίων, βέλτιστος. See ἀγαθός.

βῆμα τό, -ατος, *step,* vii. 10.

βία ἡ, *strength, force.*

βλάπτω, v.a. *impede; injure.*

βλέπω, v.a. and n. *see, look.*

βοάω, v.n. *shout.*

βοή ἡ, *shout.*

βοήθεια ἡ, *help, reinforcements.*

βοηθέω, v.n. *come to the rescue* (with dat.).

βόθρος ὁ, *pit, trench,* v. 6.

βορρᾶς ὁ, *the north wind,* v. 3; *the north.*

βουλεύω, v.a. *plan, devise;* mid. *deliberate (with oneself).*

βου-λιμιάω, v.n. *be ravenously hungry,* v. 7.

βούλομαι, v.d. *wish, be willing.*

βοῦς ὁ, ἡ, βοός, *ox, cow.*

βρέχω, v.a. *wet,* v. 2.

βρωτός, ή, όν, *eatable,* v. 5.

βωμός ὁ, *altar,* viii. 28.

γαμέω, v.a. *marry* (of the man); mid. (of the wife). v. 24.

γάρ, conj. *for.* καὶ γάρ, *for indeed, for also,* ii. 7, iii. 24.

γαστήρ ἡ, -τρός, *stomach.*

γε, particle enclitic, *at least, at any rate;* sometimes need not be translated except by an emphasis on the word to which it is attached. δέ γε, *yes and,* vi. 9.

γέλως ὁ, -ωτος, *laughter.*

γέμω, v.n. *be full* (with gen.), vi. 27.

γέρρον τό, *wicker target,* iii. 4, vii. 26.

γέρων ὁ, -οντος, *old man.*

γῆ ἡ, *earth, land; soil.*

γήλοφος ὁ, *hill,* iv. 1.

γίγνομαι, v.d., fut. γενήσομαι, aor. ἐγενόμην, pf. γέγονα and γεγένημαι, *become, come about; be made, be done; find oneself,* v. 28; *amount to,* vii. 6.

γιγνώσκω, v.a., fut. γνώσομαι, aor. ἔγνων, pf. ἔγνωκα, *observe, know; determine, decide,* vi. 10.

γόνυ τό, -ατος, *knee;* of reeds, *joint, knot,* v. 26.

γυμνής ὁ, -ῆτος, *light-armed soldier,* i. 6, vi. 17.

γυμνικός, ή, όν, *gymnastic,* viii. 25.

γυμνός, ή, όν, *naked, bare; un-protected,* iii. 6, iv. 12.
γυνή ή, -αικός, *woman; wife.*

δάκνω, v. a., fut. δήξομαι, aor. ἔδα-κον, *bite.*
δακρύω, v. n. *weep.*
δακτύλιος ὁ, *finger-ring,* vii. 27.
δάκτυλος ὁ, *finger; toe,* v. 12.
δάπεδον τό, *ground,* v. 6.
δαρεικός ὁ, *daric,* Persian gold coin, value about 16s.
δασμός ὁ, *tribute,* v. 24, 34.
δασύς, εῖα, ύ, *thick,* vii. 7, viii. 2; *shaggy,* vii. 22.
δαψιλής, ές, *abundant,* ii. 22, iv. 2.
δέ, conj. *but, and, now; on the other hand* (answering to μέν). In apodosis, δέ γε, *yes and,* vi. 9. καὶ—δέ, *yes and,* vii. 9.
δέδοικα, v. n., perf. with pres. signification, *fear.*
δεῖ, v. impers., fut. δεήσει, *it is necessary;* with gen. *there is need of;* partic. δέον, vii. 7.
δείκνυμι, v. a., fut. δείξω, *show, point out.*
δείλη ή, *afternoon,* ii. 1.
δεινός, ή, όν, *terrible, strange; clever,* vi. 16.
δειπνέω, v. n. *dine, sup.*
δεῖπνον τό, *evening meal, dinner, supper.*
δέκα, indecl. *ten.*
δένδρον τό, *tree;* dat. plur. δένδρεσι, viii. 2, or δένδροις, vii. 9.
δεξιός, ά, όν, *right, on the right hand.* Subst. ή δεξιά (χείρ), *the right hand.*
δέομαι, v. mid. *want* (with gen.), iv. 6; *request* (with gen. of person), v. 16.
δέον. See δεῖ.

δέρμα τό, -ατος, *skin,* viii. 26.
δεῦρο, adv. *hither.*
δέχομαι, v. d., fut. δέξομαι, pf. δέδεγμαι, *receive; await the attack of,* ii. 7, iii. 31.
δέω, v. a. *bind,* ii. 1, vi. 2.
δή, particle, *indeed, now;* emphasises, iii. 27, v. 4.
δῆλος, η, ον, *clear, evident.*
δηλόω, v. a. *show, explain.*
δημόσιος, α, ον, *public.* τὰ δημόσια, *public property,* vi. 16.
διά, prep.
   (1) with accus. *owing to, because of,* i. 2.
   (2) with gen. *through* (of place or time), i. 2, ii. 4; *through, by means of,* ii. 18.
διαβαίνω, v. a. *go across, traverse; stride,* iii. 8.
διάβασις ή, *crossing, ford,* viii. 3.
διαβιβάζω, v. a., fut. -βιβάσω, *make to cross, convey across,* viii. 8.
διαγίγνομαι, *continue;* with participle, v. 5.
διαγκυλόομαι, v. d. *place the finger in the thong* (of a javelin), iii. 28.
διάγω, v. a. *bring through, bring across;* absolute (βίον or χρόνον understood), *spend time, live,* ii. 6.
διαδίδωμι, v. a. *distribute,* v. 8.
διαζεύγνυμι, v. a. *disjoin, separate,* ii. 10.
διαιθριάζω, v. n. *clear* (of the sky), iv. 10.
διακελεύομαι, v. mid. *cheer on one another,* vii. 26, viii. 3.
διακονέω, v. n. *serve,* v. 33.
διακόπτω, v. a. *cut through, cut in pieces,* viii. 11.
διαλαγχάνω, v. a. *distribute by lot,* v. 23.

δια-λαμβάνω, v.a. *take separately,*
    i. 23.

δια-λέγομαι, v.d. *converse* (with
    dat.), ii. 18.

δια-λείπω, v.a. *leave intervals,*
    viii. 12; intrans. *be at intervals,*
    vii. 6. τὸ διαλεῖπον, *the space
    between,* viii. 13.

διαμπερές, adv. *right through,* i.
    18.

δια-πέμπω, v.a. *send in different
    directions,* v. 8.

δια-πράττω, v.a. *arrange, settle;*
    mid. *arrange for oneself, effect,
    gain,* ii. 23.

δια-σκηνέω, v.n. *be quartered
    apart,* iv. 8, v. 29. διασκηνη-
    τέον, verbal adj. *one must be
    quartered apart,* iv. 14.

δια-σκηνόω, v.a. *quarter apart,* iv.
    10.

δια-σπάω, v.a. *draw asunder, dis-
    perse,* viii. 10.

δια-σφενδονάω, v.a. *scatter as if
    from a sling,* ii. 3.

δια-τελέω, v.a. *accomplish,* v. 11;
    absolute, *continue* (with partic.),
    iii. 2.

δια-τήκομαι, v.mid. *melt away,*
    v. 6.

δια-τίθημι, v.a. *dispose; treat,* vii.
    4.

δια-τρέφω, v.a. *support through-
    out,* vii. 17.

δια-τρίβω, v.a. *rub away; waste,*
    vi. 9; absol. *delay.*

δια-φέρω, v.n. *differ from;* mid.
    quarrel, v. 17.

δια-φθείρω, v.a. *destroy utterly;
    mar,* v. 12.

διάφορος, ον, *different.* διάφορον
    τό, *variance,* vi. 3.

δια-χωρέω, v.n. *go through,* viii.
    20.

διδάσκω, v.a., fut. διδάξω, *teach.*

δίδωμι, v.a., fut. δώσω, aor. ἔδωκα,
    pf. δέδωκα, *give, give up.*

δι-έρχομαι, v.d. *pass through.*

δι-ηγέομαι, v.d. *describe,* iii. 8.

δι-ίημι, v.a. *send through, let pass,*
    i. 8.

δίκαιος, α, ον, *just.*

δίκη ἡ, *justice; penalty,* iv. 14.

δί-πηχυς, υ, *two cubits in length
    or width,* ii. 28.

διπλάσιος, α, ον, *double.*

δί-πλεθρος, ον, *two plethra in
    length or width,* i.e. 202 feet.

δισ-χίλιοι, αι, α, *two thousand.*

διψάω, v.n. *be thirsty,* v. 27.

διώκω, v.a. *pursue.*

δοκέω, (1) v.a., fut. δόξω, *think.*
    (2) intrans. *seem,* i. 5. Im-
    pers. δοκεῖ, *it seems good, it is
    resolved,* i. 2, 12. δόξαν, see
    note on i. 13.

δόλιχος ὁ, *long course,* viii. 27.

δόρυ τό, -ατος, *spear.* ἐπὶ δόρυ,
    see note on iii. 29.

δουλεύω, v.n. *be a slave,* viii. 4.

δοῦλος ὁ, *slave.*

δρόμος ὁ, *running,* iii. 31; *race-
    course,* viii. 26.

δύναμαι, v.d., fut. δυνήσομαι, aor.
    ἠδυνήθην, *be able.*

δύναμις ἡ, *power; military force,*
    iv. 18.

δυνατός, ή, όν, (1) of persons, *able,
    capable,* i. 12.
    (2) of things, *possible,* i. 24,
    ii. 23.

δύο, *two.*

δυσ-πάριτος, ον, *hard to pass,* i.
    25.

δυσ-πορία ἡ, *difficulty in passing,*
    iii. 7.

δώδεκα, indecl. *twelve.*

δῶρον τό, *gift.*

ἑάλωκα, ἑάλων. See ἁλίσκομαι.

ἐάν, *if* (with subj.).

ἑαυτόν, ήν, ό, reflexive pron. *himself*.

ἐάω, v.a., fut. ἐάσω, aor. εἴασα, *let, allow*.

ἑβδομήκοντα, indecl. *seventy*.

ἐγγύθεν, adv. *from near*.

ἐγγύς, comp. ἐγγυτέρω, superl. ἐγγυτάτω and ἐγγύτατα.

  (1) prep. *near* (with gen.), iv. 1.

  (2) adv. *near; nearly*, ii. 28.

ἐγείρω, v.a. *awake;* mid. *wake;* perf. ἐγρήγορα with mid. sense, vi. 22.

ἐγ-καλύπτω, v.a. *cover up*, v. 19.

ἔγ-κειμαι, v.d. *lie in; be placed in*, v. 26.

ἐγ-χειρίδιον τό, *dagger*, iii. 11.

ἐγ-χέω, v. a. *pour in*.

ἐγώ, pers. pron., ἐμοῦ or μου, *I*. ἔγωγε, *I for my part*.

ἐθελοντής ὁ, -οῦ, *volunteer*, i. 26.

ἐθέλω or θέλω, v.n., fut. ἐθελήσω, aor. ἠθέλησα, *will, be willing, be ready*.

ἔθνος τό, *tribe, nation*.

εἰ, conj. *if* (with indic. and opt.); *whether*, i. 23, 28. εἰ μή, *unless, except*. εἰ δὲ μή, *but if not, failing that*, iii. 6, vii. 20.

εἶδον. See ὁράω.

εἰκάζω, v.a. *liken; conjecture*, v. 15.

εἰκός τό, -ότος, neut. partic. of ἔοικα, *likely, reasonable*, vi. 9.

εἴκοσι, indecl. *twenty*.

εἰκότως, adv. *naturally*.

εἰμί, v.subst., fut. ἔσομαι, *be, exist*. Impers. ἔστι, *it is possible*, ii. 5, iii. 6.

εἶμι, v.n. *go ; will go*.

εἴ-περ, conj. *if at least*, vi. 16.

εἶπον, used as 2 aor. of φημί.

εἴργω, v.a. *shut in ; prevent*.

εἴρηκα, used as perf. of φημί.

εἰς, prep. with accus.

  (1) motion, *to, into; against*, v. 18.

  (2) time, *into, for, towards*, v. 13, vii. 3.

  (3) idiomatic uses, i. 28, iv. 21, v. 24, viii. 10, 15.

εἷς, μία, ἕν, *one*.

εἰσ-άγω, v.a. *bring in*.

εἰσ-δύομαι, v.mid. *enter into*, v. 14.

εἴσ-ειμι, v. n. *enter*.

εἰσ-έρχομαι, v.n. *enter*.

εἴσ-οδος ἡ, *entrance*.

εἰσ-τρέχω, v.n. *run into*.

εἰσ-φορέω, v. a. *carry into*, vi. 1

εἴτε—εἴτε, *whether—or*, vi. 8.

ἐκ (ἐξ), prep. with gen.

  (1) *out of*, v. 14 ; *from*, vi. 14.

  (2) *starting from*, i. 10, ii. 23, vii. 5 ; *after*, iv. 13.

ἕκαστος, η, ον, *each*. ἕκαστοι, see notes on ii. 8, v. 23.

ἑκάτερος, α, ον, *each of two*.

ἑκατέρωθεν, adv. *from both sides*.

ἑκατόν, indecl. *hundred*.

ἐκ-βαίνω, v. n. *get out (on to higher ground)*, ii. 1, 25.

ἐκ-βάλλω, v.a. *throw out*.

ἔκ-βασις ἡ, -εως, *outlet (on to higher ground)*, i. 20, iii. 21.

ἔκ-γονος, ον, *sprung from ;* subst. *descendant;* neut. *offspring*, v. 25.

ἐκ-δίδωμι, v.a. *give up; give in marriage*, i. 24.

ἐκ-δύω, v.a. *strip off;* mid. (and 2 aor. act.) *strip, undress*, iii. 11.

ἐκεῖ, adv. *there*.

ἐκεῖθεν, adv. *thence*.

ἐκεῖνος, η, ο, demonstr. pron. *that,
yonder; he, she, it.*

ἐκ-λείπω, v.a. *leave, desert,* i. 7;
absolute, *give up, fail,* v. 15.

ἔκ-πωμα τό, -ατος, *drinking-cup,*
iv. 21.

ἐκ-τρέπω, v.a. *turn aside;* mid.
turn aside, v. 15.

ἐκ-φεύγω, v.n. *escape.*

ἐκών, οῦσα, όν, *willing.*

ἔλαιον τό, *olive oil.*

ἐλάττων, ον, used as comp. of
μικρός.

ἐλαύνω, v.a., fut. ἐλῶ, aor. ἤλασα,
pf. ἐλήλακα, *drive;* intrans. *ride,
drive; march.*

ἐλαφρός, ά, όν, *light, nimble,* ii.
27.

ἐλάχιστος, η, ον, used as superl. of
μικρός.

ἐλέγχω, v.a., fut. ἐλέγξω, *examine,*
i. 23.

ἐλεύθερος, α, ον, *free.*

ἕλκω, v.a. *draw, pull,* v. 32.

ἐλπίζω, v.a., fut. ἐλπιῶ, *hope, expect.*

ἐλπίς ἡ, -ίδος, *hope, expectation.*

ἐμαυτόν, ήν, reflexive pron. *myself.*

ἐμ-βαίνω, v.n. *step in,* iii. 20.

ἐμ-βάλλω, v.a. *throw upon;* intrans. *attack,* vii. 20; of a river,
flow into, viii. 2.

ἐμ βολή ἡ, *inroad,* i. 4.

ἐμέω, v.n. *vomit,* viii. 20.

ἐμ-μένω, v.n. *remain in.*

ἐμός, ή, όν, possessive pron. *my,
mine.*

ἔμ-παλιν, adv. *backwards,* iii. 21.

ἔμ-πειρος, ον, *experienced,* v. 8.

ἐμ πίμπρημι, v.a. *set alight,* iv. 15.

ἐμ-πίπτω, v.n. *fall upon,* viii. 11.

ἐμ-ποδίζω, v.a. *hinder,* iii. 29.

ἐμ-ποδών, adv. *in the way of,* viii.
14.

ἔμ-προσθεν, adv. *before; earlier.*

ἐν, prep. with dat.
(1) place, *in, on,* iii. 17;
among, ii. 22.
(2) time, *during,* i. 1, vii. 12.

ἐν-αγκυλάω, v.a. *fit a strap to* (a
javelin), ii. 28.

ἐν-αντίος, α, ον, *opposite, opposed,*
iii. 28, v. 3.

ἔνατος, η, ον, *ninth.*

ἔνδον, adv. *within.*

ἐν-έδρα ἡ, *ambuscade,* vii. 22.

ἐν-εδρεύω, v.n. *lie in ambush,* i.
22.

ἔν-ειμι, v.n. *be in, be among.*

ἕνεκα and ἕνεκεν, prep. *on account
of* (with gen.), vii. 20.

ἐνεός, ά, όν, *deaf and dumb,* v. 33.

ἐν-εσθίω, v.a. *eat greedily, eat
hastily,* ii. 1, v. 8.

ἔνθα, adv. *there; where,* i. 2, v. 6;
thither; whither; thereupon, then,
v. 6.

ἔνθεν, adv. *thence; whence,* vii. 7.

ἔνθεν καὶ ἔνθεν, *on this side and
that,* vi. 12, viii. 13; (with gen.),
iii. 28.

ἔνιοι, αι, α, *some,* ii. 4.

ἐν-νοέω, v.a. *think of, apprehend,*
ii. 13.

ἐν-τάττω, v.a. *post among.*

ἐνταῦθα, adv. *there, then, thereupon.*

ἐντεῦθεν, adv. *thence, from that
time, then, therefore.*

ἐν-τυγχάνω, v.n. *light upon* (with
dat.), v. 19.

ἐν-ωμοτία ἡ, literally, *band of sworn
troops; quarter of a* λόχος, *section,* iii. 26.

ἐξ. See ἐκ.

ἕξ, indecl. *six.*

ἑξακόσιοι, αι, α, *six hundred.*

ἐξ-ανίστημι, v.a. *make to rise up:*

mid. (and pf. and 2 aor. act.)
rise up, v. 18.

ἐξ-απίνης, adv. *suddenly*, vii. 25.

ἔξ εστι, v. impers. *it is allowed, it is possible*, iii. 10. ἐξόν, accus. absolute, *it being possible*, vi. 13.

ἐξ-ηγέομαι, v.d. *guide* (with dat.), v. 28.

ἐξήκοντα, indecl. *sixty.*

ἐξ-ικνέομαι, v.d. *arrive at; reach, hit*, iii. 18, 29.

ἔξ-οδος ἡ, *way out.*

ἐξ-όν. See ἔξεστι.

ἐξ-οπλίζομαι, v. mid. *arm oneself completely*, iii. 3, vi. 9.

ἔξω, (1) adv. *outside.*
(2) prep. *outside* (with gen.), viii. 16.

ἔοικα, v. n. *seem like, seem.*

ἐπ-αγγέλλομαι, v. d. *undertake, promise*, vii. 20.

ἐπ-ακολουθέω, v.n. *follow closely on* (with dat.), i. 1.

ἐπάν (ἐπεί, ἄν), *whenever* (with subj.), vi. 9.

ἐπ-εγείρω, v.a. *rouse up*, iii. 10.

ἐπεί, conj. *when, since.*

ἐπειδάν, conj. *whenever, as soon as* (with subj.).

ἐπειδή, conj. *when, since.*

ἔπ-ειμι, v. n. *be upon* (εἰμί).

ἔπ-ειμι, v. n. *come upon* (εἶμι). ἡ ἐπιοῦσα (sc. ἡμέρα), *the next day.*

ἔπειτα, adv. *then, next.*

ἐπ-ήκοος, ον, *within hearing*, iv. 5.

ἐπί, prep.
(1) with accus. *to*, iii. 11; *against*, iii. 31; *over*, vi. 11.
(2) with gen. *upon*, iii. 17, vii. 10.
(3) with dat. *upon*, iii. 3; *in charge of*, iv. 19; idiomatic uses, ii. 19, iv. 6, 17.

ἐπι-βάλλω, v.a. *throw upon, lay upon;* mid. *lay (an arrow) on (the string)*, iii. 28.

ἐπι-δείκνυμι, v.a. *show off;* mid. *show off oneself*, vi. 15.

ἐπι-διώκω, v.a. *pursue after.*

ἐπί-θεσις ἡ, -εως, *attack*, iv. 22.

ἐπι-θυμέω, v. n. *desire* (with gen. or infin.).

ἐπι-καταρριπτέω, v.a. *throw down after*, vii. 13.

ἐπί-κειμαι, v.d. *attack*, iii. 7.

ἐπι-κούρημα τό, -ατος, *defence*, v. 13.

ἐπι-κύπτω, v.n. *stoop over*, v. 32.

ἐπι-λαμβάνομαι, v. mid. *catch hold of* (with gen.), vii. 12.

ἐπι-λείπω, v.n. *fail*, v. 14, vii. 1.

ἐπι-μαρτύρομαι, v.d. *call to witness*, viii. 7.

ἐπι-μέλομαι, v.d. *take care of* (with gen.), iii. 30, viii. 25.

ἐπι-πίπτω, v.n. *fall upon*, i. 10.

ἐπι-σιτίζομαι, v. mid. *get provisions*, vii. 18.

ἐπι-σπάω, v.a. *draw after one*, vii. 14.

ἐπι-τελέω, v.a. *accomplish*, iii. 13.

ἐπιτήδειος, α, ον, *fitting, proper, necessary.* τὰ ἐπιτήδεια, *provisions*, ii. 22.

ἐπι-τίθημι, v.a. *put upon, inflict*, ii. 8; mid. *attack* (with dat.), iii. 24.

ἐπι-τρέχω, v.n. *run upon.*

ἐπι-τυγχάνω, v.n. *light upon* (with dat.), i. 9.

ἐπι-φθέγγομαι, v.d. *sound* (of a trumpet), ii. 7.

ἐπι-χειρέω, v.a. *attempt.*

ἐπι-χέω, v.a. *pour upon.*

ἐπι-χωρέω, v.n. *advance upon.*

ἕπομαι, v.d., impf. εἱπόμην, aor. ἐσπόμην, *follow* (with dat.).

ἔραμαι, v.d. *love*, vi. 3.

ἔργον τό, *work, deed.*

ἐρημία ἡ, *solitude.*

ἔρημος, ον, *deserted, abandoned.*

ἐρίζω, v.n. *strive, quarrel.*

ἐρίφειος, ον, *of kid*, v. 31.

ἑρμηνεύς ὁ, -έως, *interpreter*, ii. 18, iv. 5.

ἔρομαι, v.d. *ask.*

ἔρυμα τό, *defence, fort*, v. 9.

ἔρχομαι, v.d., fut. ἐλεύσομαι, aor. ἦλθον, pf. ἐλήλυθα, *come, go.*

ἐρῶ, v.a. used as fut. of φημί, *say.*

ἐρωτάω, v.a. *ask.*

ἐσθής ἡ, -ῆτος, *clothing*, iii. 25.

ἐσθίω, v.a., fut. ἔδομαι, aor. ἔφαγον, *eat.*

ἑσπέρα ἡ, *evening*, vii. 27; *the west*, iv. 4.

ἔστε, (1) adv. *as far as*, v. 6.
  (2) conj. *while; until*, v. 28.

ἔσωθεν, adv. *from within.*

ἑταῖρος ὁ, *comrade.*

ἕτερος, α, ον, *one of two*, i. 23; *another*, i. 24.

ἔτι, adv. *still; further;* with negative, *any longer.*

ἕτοιμος, η, ον, *ready.*

εὖ, adv. *well.*

εὐ-δαίμων, ον, *prosperous*, vii. 19.

εὔ-ζωνος, ον, *well-girt, active*, ii. 7, iii. 20.

εὐ-θυμέομαι, v.d. *be cheerful*, v. 30.

εὐθύς, adv. *immediately;* with partic., vii. 2.

εὐ-μενής, ές, *favourable*, vi. 12.

εὔ-νοια ἡ, *goodwill.*

εὔ-οδος, ον, *easy to pass*, ii. 9, viii. 10, 12.

εὐ-πετῶς, adv. *easily* (εὖ, πίπτω), iii. 21.

εὑρίσκω, v.a., fut. εὑρήσω, aor. εὗρον, pf. εὕρηκα, *find;* mid. *find for oneself, obtain.*

εὖρος τό, *breadth.*

εὐρύς, εῖα, ύ, *broad.*

εὔχομαι, v.d. *pray; vow*, viii. 16, 25

εὐ-ώδης, ές, *fragrant*, iv. 9.

εὐ-ώνυμος, ον, *left*, viii. 4.

εὐωχέομαι, v.mid. *feast*, v. 30.

ἐφ-έπομαι, v.d. *follow after, pursue*, i. 6, 7.

ἐφ-ίστημι, v.a. *set over; make to halt;* mid. (and 2 aor. and pf. act.) *stand on; halt; be set over.*

ἔφ-οδος ἡ, *approach*, ii. 6; *advance, attack.*

ἐφ᾽ ᾧ. See notes on ii. 19, iv. 6.

ἔχω, v.a., fut. ἕξω or σχήσω, aor. ἔσχον, pf. ἔσχηκα, *hold, have; hold oneself, be*, esp. with adverbs, i. 19, iii. 16.

ἕωθεν, adv. *in the morning*, iv. 8.

ἕως ἡ, ἕω, *dawn, morning.*

ἕως, conj. *while* (with indic.); *until* (with opt.).

ζάω, v.n., infin. ζῆν, fut. ζήσω, *live.*

ζεύγνυμι, v.a., fut. ζεύξω, *join.*

ζωγρέω, v.a. *capture alive*, vii. 22.

ζώνη ἡ, *girdle, belt*, vii. 16.

ἤ, conj. *either, or; than.*

ἦ, particle, *surely.*

ᾗ (sc. ὁδῷ), *by which way, where*, viii. 12.

ἡβάσκω, v.n. *grow to manhood*, vi. 1.

ἡγεμονία ἡ, *lead*, vii. 8; *command.*

ἡγεμόσυνα τά, *rewards for guidance*, viii. 25.

ἡγεμών ὁ, -όνος, *guide, leader*, i. 21, ii. 1.

ἡγέομαι, v.d. *lead, guide* (absol. or with gen.), i. 6.

ᾔδειν. See οἶδα.

ἡδέως, adv. *pleasantly*, comp. ἥδιον, superl. ἥδιστα.

ἤδη, adv. *now, already,* vii. 6.

ἥδομαι, v.d. *rejoice.*

ἡδονή ἡ, *pleasure.*

ἡδύς, εῖα, ύ, *sweet, pleasant.*

ἥκω, v.n. *have come, have arrived.*

ἥλιος ὁ, *sun.*

ἥλωκα, contr. for ἑάλωκα, ii. 13.

ἥλων, contr. for ἑάλων, iv. 21, v. 24.

ἡμεῖς, nom. plur. of ἐγώ.

ἡμέρα ἡ, *day.* ἅμα τῇ ἡμέρᾳ, *at daybreak,* i. 5.

ἡμέτερος, a, ον, possessive pron. *our.*

ἡμί-πλεθρον τό, *half a plethrum,* vii. 6.

ἥμισυς, -εια, υ, *half,* ii. 9, iii. 15.

ἦν, contr. for ἔην.

ἡνίκα, conj. *when,* i. 5.

ᾖ-περ, adv. *by which way,* ii. 9.

ἡσυχία ἡ, *quietness.*

ἦτρον τό, *abdomen,* vii. 15.

ἡττάομαι, v.d., fut. ἡττήσομαι, *be inferior, be worsted,* vi. 36.

ἧττον, comp. adv. *less.*

θάλαττα ἡ, *sea.*

θαμινά, adv. *frequently,* i. 16.

θάπτω, v.a. *bury.*

θαρραλέος, a, ον, *brave, confident,* vi. 9.

θαρρέω, v.n. *have courage,* v. 28.

θάττων, ον, comp. of ταχύς.

θαυμάζω, (1) v.n. *wonder.*

(2) v.a. *wonder at.*

θαυμαστός, ή, όν, *wonderful.*

θέα, ἡ, *spectacle,* viii. 27.

θέαμα τό, *spectacle.*

θεάομαι, v.d. *be a spectator,* vii. 11.

θέλω. See ἐθέλω.

θεός ὁ, *god.*

θέω, v.n. *run,* iii. 29, v. 24.

θηράω, v.a. *hunt,* v. 24.

θνήσκω, v.n., fut. θανοῦμαι, aor. ἔθανον, pf. τέθνηκα, *die, be killed.* τεθνάναι, pf. inf. *lie dead,* i. 19, ii. 17, vii. 20.

θόρυβος ὁ, *disorder, tumult.*

θρασέως, adv. *boldly.*

θυγάτηρ ἡ, -τρός, *daughter.*

θυμο-ειδής, ές, *spirited,* v. 36.

θυσία ἡ, *sacrifice.*

θύω, v.a. *sacrifice;* mid. *have a sacrifice offered,* iii. 9, vi. 23.

θώραξ ὁ, *breastplate, cuirass,* ii. 28, vii. 15.

ἱερεῖον τό, *victim, animal,* iv. 9.

ἱερός, ά, όν, *sacred;* with gen., v. 35; τὰ ἱερά, *victims,* iii. 9.

ἵημι, v.a., fut. ἥσω, aor. ἧκα, pf. εἷκα, *send; throw,* v. 18; *shoot;* mid. *attack,* ii. 7, 20.

ἱκανός, ή, όν, *sufficient; competent.*

ἱμάς ὁ, -άντος, *strap,* v. 14.

ἱμάτιον τό, *cloak.*

ἵνα, conj. *in order that* (with subj. and opt.).

ἱππεύς ὁ, *horseman;* plur. ἱππεῖς, *cavalry.*

ἵππος ὁ, *horse.*

ἴσος, η, ον, *equal.* εἰς τὸ ἴσον, vi. 18. ἴσως, adv. *equally.*

ἰσο-χειλής, ές, *level with the edge,* v. 26.

ἵστημι, v.a., fut. στήσω, 1 aor. ἔστησα, *make to stand, make to halt, set up, place;* mid. (and 2 aor. ἔστην and pf. ἕστηκα), *stand, halt.*

ἰσχυρός, ά, όν, *strong.* ἰσχυρῶς, adv. *strongly, exceedingly,* ii. 26, viii. 28.

ἴτυς ἡ, -vos, *rim of shield,* vii. 12.

καθ-εύδω, v.n. *sleep.*

καθ-ήκω, v.n. *reach down,* iii. 11.

κάθ-ημαι, v.d. *sit down; be encamped*.

καθ-ίστημι, v.a. *place*, viii. 8; of troops, *draw up;* mid. (and 2 aor. and pf. act.), *place oneself,* v. 19.

καθ-οράω, v.a. *catch sight of,* iii. 11, iv. 20.

καί, conj. *and; also, too; even, actually*. καὶ—καί or τε—καί, *both—and*. καὶ—δέ, *yes and,* vii. 9. καὶ γάρ, *fór indeed, for also,* ii. 7, iii. 24.

καιρός ὁ, *opportunity, right time*.

καί-τοι, conj. *and yet*.

καίω, v.a., fut. καύσω, *burn*.

κακός, ή, όν, comp. κακίων, superl. κάκιστος, *bad, wicked, cowardly*. κακόν τό, *misfortune, evil*. κακῶς, adv. *ill, wickedly*.

κακόω, v.a. *injure,* v. 35.

κάκωσις ἡ, -εως, *ill-treatment,* vi. 3.

κάλαμος ὁ, *reed,* v. 26.

καλέω, v. a., fut. καλέσω or καλῶ, aor. ἐκάλεσα, pf. κέκληκα, *call, summon;* mid. *call for oneself*.

καλινδέω, v.a. *roll;* mid. *roll over,* viii. 28.

καλός, ή, όν, comp. καλλίων, superl. κάλλιστος, *beautiful, noble, honourable; excellent,* viii. 26. καλῶς, adv., comp. κάλλιον, superl. κάλλιστα, *well, nobly*. καλὸς κἀγαθός, i. 19.

κάμνω, v.n., fut. καμοῦμαι, aor. ἔκαμον, pf. κέκμηκα, *be weary, toil*.

καρβάτιναι αἱ, *brogues,* v. 14.

κατά, prep.

(1) with accus. *down, over, along,* iii. 12, vi. 11, 23; *over against, at,* iii. 17, iv. 8, vi. 23; *according to,* idiomatic uses, iii. 26, vi. 6, vii. 8.

(2) with gen. *down over,* v. 18, vii. 14.

κατα-βαίνω, v.n. *go down, descend,* i. 10, viii. 27.

κατά-βασις ἡ, *going down, descent,* i. 10.

κατά-γειος ον, *underground,* v. 25.

κατ-άγνυμι, v.a. *break down,* ii. 20.

κατα-διώκω, v.a. *chase down,* ii. 5.

κατα-δύω, v. n., fut. -δύσομαι, *sink;* mid., v. 36.

κατα-θύω, v. a. *sacrifice,* v. 35.

κατα-καίνω, v.a., aor. -έκανον, *slay,* ii. 5, viii. 25.

κατά-κειμαι, v.d. *lie down*.

κατα-κτείνω, v.a. *kill*.

κατα-λαμβάνω, v.a. *seize,* vi. 17; *overtake,* v. 7; *find,* v. 9, 30.

κατα-λείπω, v.a. *leave behind*.

κατα-πέμπω, v.a. *send down*.

κατα-σκευάζω, v.n. *train, equip, furnish,* i. 8; mid. *equip oneself, prepare*.

κατα-στρατοπεδεύομαι, v. mid. *form a camp,* v. 1.

κατα-σφάττω, v. a. *slaughter,* i. 23.

κατα-τέμνω, v.a. *cut up*.

κατα-τιτρώσκω, v.a. *wound severely,* i. 10.

κατα-φεύγω, v. n. *flee for refuge*.

κατ-εσθίω, v.a. *eat up*.

κατ-έχω, v.a. *hold,* ii. 1, 5, 12.

κατ-ορύττω, v.a. *dig down, bury,* v. 29.

κάτω, adv. *downwards, below*. τὸ κάτω, *the lower part,* ii. 28.

κεῖμαι, v.d., fut. κείσομαι, *lie; be laid, be set,* ii. 20.

κελεύω, v.a. *order, command*.

κενός, ή, όν, *empty*.

κέρας τό, κέρατος, κέρως, *horn; wing* (of an army), vi. 6.

κεφαλή ἡ, *head*.

κηρίον τό, *honey-comb*, viii. 20.
κῆρυξ ὁ, -υκος, *herald.*
κηρύττω, v.a., fut. κηρύξω, *proclaim*, i. 13.
κινδυνεύω, v. n. *be in danger;* with infin., i. 11.
κίνδυνος ὁ, *danger.*
κινέω, v.a. *move;* mid., v. 13.
κλέπτω, v.a. *steal*, vi. 11, 15; *smuggle*, i. 14.
κλῖμαξ ὁ, -ακος, *ladder*, v. 25.
κλίνη ἡ, *couch*, iv. 21.
κλοπή ἡ, *theft*, vi. 14.
κλώψ ὁ, -ωπός, *thief*, vi. 17.
κνέφας τό, *darkness*, v. 9.
κνημίς ἡ, -ῖδος, *greave*, vii. 16.
κοιμάομαι, v.mid. *go to sleep.*
κοινός, ή, όν, *common.* κοινῇ, adv. *in common*, v. 34. ἀπὸ κοινοῦ, *from the common stock*, vii. 27.
κολωνός ὁ, *cairn.*
κομίζω, v.a., fut. κομιῶ, *carry, convey.*
κονιατός, όν, *made of cement*, ii. 22.
κόπτω, v.a. *cut, cut up; knock.*
κόρη ἡ, *maiden.*
κορυφή ἡ, *head, top, crest.*
κράνος τό, -ους, *helmet*, vii. 16.
κρατέω, v.n. *be powerful, be conqueror;* with gen. *be master of, overcome.*
κρατήρ ὁ, -ῆρος, *mixing-bowl*, v. 32.
κράτιστος, η, ον (superl. of κρατερός), *strongest, chief; best*, vi. 16. κράτιστα, adv. *most stoutly*, vi. 10.
κράτος τό, -ους, *strength.*
κραυγή ἡ, *shout, noise.*
κρέας τό, κρέως, *meat*, v. 31.
κρείττων, ον (comp. of κρατερός), *stronger; better.*
κρέμαμαι, v.d. *hang*, i. 2.

κρήνη ἡ, *spring, fountain.*
κριθή ἡ, *barley;* plur., v. 26.
κρίθινος, η, ον, *made of barley*, v. 26, 31.
κρίνω, v.a., fut. κρινῶ, aor. ἔκρινα, pf. κέκρικα, *choose, decide.*
κρούω, v.a. *knock, clash*, v. 18.
κτείνω, v.a., fut. κτενῶ, aor. ἔκτεινα, pf. ἔκτονα, *kill.*
κτῆνος τό, *possession;* plur. *cattle*, v. 25, vii. 2.
κύκλος ὁ, *circle.* κύκλῳ, *round about*, vii. 2.
κυκλόω, v.a. *encircle*, ii. 15.
κυλίνδω, v.a. *roll*, vii. 4.
κωλύω, v.a. *hinder, prevent.*
κωμάρχης ὁ, -ου, *village-chief, headman*, v. 10.
κώμη ἡ, *village.*
κωμήτης ὁ, *villager.*

λαγχάνω, v.a., fut. λήξομαι, aor. ἔλαχον, pf. εἴληχα, *obtain by lot, get*, v. 24.
λαγώς ὁ, -ώ, *hare*, v. 24.
λάκκος ὁ, *cistern*, ii. 22.
λαμβάνω, v.a., fut. λήψομαι, aor. ἔλαβον, pf. εἴληφα, *take, seize, catch.*
λανθάνω, v.a. and n., fut. λήσομαι, 2 aor. ἔλαθον, pf. λέληθα, *escape notice;* often with partic., i. 4, ii. 7.
λέγω, v.a., fut. λέξω, *say, speak; mean.*
λεῖος, α, ον, *smooth*, iv. 1.
λείπω, v.a., fut. λείψω, aor. ἔλιπον, pf. λέλοιπα, *leave.*
λήγω, v.n. *cease.*
ληίζω, v.a. *plunder;* also mid., viii. 22.
λίθος ὁ, *stone.*
λινοῦς, ᾶ, οῦν, *made of linen*, vii. 15.

λόγος ὁ, word, speech; narrative,
i. 1.
λόγχη ἡ, spear-head, vii. 16; spear,
viii. 3.
λοιπός, ή, όν, remaining.
λόφος ὁ, ridge, crest.
λοχᾱγός ὁ, captain of a λόχος.
λόχος ὁ, company of 100 foot-
soldiers. λόχοι ὄρθιοι, company
columns, ii. 11, iii. 17, viii. 12.
λύω, v.a., fut. λύσω, loose, iii. 8,
10; break, ii. 25; weary, vi. 2.
λωφάω, v.n. cease, have respite,
vii. 6.

μαίνομαι, v.d., aor. ἐμάνην, pf.
μέμηνα, be mad, viii. 20.
μακρός, ά, όν, long.
μάλα, adv. much, very, vi. 15;
comp. μᾶλλον, more, rather;
superl. μάλιστα, most, especially.
μανθάνω, v.a., fut. μαθήσομαι, aor.
ἔμαθον, pf. μεμάθηκα, learn, find
out.
μάντις ὁ, -εως, prophet; soothsayer,
v. 4.
μάρσιπος ὁ, bag, iii. 11.
μαστιγόω, v.a. scourge, vi. 15.
μαστός ὁ, breast; breast-like hill
(French mamelon), ii. 18.
μαχαίριον τό, small knife, vii. 16.
μάχη ἡ, battle.
μάχομαι, v.d., fut. μαχοῦμαι, fight.
μέγας, μεγάλη, μέγα, great, important, comp. μείζων, superl.
μέγιστος.
μέγεθος τό, -ους, size.
μεθύω, v.n. be drunk, viii. 20.
μείων, used as comp. of ὀλίγος,
fewer, less.
μέλας, αινα, αν, black.
μελετάω, v.a. practise.
μέλι τό, -ιτος, honey, viii. 20.

μέλλω, (1) v.n. be likely, be about
to, intend, v. 1, vii. 16.
(2) v.a. intend, delay.
μέν, particle, indeed, on the one
hand, answered by δέ.
μέντοι, however. See note on vi. 15.
μένω, (1) v.n. remain, stay; stand
one's ground, vi. 18.
(2) v.a. wait for.
μέρος τό, part, share.
μέσος, η, ον, middle.
μεστός, ή, όν, full (with gen.).
μετά, prep.
(1) with accus. after, iv. 14;
next to, in course of, vi. 12.
(2) with gen. with, iii. 25.
μετα-δίδωμι, v.a. give a share,
v. 5.
μετρέω, v.a. measure, v. 6.
μέχρι, (1) conj. until (with indic.), ii. 4.
(2) prep. as far as (with gen.),
v. 36, vii. 15.
μή, neg. particle, not; do not; lest,
after verbs of fearing, etc., iii.
21, vi. 35. See notes on i. 6,
ii. 7, 13, iv. 15, v. 11, 12, vi.
14. οὐ μή, see note on viii. 13.
μὴ οὔ, see note on vii. 11.
μηδέ, conj. nor, not even.
μηδ-είς, μηδεμία, μηδέν, not one,
none.
μηδέ-ποτε, adv. never.
μήν, particle, verily, indeed.
μή-ποτε, adv. never.
μή-πω, adv. not yet.
μή-τε, conj. neither, nor.
μηχανάομαι, v.d. contrive, vii. 10.
μηχανή ἡ, engine; contrivance,
means, v. 16.
μικρός, ά, όν, small, little.
μιμνήσκω, v.a., fut. μνήσω, re-
mind; mid. remember, pf. μέμ-
νημαι.

μισθο-φόρος ὁ, *mercenary*, iii. 4, iv. 18.

μνημονεύω, v. n. *remember* (with gen.), iii. 2.

μόγις, adv. *painfully, hardly.*

μόλις, adv. *scarcely, with difficulty,* viii. 28.

μοναχῇ, adv. *by one way only,* iv. 18.

μόνος, η, ον, *alone, only.* μόνον, adv. *only.*

μόσχειος, ον, *of calf,* v. 31.

μύζω, v.a. *suck,* v. 27.

μύριοι, αι, α, *ten thousand.*

μύρον τό, *perfume,* iv. 13.

μύχος ὁ, *recess,* i. 7.

νάπη ἡ, *glen,* v. 15.

νεανίσκος ὁ, *young man*, iii. 13.

νεκρός, ά, όν, *dead.*

νέμω, v.a. *distribute ;* mid. *feed on, enjoy ;* pass. *be grazed on,* vi. 17.

νεό-δαρτος, ον, *newly flayed,* v. 14.

νέος, α, ον, *young, new.*

νευρά ἡ, *bow-string,* ii. 28.

νέω, v.n., fut. *νεύσομαι* or *νευσοῦμαι, swim,* iii. 12.

νεωστί, adv. *lately.*

νικάω, v.a. *conquer ; be conqueror.*

νίκη ἡ, *victory.*

νοέω, v.a. *think, conceive.*

νομίζω, v.a., fut. *νομιῶ, think, consider ;* pass. *to be customary,* iii. 23.

νόμιμος, η, ον, *customary,* vi. 15.

νόμος ὁ, *law, custom.*

νυκτερεύω, v.n. *pass the night,* iv. 11.

νύκτωρ, adv. *by night,* vi. 12.

νῦν, adv. *now.*

νύξ ἡ, *νυκτός, night.*

ξένιος, α, ον, *hospitable.* τὸ ξένιον, *pledge of friendship,* viii. 23.

ξένος ὁ, *stranger ; guest-friend.*

ξηρός, ά, όν, *dry.*

ξίφος τό, -ους, *sword.*

ξυήλη ἡ, *scimitar,* vii. 16.

ξύλον τό, *wood.*

ὁ, ἡ, τό, article, *the ;* also used as demonstr. pron., e.g. οἱ μὲν—οἱ δέ, *the one—and the other.* τῇ μὲν—τῇ δέ, *partly—partly.*

ὀγδοήκοντα, indecl. *eighty.*

ὄγδοος, η, ον, *eighth.*

ὅδε, ἥδε, τόδε, demonstr. pron., *this, this one here.*

ὁδο-ποιέω, v. a. *make a road,* viii. 8.

ὁδός ἡ, *way, road, march.*

ὅθεν, adv. *whence.*

οἷ, adverb, *whither.*

οἶδα, perf. with pres. meaning, *know,* plup. ἤδειν, fut. εἴσομαι.

οἴκαδε, adv. *homewards.*

οἰκέτης ὁ, -ου, *house-servant,* v. 35.

οἰκέω, (1) v.a. *inhabit,* vii. 19. (2) v.n. *dwell,* vii. 17.

οἰκία ἡ, *house.*

οἴκοθεν, adv. *from home,* viii. 25.

οἶκος ὁ, *house, home.*

οἶνος ὁ, *wine.*

οἴομαι, contr. οἶμαι, v.d. *think.*

οἷος, α, ον, *what kind of ; such as.* οἷός τε, *able ; possible.*

ὄϊς ὁ, ἡ, ὄϊος, *sheep.*

οἴχομαι, v.d. *be gone, be off,* vi. 3.

ὄκνος ὁ, *hesitation, fear.*

ὀλίγος, η, ον, *small ;* plur. *few.*

ὀλισθηρός, ά, όν, *slippery.*

ὀλοίτροχος ὁ, *boulder,* ii. 3.

ὅλος, η, ον, *whole.*

ὁμαλής, ές, *level.*

ὁμαλός, ή, όν, *level.* τὸ ὁμαλόν, *level ground,* ii. 16.

ὁμίχλη ἡ, *mist,* ii. 7.

ὄμνυμι, v. a., fut. ὀμοῦμαι, aor. ὤμοσα, pf. ὀμώμοκα, swear.

ὅμοιος a, ον, like. οἱ ὅμοιοι, the peers (at Sparta), vi. 14.

ὁμοῦ, adv. together.

ὀμφαλός ὁ, navel, the middle, v. 2.

ὅμως, conj. nevertheless.

ὄναρ τό, ὀνείρατος, dream, iii. 8.

ὀνίνημι, v. a., fut. ὀνήσω, aor. ὤνησα, benefit.

ὄνομα τό, -ατος, name.

ὄνος ὁ, ἡ, ass.

ὅπῃ, adv. in whatever way, how, v. i.; where, ii. 24.

ὄπισθεν, adv. behind.
(1) of place, in the rear.
(2) of time, after.

ὀπισθο-φυλακέω, v. a. guard the rear, bring up the rear, ii. 4.

ὀπισθοφυλακία ἡ, command of the rear-guard.

ὀπισθο-φύλαξ ὁ, -ακος, one who guards the rear, ii. 2.

ὁπλίζω, v. a. arm; mid. arm oneself.

ὁπλίτης ὁ, -ου, heavy-armed soldier, hoplite.

ὁπλιτικός, ἡ, όν, belonging to hoplites. τὸ ὁπλιτικόν, heavy-armed force, viii. 18.

ὅπλον τό, weapon; usually in plur. ὅπλα, arms; the place where the arms were piled; hoplites, heavy-armed troops, see note on ii. 20.

ὅποι, adv. whither.

ὁπόσος, η, ον, how great, iv. 17; plur. as many as.

ὁπόταν, conj. whenever (with subj.).

ὁπότε, conj. whenever (with ind. and opt.); now that, since.

ὅπου, adv. where.

ὅπως, (1) adv. as; how.

(2) conj. that, in order that (with subj. and opt.).

ὁράω, v. a., fut. ὄψομαι, aor. εἶδον, pf. ἑώρακα, see, perceive.

ὀργή ἡ, temper, anger.

ὀργίζομαι, v. d. be angry.

ὀργυιά ἡ, a measure of length, about 6 feet, v. 4.

ὄρθιος, a, ον, straight, steep, i. 20, ii. 14. ὄρθιοι λόχοι, company columns, ii. 11, iii. 17, viii. 12. πρὸς τὸ ὄρθιον, uphill, ii. 3.

ὀρθός, ἡ, όν, straight, upright, viii. 20; right.

ὄρθρος ὁ, dawn.

ὁρίζω, v. a. bound, iii. 1.

ὅριον τό, boundary, viii. 8.

ὁρμάω, act. set in motion; neut. start, iii. 31; pass. and mid. start, viii. 23; hasten.

ὀρνίθειος ον, belonging to birds, v. 31.

ὄρνις ὁ, ἡ, -ιθος, bird.

ὄρος τό, mountain; gen. plur. uncontr. ὀρέων, i. 2.

ὀρυκτός, ἡ, όν, dug, v. 23.

ὀρύττω, v. a. dig.

ὅς, ἥ, ὅ, relative pron. who, which.

ὅσος, η, ον, how great, as great as; plur. how many, as many as. ὅσον, adv. as much as, about (with numerals), vii. 6.

ὅσ-περ, ἥπερ, ὅπερ, relative pron. who, which.

ὄσπριον τό, pulse, iv. 9.

ὅσ-τις, ἥτις, ὅ τι, who, whosoever; he who, inasmuch as he. ὅ τι, sometimes why (indirect).

ὅταν, conj. whenever (with subj.).

ὅτε, conj. when.

ὅτι, conj. that; because. ὅτι πλεῖστοι, as many as possible, i. 45.

ὅτου, ὅτῳ, gen., dat. (contr.) of
   ὅστις, i. 9, iv. 11.
οὐ (οὐκ, οὐχ), neg. particle, *not.*
οὗ, adv. *where.*
οὐδαμῇ, adv. *nowhere, in no wise.*
οὐδαμόθεν, adv. *from no quarter*,
   v. 30.
οὐδαμοῦ, adv. *nowhere.*
οὐδέ, conj. *nor; nor yet; not even.*
οὐδ-είς, οὐδεμία, οὐδέν, *no one,
   none.* οὐδέν, also adv. *not at
   all*, ii. 4.
οὐδέ-ποτε, adv. *never.*
οὖν, particle, *therefore, then.*
οὔ-ποτε, adv. *never.*
οὔ πω, adv. *not yet.*
οὐ-πώ-ποτε, adv. *never yet.*
οὐρά ἡ, *tail; rear* (of an army).
οὐραγός ὁ, *rear-rank man*, iii. 29.
οὐρανός ὁ, *sky.*
οὔτε, conj. *neither, nor.*
οὗτος, αὗτη, τοῦτο, demonstr. pron.
   this. On its 'deictic' force see
   note on vii. 5.
οὕτω (οὕτως), adv. *thus, so;* idiomatic use, i. 11, v. 29.
ὀφθαλμός ὁ, *eye.*
ὄχθη ἡ, *bank*, iii. 3.
ὄχλος ὁ, *throng*, i. 20; esp. of
   camp-followers, iii. 15, 26.
ὀχυρός, ά, όν, *strong;* neut. plur.
   strongholds, vii. 17.
ὀψέ, adv. *late.*
ὀψίζω, v. n. *be late*, v. 5.
ὄψομαι. See ὁράω.

παγκράτιον τό, *pancratium*, a com-
   petition combining boxing and
   wrestling, viii. 27.
πάθος τό, -ους, *experience, misfortune*, v. 7.
παιανίζω, v. n. *sing a paean* or
   war-song.
παιδεία ἡ, *education.*

παιδίον τό, *child.*
παιδίσκη ἡ, *maiden*, iii. 11.
παῖς ὁ, ἡ, παιδός, *child, boy.*
παίω, v. a. *strike, wound.*
πάλαι, adv. *long ago.*
παλαιός, ά, όν, *ancient, old.*
παλαίω, v. n. *wrestle*, viii. 26.
πάλη ἡ, *wrestling*, viii. 27.
πάλιν, adv. *back; again.*
πάμ-πολυς, -πόλλη, -πολυ, *very
   much, very many*, i. 8.
παντάπασι, adv. *wholly, altogether*, i. 2.
πανταχοῦ, adv. *everywhere.*
παντο-δαπός, ή, όν, *of every kind*,
   iv. 9.
πάνυ, adv. *altogether, very.*
παρά, prep.
   (1) with accus. **to** *the side of,
   to*, iii. 27; *alongside of*, iii. 1,
   vii. 16.
   (2) with gen. **from** *the side
   of, from*, vii. 27.
   (3) with dat. **at** *the side of,
   near, with*, i. 24.
παρα-βαίνω, v. a. *pass; transgress*,
   i. 1.
παρα-βοηθέω, v. n. *come up to aid.*
παρ-αγγέλλω, v. a. *pass orders a-
   long (the line)*, i. 16, vii. 9.
παρ-άγγελσις ἡ, -εως, *passing of
   orders along the line*, i. 5.
παρ-άγω, v. a. *lead alongside, wheel
   round*, iii. 36.
παρα-δίδωμι, v. a. *deliver up.*
παρα-θέω, v. n. *run along*, vii.
   12.
παρα-καλέω, v. a. *summon; ex-
   hort.*
παρα-κέλευσις ἡ, -εως, *encourage-
   ment*, viii. 28.
παρα-κελεύω, v. a. and mid. *en-
   courage*, ii. 9.
παρ-ακολουθέω, v. n. *accompany.*

παρα-λαμβάνω, v.a. *receive, take on.*

παρα-πέμπω, v.a. *send along.*

παραρρέω, v.n. *flow past; slip off,* iv. 11.

παρασάγγης ὁ, *parasang,* a Persian measure; N.B. not a fixed unit of measurement, but varying according to the character of the country traversed. See note on iv. 1.

παρα-σκευάζω, v.a. *prepare, provide.*

παρα-τάττω, v. n. *draw up in line.*

παρα-τείνω, v.a. *stretch along.*

παρα-τίθημι, v.a. *set before,* v. 30.

παρα-τρέχω, v.n. *run past.*

παρ-εγγυάω, v.a. *pass word along,* vii. 24, viii. 16.

πάρ-ειμι, v.n. *be present, be at one's side* (εἰμί). πάρεστι, impers. *it is possible,* v. 6.

πάρ-ειμι, v.n. *pass by, advance* (εἶμι), ii. 13.

παρ-έρχομαι, v.d. *pass,* ii. 12, iii. 2.

παρ-έχω, v.a. *provide, offer,* viii. 8 ; *render, cause,* i. 22.

παρ-ίστημι, v. a. *place beside;* mid. (and 2 aor. and pf. act.) *stand beside.*

πάρ-οδος ἡ, *passage,* i. 2.

πᾶς, πᾶσα, πᾶν, *all, every.*

πάσχω, v.a., fut. πείσομαι, aor. ἔπαθον, pf. πέπονθα, *experience, suffer; be treated.*

πατάσσω, v.a. *strike.*

πατήρ ὁ, -τρός, *father.*

πατρίς ἡ, -ίδος, *fatherland.*

παύω, v.a. *stop,* viii. 10; mid. *cease.*

παχύς, εῖα, ύ, *thick.*

πέδη ἡ, *fetter.*

πεδίον τό, *plain.*

πεζός, ή, όν, *on foot.* οἱ πεζοί, *infantry.* πεζῇ, adv. *on foot.*

πείθω, v. a., fut. πείσω, aor. ἔπεισα, pf. πέπεικα, *persuade;* 2 pf. πέποιθα, and mid. *obey, trust* (with dat.).

πειράω and πειράομαι, *attempt, make trial of.*

πελάζω, v.n. *approach* (with dat.).

πελταστής ὁ, -οῦ, *peltast, targeteer,* armed with the πέλτη, a crescent-shaped wicker shield, i. 26.

πέμπω, v.a., fut. πέμψω, aor. ἔπεμψα, pf. πέπομφα, *send.*

πέντε, indecl. *five.*

πεντε-καί-δεκα, indecl. *fifteen.*

πέραν, (1) adv. *on the other side,* iii. 33.

(2) prep. *beyond* (with gen.), iii. 3.

περάω, v.a. *cross.*

περί, prep.

(1) with accus. *around; about* (of time and number).

(2) with gen. *about, concerning,* ii. 18.

περι-βάλλω, v. a. *throw round; embrace,* vii. 25.

περι-ειλέω, v. a. *wrap round,* v. 36.

περί-ειμι (εἰμί), *be superior, get the best of it.*

περί-ειμι (εἶμι), *go round* (in fut. sense), i. 3.

περι-ίστημι, v.a. *place round;* mid. (and 2 aor. and pf. act.) *stand round.*

περι-μένω, v. a. *await.*

πέριξ, adv. *round about,* iv. 7.

περί-οδος ἡ, *circuit.*

περι-πήγνυμαι, v.mid. *freeze round,* v. 14.

περιρρέω, v.a. *flow round;* 2 aor. περιερρύην, *slipped from around,* iii. 8.

περι-τρέχω, v. n. *run round*, v. 8.
περιττεύω, v. n. *surpass in numbers*,
viii. 11.
περιττός, ή, όν, *excessive, superfluous*, viii. 11.
περιφανῶς, adv. *manifestly*, v. 4.
περσίζω, v. n. *speak Persian*, v. 34.
περσιστί, adv. *in Persian*, v. 10.
πέτομαι, v. d. *fly*.
πέτρα ή, *rock*.
πέτρος ὁ, *stone*, ii. 20.
πῃ, adv. *somewhere, somehow*, viii.
11, 13.
πηγή ή, *spring, source*, i. 3.
πήγνυμι, v. a., fut. πήξω, pf. πέ-
πηγα (with passive meaning),
freeze, v. 3.
πῆχυς ὁ, -εως, *elbow; cubit*, vii.
16.
πιέζω, v. a. *press, press hard*.
πικρός, ά, όν, *bitter*, iv. 13.
πίνω, v. a., fut. πίομαι, aor. ἔπιον,
pf. πέπωκα, *drink*.
πίπτω, v. n., fut. πεσοῦμαι, aor.
ἔπεσον, pf. πέπτωκα, *fall*.
πιστός, ή, όν, *faithful*. τὰ πιστά,
pledges, viii. 7.
πίτυς ή, -υος, *fir*.
πλανάομαι, v. mid. *wander*.
πλέθρον τό, *plethrum*, a Greek
measure of length, one sixth of
a stade, 100 Greek feet = 101
English, vii. 6.
πλεθριαῖος, α, ον, *measuring a
plethrum*, vi. 4.
πλεῖστος, η, ον}
πλείων, ον   } See πολύς.
πλευρά ή, *side, flank*.
πληγή ή, *blow*.
πλῆθος τό, *number*, ii. 2; *quantity*,
iv. 8.
πλήν, (1) prep. *except* (with gen.),
vi. 1.
    (2) adv. *except*, i. 14.

πλησιάζω, v. n. *approach* (with
dat.), vi. 6.
πλησίον, adv. *near*. ὁ πλησίον,
the neighbouring, v. 34, viii. 24.
πνεῦμα τό, -ατος, *wind*.
πνέω, v. n. *breathe; blow*.
ποδαπός, ή, όν, *of what country*,
iv. 17.
ποιέω, v. a. *make, render, do*; mid.
make for one's self, i. 1, viii. 15.
κακῶς ποιέω, *injure*.
πολεμέω, v. n. *carry on war*, i. 1.
πολεμικός, ή, όν, *belonging to war*,
iii. 29; *apt for war*.
πολέμιος, α, ον, *hostile;* subst.
enemy. ή πολεμία (sc. χώρα),
the enemy's country.
πόλεμος ὁ, *war*.
πολιορκέω, v. a. *besiege*.
πόλις ή, *city, state*.
πόλισμα τό, -ατος, *town*, vii. 16.
πολλάκις, adv. *often*.
πολλαχοῦ, adv. *in many places*,
i. 28.
πολύς, πολλή, πολύ, comp. πλείων;
superl. πλεῖστος, *much; great*,
i. 15; plur. *many*. οἱ πολλοί, *the
many, the majority*. πολύ, *far,
considerably*.
πόνος ὁ, *toil*.
πορεία ή, *journey, march*.
πορευτέον, verbal adj. *one must
go*, i. 2, v. 1.
πορεύω, v. a. *convey;* mid. and
pass. *go, march*.
πορίζω, v. a., fut. ποριῶ, *provide,
supply;* mid. *provide for one's
self*, i. 13.
πόρος ὁ, *ford*.
πόρρω or πρόσω, adv. *forwards;
far*, i. 3.
ποταμός ὁ, *river*.
ποτε, enclitic, *at some time, ever*.
ποῦ, adv. *where?*

που, enclitic, *somewhere.*

πούς ὁ, *ποδός, foot.*

πρᾶγμα *τό,* -ατος, *thing, matter;* sing. and plur. *trouble,* i. 17, 22.

πρανής, ές, *steep.*

πράττω, v.a., fut. πράξω, aor. ἔπραξα, pf. πέπραχα, *do, perform;* intrans. *fare* (2 pf. πέπρᾱγα).

πρίν, (1) adv. *before, formerly.*
(2) conj. *before that, until,* i. 4, v. 1.

πρό, prep. *before, in front of* (with gen.), ii. 21, v. 13.

προ-άγω, v.a. *lead forward;* abs. *advance.*

προ-βάλλω, v.a. *throw before;* mid. *throw before oneself,* ii. 21.

πρόβατον *τό, sheep.*

προ-διώκω, v.a. *pursue forwards.*

προ δρομή *ἡ, sally,* vii. 10.

προ-ελαύνω, v.a. *drive in front;* abs. *ride in front.*

προ-θυμέομαι, v.d. *be eager,* i. 22.

προ-θυμία *ἡ, eagerness.*

προ-κατα-λαμβάνω, v.a. *seize beforehand,* i. 25.

προ-πέμπω, v.a. *send forward.*

προ-πίνω, v.n. *drink to the health of* (with dat.), v. 32.

πρός, prep.
(1) with accus. *to, towards,* iv. 4, v. 18; *against,* iv. 1 ; *with a view to,* iii. 10, 31.
(2) with gen. *from; on the side of,* iii. 26.
(3) with dat. *close to; at,* v. 9, 22; *in addition to.*

προσ-άγω, v.a. *bring to,* i. 23; abs. *move up to attack,* vi. 21.

προσ-βαίνω, v.n. *step against,* ii. 28.

προσ-βάλλω, v.a. *throw against;* abs. *attack,* ii. 11.

προσ-βατός, ή, όν, *accessible,* iii. 12.

προσ-γίγνομαι, v.d. *be added to, join,* vi. 6.

προσ-ελαύνω, v.a. *drive up to;* absolute, *ride up,* iv. 5.

προσ-έρχομαι, v.d. *come to.*

πρόσ-ετι, adv. *further, besides.*

προσ ἔχω, v.a. *apply,* ii. 2.

προσ-ήκω, v.n. *reach,* iii. 23.

πρόσθεν, (1) adv. *before* (both of time and place). ὁ **πρόσθεν,** *previous; that which is in front.*
(2) prep. (both of time and place) *before.*

προσ-ίημι, v.a. *send to; admit,* v. 5; mid. *suffer to come near one,* ii. 12.

προσ-λαμβάνω, v.a. *take besides.*

προσ-μίγνυμι, v.a. *mix with;* abs. *join,* ii. 16.

προσ-ποιοῦμαι, v.mid. *claim; pretend,* iii. 20.

προ-στατέω, v.n. *preside over* (with gen.), viii. 25.

προσ-τρέχω, v.a. *run up to.*

πρόσω. See **πόρρω.**

πρότερος, a, ον, *before, earlier, former.*

προ-τρέχω, v.n. *run forward,* vii. 10.

πρῶτος, η, ον, *first; foremost.* **πρῶτον,** adv. *first.* τὰ **πρῶτον,** *in the first place.*

πταίω, v.n. *stumble.*

πτέρυξ *ἡ,* -υγος, *wing; flap,* vii. 16.

πυγμή *ἡ, boxing,* viii. 27.

πυκνός, ή, όν, *dense,* viii. 2.

πυνθάνομαι, v.d., fut. πεύσομαι, aor. ἐπυθόμην, pf. πέπυσμαι, *learn, hear of.*

πῦρ *τό, πυρός, fire.* **πυρά,** *watch-fires,* i. 11.

πύρινος, η, ον, *wheaten*, v. 31.
πυρός ὁ, *wheat*, usually in plur., v. 26.
πω, enclitic, *some time, yet.*
πῶλος ὁ, *colt.*
πῶμα τό, *draught*, v. 27.
πώ-ποτε, adv. *ever yet.*
πῶς, adv. *how?*
πως, enclitic, *in any way; somehow.*

ῥᾴδιος, α, ον, *easy;* comp. ῥᾴων, superl. ῥᾷστος. ῥᾳδίως, adv. *easily.*
ῥᾷστος, η, ον. See ῥᾴδιος.
ῥίπτω or ῥιπτέω, v. a., fut. ῥίψω, *throw, hurl.*
ῥοφέω, v. a. *gulp down*, v. 32.

σάγαρις ἡ, -εως, *battle-axe*, iv. 16.
σακίον τό, *small bag*, v. 36.
σάλπιγξ ἡ, -ιγγος, *trumpet*, ii. 1.
σαλπικτής ὁ, -οῦ, *trumpeter*, iii. 32.
σατράπης ὁ, -ου, *satrap*, Persian viceroy, iv. 2.
σαφής, ές, *clear, sure.*
σαφῶς, adv. *clearly.*
σεαυτόν, contr. σαυτόν, -ήν, reflexive pron. *thyself.*
σημαίνω, v. a., fut. σημανῶ, aor. ἐσήμηνα, *signify; give a signal,* ii. 1, iii. 29.
σησάμινος, η, ον, *made of sesame,* iv. 13.
σιγή ἡ, *silence.* σιγῇ, *silently,* ii. 7.
σῖτος ὁ, *corn; food;* plur. σῖτα τά, *provisions.*
σκεδάννυμι, v. a., fut. σκεδῶ, aor. ἐσκέδασα, *scatter.*
σκέλος τό, -ους, *leg.*
σκεπτέος, α, ον, *to be considered,* vi. 10.

σκευή ἡ, *equipment*, vii. 27.
σκεῦος τό, *vessel;* plur. *baggage,* iii. 30.
σκευο-φόρος, ον, *carrying baggage.*
οἱ σκευοφόροι, *porters.* τὰ σκευοφόρα, *baggage animals*, iii. 25.
σκηνέω, v.n. *encamp*, v. 33, vii. 27.
σκηνή ἡ, *tent, hut.* σκηναί, *quarters* generally.
σκηνόω, v.a. *make to encamp*, v. 23.
σκληρός, ά, όν, *hard.*
σκοπέω, v.a., fut. σκέψομαι, aor. ἐσκεψάμην, pf. ἔσκεμμαι, *view, consider;* intrans. *watch, spy.*
σκοταῖος, α, ον, *in the dark*, i. 10.
σκότος ὁ and τό, -ου and -ους, *darkness.*
σμῆνος τό, -ους, *bee-hive*, viii. 20.
σός, σή, σόν, possessive pron. *thy.*
σπάρτον τό, *rope*, vii. 15.
σπένδω, v.a., fut. σπείσω, *pour a libation;* mid. *make a truce*, iv. 6.
σπεύδω, (1) v.a. *urge on*, i. 21.
  (2) v.n. *hasten*, viii. 14.
σπολάς ἡ, -άδος, *leather cuirass, buff jerkin*, i. 18.
σπονδή ἡ, *libation;* plur. σπονδαί, *truce, treaty*, i. 1.
σπουδή ἡ, *haste.*
στάδιον τό (plur. στάδιοι οἱ), *stade* = 600 Greek feet or 606 English; lit. *race-course*, viii. 27.
σταθμός ὁ, *halting-place, encampment*, i. 19; *stage, day's march*, iv. 3.
στέγασμα τό, *covering.*
στέγη ἡ, *roof, shelter*, iv. 13.
στέλλω, v.a., fut. στελῶ, aor. ἔστειλα, *send; arrange; equip.*
στενός, ή, όν, *narrow*, comp. στενότερος, superl. στενότατος.
τὸ στενόν, *defile*, i. 14, iv. 18.

στερέω, v. a. *deprive.*

στέρομαι, v. d. *be deprived of, lack* (with gen. of thing), v. 28.

στέφανος ὁ, *wreath*, v. 33.

στεφανόω, v. a. *wreathe ;* mid. *wreathe oneself*, iii. 17.

στολή ἡ, *dress, robe*, v. 33.

στόμα τό, -ατος, *mouth,* v. 27; *entrance,* v. 25.

στρατεύω, v. n. and στρατεύομαι, v. mid. *serve as a soldier, march, go on an expedition.*

στρατηγός ὁ, *general.*

στρατιά ἡ, *army.*

στρατιώτης ὁ, -ου, *soldier.*

στρατοπεδεύομαι, v. d. *encamp.*

στρατόπεδον τό, *camp; army.*

στρατός ὁ, *army.*

στρέφω, v. a., fut. στρέψω, *turn; twist*, vii. 15; abs. *wheel round*, iii. 26, 32.

σύ, personal pron. *thou, you.* σύ-γε, *you at least.*

συγ-γενής, ές, *akin.*

συγ-γίγνομαι, v. d. *join, converse with*, v. 23.

συγ-καλέω, v. a. *call together.*

σύειος, a, ον, *of swine,* iv. 13.

συλ-λαμβάνω, v. a. *seize.*

συλ-λέγω, v. a. *collect.*

συμ-βάλλω, v. a. *throw together*, mid., vi. 14.

συμ-βοηθέω, v. n. *join in aiding* (with dat.).

συμ-μανθάνω, v. a. *learn with; become accustomed to*, v. 27.

συμ-μίγνυμι, v. a. *mix together;* abs. *meet, join*, vi. 24.

σύμ-πας, -ασα, -αν, *all together*, iii. 2.

συμ-πέμπω, v. a. *send together.*

συμ-ποδίζω, v. a. *hamper*, iv. 11.

συμ-πορεύομαι, v. d. *go with.*

σύν (rare in Attic Prose except in Xen.), prep. with dat.
  (1) *together with*, i. 1.
  (2) *with the aid of*, i. 23, 42, ii. 8, 16.

συν-άγω, v. a. *bring together, collect.*

σύν-δειπνος ὁ, *guest at dinner*, v. 28.

συν-δια-πράττομαι, v. mid. *negotiate with*, viii. 24.

συν-εισ-έρχομαι, v. d. *go in with.*

συν-εκ-βαίνω, v. n. *go out with*, iii. 29.

συν-εκ-κόπτω, v. a. *help in cutting down*, viii. 8.

συν-έπομαι, v. d. *follow along with.*

συν-έρχομαι, v. d. *come together, meet.*

συν-εφ-έπομαι, v. d. *follow up along with.*

σύν-θημα τό, -ατος, *agreement*, vi. 20.

συν-ίστημι, v. a. *place together, bring together;* mid. (and 2 aor. and pf. act.) *come together.*

σύν-οιδα, v. a. *be conscious of.*

συν-ολολύζω, v. n. *cry out together*, iii. 19.

συν-ομολογέω, v. n. *agree together*, ii. 19.

συν-οράω, v. a. *see at the same time,* i. 11.

συν-τάττω, v. a. *draw up together;* mid. iv. 1.

συν-τίθημι, v. a. *put together;* mid. *make an agreement*, ii. 1.

συν-τρίβω, v. a. *rub together, crush*, vii. 7.

συρρέω, v. n. *flow together, flock together*, ii. 19.

σῦς ὁ, ἡ, *pig, sow.*

συ-σκευάζω, v. a. and συσκευάζομαι, v. mid. *pack up*, iii. 14.

σφαγιάζω, v.a. *sacrifice*, v. 4; mid. *sacrifice for oneself*, v. 4.

σφάγιον τό, *victim*, iii. 19.

σφάττω, v.a., fut. σφάξω, *slaughter*, v. 16.

σφεῖς, σφῶν, reflexive pron. plur. *themselves*.

σφενδονάω, v. n. *sling*, i. 16.

σφενδόνη ἡ, *sling*.

σφόδρα, adv. *exceedingly*.

σχεδόν, adv. *near; nearly*.

σχίζω, v.a. *cleave*, iv. 12.

σχολαῖος, α, ον, *leisurely*, i. 12.

σχολή ἡ, *leisure*, i. 17. σχολῇ, *leisurely*, i. 16.

σῴζω, v. a., fut. σώσω, pf. σέσωκα, *save; bring in safety*.

σωτήρ ὁ, *saviour, preserver*.

σωτηρία ἡ, *safety*.

σωτήριος, ον, *saving*. Subst. σωτήρια τά, *thank-offerings for safety*, viii. 25.

ταξίαρχος ὁ, *taxiarch, commander of a τάξις*.

τάξις ἡ, *rank*, iii. 29; *company* (of troops), iii. 22.

τάττω, v. a., fut. τάξω, aor. ἔταξα, pf. τέταχα, aor. pass. ἐτάχθην, *draw up, arrange*.

ταύτῃ, adv. *in this way*, ii. 4.

ταχύς, εῖα, ύ, *quick*, comp. θάττων, superl. τάχιστος. Adverbial neut. accus. ταχύ, *quickly*. ταχέως, adv. *quickly*.

τε, conj. enclitic, *both, and*.

τείνω, v.a., fut. τενῶ, aor. ἔτεινα, pf. τέτακα, *stretch ;* abs. *press forward*, iii. 21.

τεκμαίρομαι, v.d. *infer, conclude*, ii. 4.

τέκνον τό, *child*.

τελευταῖος, α, ον, *last*, ii. 16.

τελευτάω, v. a. *end;* absolute, *come to an end, die*. partic. τελευτῶν, *at last*, v. 16.

τερμίνθινος, η, ον, *of the turpentine tree*, iv. 13.

τέταρτος, η, ον, *fourth*.

τέτταρες, α, *four*.

τέχνη ἡ, *art, device*, v. 16.

τέως, adv. *meanwhile*, ii. 12.

τήκω, v.n., fut. τήξω, pf. τέτηκα, *melt*, v. 15.

τήμερον, adv. *to-day*.

τηνικαῦτα, adv. *then*, i. 5, ii. 3.

τί, interrogative particle, *why?*

τίθημι, v.a., fut. θήσω, aor. ἔθηκα, pf. τέθεικα, *place;* mid *place for oneself*. ὅπλα τίθεσθαι, *pile arms*, iii. 16, 26.

τις, τι, indefinite pron. enclitic, *some one, some*, a. τι, *in some way*, i. 14.

τίς, τί, interrogative pron. *who? what?* τί, *why?*

τιτρώσκω, v.a., fut. τρώσω, aor. ἔτρωσα. pf. τέτρωκα, *wound*.

τοιόσδε, άδε, όνδε, *such* (referring to what follows).

τοιοῦτος, -αύτη, -οῦτο, *such*.

τολμάω, v. a. *dare*.

τόξευμα τό, -ατος, *arrow*.

τοξεύω, v.a. *shoot with a bow*.

τόξον τό, *bow*.

τοξότης ὁ, -ου, *archer*.

τόπος ὁ, *place*.

τόσος, η, ον, *so great, so much*.

τοσοῦτος, -αύτη, -οῦτο(ν), *so great, so much;* plur. *so many*.

τότε, adv. *then, at that time; on the previous occasion*, iv. 20.

τράπεζα ἡ, *table*.

τραῦμα τό, -ατος, *wound*.

τραχύς, εῖα, ύ, *rough*.

τρεῖς, τρία, *three*.

τρέπω, v.a., fut. τρέψω, aor. ἔτρεψα, turn; put to flight; mid. turn oneself, v. 13.

τρέφω, v.a., fut. θρέψω, pf. τέτροφα, pf. pass. τέθραμμαι, nourish, rear.

τρέχω, v.n., fut. δραμοῦμαι, aor. ἔδραμον, run.

τριάκοντα, indecl. thirty.

τριακόσιοι, αι, α, three hundred.

τρί-πηχυς, υ, three cubits in length, ii. 28.

τρίτος, η, ον, third.

τριχῇ, adv. in three ways, in three parts, viii. 15.

τρίχινος, η, ον, of hair, viii. 3.

τρόπαιον τό, trophy, vi. 27.

τροπή ἡ, rout, viii. 21.

τρόπος ὁ, way, manner; character.

τυγχάνω, v.n., fut. τεύξομαι, aor. ἔτυχον, pf. τετύχηκα, hit, meet with, obtain (with gen.); happen; happen to be, with partic., i. 24.

τύρσις ἡ, -εως, tower, iv. 2.

ὑγιαίνω, v.n. be healthy, v. 18.

ὑδρο-φορέω, v.n. carry water, v. 9.

ὑδρο-φόρος, ον, carrying water, v. 10.

ὕδωρ τό, -ατος, water, v. 27; rain, ii. 2.

υἱός ὁ, son.

ὑμεῖς, plur. of σύ.

ὑμέτερος, α, ον, possessive pron. your.

ὑπ-άγω, v.a. lead on; absolute, advance slowly, ii. 16.

ὑπ-ακούω, v.n. listen to; answer, i. 9.

ὑπ-αντάω, v.n. go to meet (with dat.), iii. 34.

ὕπ-αρχος ὁ, lieutenant-governor, iv. 4.

ὑπ-ασπίστης ὁ, -ου, shield-bearer, ii. 20.

ὑπέρ, prep,
(1) with accus. beyond, over.
(2) with gen. above, over, iii. 1, 23; on behalf of, viii. 24.

ὑπερ-βάλλω, v.a. throw over; abs. pass over, i. 7.

ὑπερ-βολή ἡ, crossing over, iv. 18, vi. 5 ; pass, i. 21.

ὑπερ-έρχομαι, v.d. come over.

ὑπ-ισχνέομαι, v.d., fut. ὑποσχήσομαι, aor. ὑπεσχόμην, pf. ὑπέσχημαι, promise.

ὑπό, prep.
(1) with accus. under (motion to), vii. 8.
(2) with gen. from under; by (agent); from (cause), v. 35, vii. 6.
(3) with dat. under (rest under).

ὑπο-δέομαι, v. mid. bind (sandals) under one's feet, v. 14.

ὑπό-δημα τό, sandal, v. 14.

ὑπο-ζύγιον τό, beast of burden, lit. animal under the yoke (ζυγόν), i. 13.

ὑπο-λείπω, v.a. leave behind, iii. 25, v. 15.

ὑπο-λύομαι, v. mid. loose (sandals) from off one's feet, v. 13.

ὑπο-μένω, (1) v.n. stay behind, i. 19.
(2) v.a. wait for.

ὑπ-οπτεύω, v.a. suspect.

ὑπο-φαίνω, v.a. show under, show slightly; intrans. shine slightly, break (of the day), ii. 7, iii. 9.

ὑπο-φείδομαι, v. dep. spare a little, i. 8.

ὑπο-χωρέω, v.n. fall back, v. 20.

ὑστεραῖος, α, ον, belonging to the next day. ἡ ὑστεραία (sc. ἡμέρα), the next day, i. 15.

ὕστερος, a, ον, *later; behind, in the rear.* Superl. ὕστατος. ὕστερον, adv. *after, afterwards.*

ὑφ-ηγέομαι, v.d. *lead on slowly,* i. 7.

ὑφ-ίστημι, v.a. *place under,* vii. 9; mid. (and 2 aor. and pf. act.) *undertake,* i. 14, 26.

φαίνω, v.a., fut. φανῶ, aor. ἔφηνα, 2 pf. πέφηνα (intrans.), aor. pass. ἐφάνην, *show;* intrans. *give light,* iv. 9; mid. and pass. *be shown, appear.*

φάλαγξ ἡ, -γγος, *line of battle* (to be distinguished from the Macedonian phalanx), iii. 26.

φανερός, ά, όν, *visible, manifest,* ii. 1, with partic. φανερῶς, adv. *clearly.*

φαρέτρα ἡ, *quiver,* iv. 16.

φαρμακο-ποσία ἡ, *drinking of poison,* viii. 21.

φάσκω, v.a. *say.*

φέρω, v.a., fut. οἴσω, aor. ἤνεγκον, pf. ἐνήνοχα, *bear, bring; plunder,* i. 8.

φεύγω, v.a. and n., fut. φεύξομαι or φευξοῦμαι, aor. ἔφυγον, pf. πέφευγα, *flee, escape; go into exile,* viii. 25.

φημί, v.a., fut. φήσω, *say.*

φθάνω, v.a., fut. φθάσω or φθήσομαι, aor. ἔφθασα or ἔφθην, pf. ἔφθακα, *anticipate, be beforehand,* i. 4, 21.

φθέγγομαι, v.d., fut. φθέγξομαι, *sound,* ii. 7, v. 18.

φθείρω, v.a., fut. φθερῶ, aor. ἔφθειρα, pf. ἔφθαρκα, *destroy, lay waste.*

φιάλη ἡ, *saucer, cup,* vii. 27.

φιλικός, ή, όν, *friendly,* i. 9.

φίλιος, a, ον, *friendly.*

φιλο-νεικία ἡ, *rivalry,* viii. 27.

φίλος, η, ον, *beloved, dear;* subst. φίλος ὁ, *friend.*

φιλο-φρονέομαι, v.d. *be kindly disposed,* v. 28.

φοβέω, v.a. *frighten;* mid. and pass. *fear, be afraid.*

φόβος ὁ, *fear.*

φράζω, v.a., fut. φράσω, *point out,* v. 29, 34; *tell.*

φρέαρ τό, -ατος, *well,* v. 25.

φρονέω, v.n. *think, have sense.*

φρύγανα τά, *firewood.*

φυγάς ὁ, -άδος, *exile.*

φυγή ἡ, *flight.*

φυλακή ἡ, *guard, watch, outpost.*

φύλαξ ὁ, -ακος, *guard.*

φυλάττω, v.a., fut. φυλάξω, *guard;* mid. *be on one's guard,* vii. 28.

φωνή ἡ, *voice; language,* viii. 4.

χαλεπαίνω, v.n. *be indignant,* v. 16; also in pass., v. 16, vi. 2.

χαλεπός, ή, όν, *hard, severe, cruel.* τὸ χαλεπόν, *severity;* v. 4.

χάλκωμα τό, *bronze vessel.*

χαράδρα ἡ, *ravine,* ii. 3.

χειμών ὁ, -ῶνος, *winter; storm.*

χείρ ἡ, χειρός, *hand.*

χειρο-ποίητος, ον, *made by hand, artificial,* iii. 5.

χιλός ὁ, *grass,* v. 25.

χιτών ὁ, -ῶνος, *tunic, shirt,* viii. 3.

χιών ἡ, -όνος, *snow,* v. 1.

χοίρειος, -α, -ον, *of swine,* v. 31.

χορεύω, v.n. *dance,* vii. 16.

χράομαι, v.d., pres. inf. χρῆσθαι, fut. χρήσομαι, *use, enjoy* (with dat.); *experience,* vi. 3, 13.

χρῄζω, v.n. *desire,* viii. 5.

χρῖμα τό, *anointing-oil,* iv. 13.

χρίομαι, v.mid. *anoint oneself,* iv. 12.

χρόνος ὁ, *time.*

χώρα ἡ, *country, district; position,*
  viii. 15.
χωρέω, v.n. *go, advance.*
χωρίον τό, *place, position.*

ψιλόω, v.a. *strip, deprive of* (with
  gen.), iii. 26.
ψοφέω, v.n. *sound,* iii. 29.
ψοφός ὁ, *sound,* ii. 5.
ψῦχος τό, *cold,* v. 12.

ᾠδή ἡ, *song,* iii. 27.
ὠμο-βόειος, a, ον, *of raw ox-hide,*
  vii. 22, 26.
ὠμός, ή, όν, *raw,* viii. 14.
ὠφέλιμος, η, ον, *useful,* i. 23.

ὥρα ἡ, *season, proper time; time,*
  viii. 21.
ὡς, (1) adv. *how,* i. 20; *as; as if,*
  iii. 11; with numerals, *about,*
  iii. 1.
  (2) conj. *when, since,* iii. 27;
  that (introducing statements);
  in order that (with subj. and
  opt.); *so that* (with infin. =
  ὥστε), iii. 29, vi. 13.
ὡσ-αύτως, adv. *in like manner,*
  vii. 13.
ὥσ-περ, adv. *just as.*
ὥστε, conj. *so that* (with indic.
  or infin.), i. 16, 17, ii. 15, 22,
  27.

LIST OF UN-ATTIC WORDS.

The following words which occur in the Fourth Book of the Anabasis are not found in any other Attic Prose writer:—

αἴθω, vii. 20.
ἄλκιμος, iii. 4.
ἀμαξιαῖος, ii. 3.
ἀναχάζω, i. 16, vii. 10.
ἀνιμάω, ii. 8.
ἀντίπορος, ii. 18.
ἀτασθαλία, iv. 14.
βατός, vi. 17.
βουλιμιάω, v. 7.
δάπεδον, v. 6.
δασμός, v. 24.
δαψιλής, ii. 22, iv. 2.
θαμινά, i. 16.
κατακαίνω, ii. 5, viii. 25.
κλώψ, vi. 17.
κνέφας, v. 9.
μαστός, ii. 6.
ὀλοίτροχος, ii. 3.
ὀχυρός, vii. 17.
σακίον, v. 36.
ὠμοβόειος, vii. 22.

INDEX OF PROPER NAMES.

Ἀγασίας, *Agasias*, a Greek captain. i. 27, vii. 9.
Ἀθηναῖος, *Athenian*. ii. 13, vi. 16.
Ἀθήνησι, locative, *at Athens*. viii. 4.
Αἰνέας, *Aeneas*, a Greek captain. vii. 13.
Αἰσχίνης, *Aeschines*, a Greek captain. viii. 18.
Ἀκαρνάν, -ᾶνος, *Acarnanian*, belonging to Acarnania, a district in the west of Greece proper. viii. 18.
Ἀμαζόνες, *Amazons*, a legendary race of female warriors. iv. 16.
Ἀμφικράτης, *Amphicrates*, a Greek captain. ii. 13, 17.
Ἀμφιπολίτης, *belonging to Amphipolis*, a town on the Strymonic gulf. vi. 1.
Ἀργεῖος, *Argive*, belonging to Argos, a town on the east of the Peloponnese. ii. 13.
Ἀριστέας, *Aristeas*, a Greek captain. i. 29, vi. 20.
Ἀριστώνυμος, *Aristonymus*, a Greek captain. i. 27, vi. 20, vii. 9.
Ἀρκαδικός, *Arcadian*, belonging to Arcadia, the central district of the Peloponnese. viii. 18.
Ἀρκάς, -άδος, *Arcadian*. i. 18, 27.
Ἀρμενία, *Armenia*, a province to the north-east of Asia Minor. i. 2, iii. 1, iv. 1, v. 34.
Ἀρμένιος, *Armenian*. iii. 4, 20.

Ἅρπασος, *Harpasus*, a river flowing into the Euxine sea. vii. 18.
Ἀρτούχας, *Artuchas*, a Persian commander. iii. 4.
Ἀρχαγόρας, *Archagoras*, a Greek captain. ii. 13.

Βασίας, *Basias*, a Greek soldier. i. 18.

Γυμνίας, *Gymnias*, a town in Pontus, near the Euxine sea. vii. 19.

Δημοκράτης, *Democrates*, a Greek soldier. iv. 15.
Δρακόντιος, *Dracontius*, a Greek soldier. viii. 25.

Ἕλλην, *a Greek*. i. 1, etc.
Ἑλληνικός, *Greek*. i. 10, ii. 22.
Ἑλληνίς, fem. adj., *Greek*. viii. 22.
Ἐπισθένης, *Episthenes*, a Greek captain. vi. 1.
Εὔξεινος Πόντος, *Euxine sea*, the Black sea. viii. 22.
Εὐρύλοχος, *Eurylochus*, a Greek soldier. ii. 21, vii. 11.
Εὐφράτης, *Euphrates*, a great river of Western Asia. i. 2, v. 2.

Ζεύς, gen. Διός, *Zeus*, king of the gods. viii. 25.

Ἥλιος, *Helios*, the Sun-god. v. 35.

GRAMMATICAL INDEX.

MOODS :
  Optative:
    after εἰ πως (in final sense), i.
      8.
    after ὅπως ἄν, vi. 13.
    frequentative, i. 9, 14, 16, ii.
      24, 28, iv. 11.
    with ἄν (in dependent question), viii. 7.
    without ἄν, vi. 13.
  Subjunctive:
    vivid use, i. 3, iii. 29, vi. 6,
      vii. 11.
NEGATIVES :
    see *Vocabulary* under οὐ and
      μή.
    accumulation of, i. 9, v. 18,
      19.
ORATIO OBLIQUA :
    change of mood, i. 3, v. 10,
      28.
    future optative in, i. 25, iii.
      29, v. 28.
    transition in, iii. 12.
PARTICIPLE :
    denotes concession, i. 10, 23.
    denotes reason, i. 13.
    future, denotes purpose, iii. 3,
      v. 22, 24.
    imperfect, i. 7, iii. 25.
    present, iii. 30, v. 8.
    stress of sentence on, ii. 3, v.
      28, viii. 6.
    with διατελέω, iii. 2.
    with εἰμί, iii. 5, iv. 18, v. 15,
      vii. 2.
    with κινδυνεύω, i. 11.
    with λανθάνω, i. 4.
    with φαίνομαι and like words,
      ii. 4, iii. 33, v. 28, vi. 11.
    with φθάνω, i. 4.

PARTICLES :
    see *Vocabulary* under various
      Particles.
    omission of connecting particle, i. 20, 27.
PREPOSITIONS :
    see *Vocabulary* under various
      Prepositions.
PRONOUNS :
    demonstrative, in 'deictic'
      sense, vii. 5.
    relative, attracted, v. 16, 17,
      vii. 15.
SUBJECT :
    changed, ii. 20, viii. 19.
    dual, with plural verb, iii. 10.
    neuter plural, with plural verb,
      i. 13, ii. 20, v. 14, 25.
    two, with singular verb, i. 27.
SUBSTANTIVE :
    used as epithet, i. 6, 26.
TENSES :
  Aorist :
    infinitive, vi. 19.
    subjunctive with ἐπειδάν, vi.
      17.
  Future :
    after εἰ, vi. 9, vii. 3, viii. 11.
    after ὅπως, vi. 7, 10.
    optative, i. 25, iii. 29, v. 28.
  Imperfect :
    force of, iii. 6.
    with ἄν, vii. 16.
  Perfect :
    force of, ii. 10, 17, vii. 20.
    passive in mid. sense, iii. 28,
      vii. 1, 17.
  Present :
    historic, i. 4, 7.
    infinitive, v. 15.
    with πάλαι, viii. 14.

9 781107 600218